WATERPOWER

❧

Mills, Factories, Machines & Floods
at Harpers Ferry, West Virginia
1762-1991

David T. Gilbert

First Edition

WATERPOWER
Mills, Factories, Machines & Floods at Harpers Ferry, West
Virginia, 1762-1991

Copyright © 1999 by David T. Gilbert

ISBN 0-9674033-0-8

Published by the Harpers Ferry Historical Association,
P.O. Box 197, Harpers Ferry, WV 25425

Typography and page composition by the author.

Front cover: "Stock House, End Elevation," drawn by
Armistead Ball, Master Machinist of the Harpers Ferry
Armory, July 17, 1858 (*Burton Drawings,* Harpers Ferry
NHP, Catalog No. 13694); illustration of a "Fourneyron
or outward discharge turbine water-wheel" from a Kilburn,
Lincoln, & Co. 1874 catalog (courtesy The American
Textile History Museum).

Back cover (left to right): "New American" turbine runner,
from the patent drawings of William Mills, February 19,
1884 (United States Patent Office, No. 293,904); water
intake arch ruins on Virginius Island (October 1994 photo
by the author); Leffel turbine drive shafts in the cotton
factory ruins on Virginius Island (February 1987 photo by
the author).

TABLE OF CONTENTS

*New American turbine runner, from **Water Power Engineering** by Daniel W. Mead, 1920 edition.*

ACKNOWLEDGEMENTS

Many people have made this book possible. I am deeply indebted to Patricia Chickering, former Lead Historian at Harpers Ferry NHP, who thoroughly reviewed my manuscript and provided indispensible editorial comments. I would also like to thank Bruce J. Noble, Jr., Chief of Interpretation and Cultural Resources Management, Harpers Ferry NHP; Nancy Hatcher, Museum Technician, Harpers Ferry NHP; John Zimmerman, Interpretive Park Ranger, Harpers Ferry NHP; Marsha Starkey, Public Relations & Education Specialist, Harpers Ferry NHP; Deborah Piscitelli, Executive Director, Harpers Ferry Historical Association; Dean Herrin, Historian, Historic American Engineering Record (HAER), Washington, D.C.; Dru Bronson-Geoffroy, Archives Technician, Springfield Armory NHS, Springfield, Mass.; Eric Long, Photographer, Gaithersburg, Md.; Nick Blanton, The Rumseian Society, Shepherdstown, W.Va.; William E. Worthington, Jr., Division of Engineering & Industry, National Museum of American History, Washington, D.C.; Jon M. Williams, Curator of Prints and Photographs, Hagley Museum and Library, Wilmington, Del.; Robt Cox, Curator of Manuscripts, American Philosophical Society, Philadelphia, Pa.; Judith Ann Schiff, Chief Research Archivist, Manuscripts and Archives, Yale University Library, New Haven, Conn.; and Bill Trout, Virginia Canals and Navigations Society, Richmond, Va.

SPECIAL PLATES

PREFACE

VESTIGES OF AMERICA'S INDUSTRIAL PAST are rapidly fading from the national landscape. To the extent that industrial artifacts remain evident to the modern observer, they are most often thought of in connection with large "rust belt" cities like Pittsburgh, Cleveland, and Detroit. Less well known today is the fact that industry in early 19th century America was largely a rural phenomenon made possible by the ready availability of water power in the countryside. Situated at the picturesque junction of the Shenandoah and Potomac rivers, Harpers Ferry was perfectly positioned to develop into one of the leading centers of early industry in the United States. In the pages of this book, David T. Gilbert provides a compelling portrait of a town that rose to industrial prominence based on a combination of factors including proximity to water power, the creativity of technological innovators, the capital of cagey entrepreneurs, and the stability provided by a government-sponsored arms manufacturing operation.

In 1977, Merritt Roe Smith drew attention to Harpers Ferry's industrial significance when he published *Harpers Ferry Armory and the New Technology*. In his book, Smith found Harpers Ferry to be a place of resistance to the changes ushered in by the age of industry. According to this portrayal, a traditional commitment to the skills of the craftsman and a more abiding interest in an agrarian lifestyle prevented Harpers Ferry from readily acquiescing to the demands of mass production in an age of capitalist expansion. Smith's Harpers Ferry was more imitative than innovative, especially when compared with America's "northern armory" located in Springfield, Mass.

Gilbert presents a different view of Harpers Ferry. He does not attribute the town's decline as an industrial center to an unwillingness to embrace new technologies. In fact, he notes that local manufacturers adopted the most innovative technologies of their day. Instead, he connects the community's industrial demise with the lack of a consistent water supply. Modern day rafters and kayakers will attest to the fact that the two local rivers tend to vacillate dramatically between low and high water. For the manufacturer, this produced an ongoing series of frustrating shifts from insufficient water that forced operators to shut down machines, to raging torrents that damaged industrial facilities. Faced with the cyclical nature of water-powered production, the unwavering dependability of steam power fueled the rise of America's great industrial cities in the late 19th century, and led to the obsolescence of rural industry in places like Harpers Ferry.

Visitors to Harpers Ferry today are often most visibly impressed by the natural beauty of the precipitous hills towering one thousand feet above the rivers below. Gone is the major armory complex along the Potomac River. Gone too are the many small factories on Virginius Island and the rifle factory along the Shenandoah River where John Hall did his pioneering work with interchangeable parts. Careful observation along the rivers, however, will yield results for those seeking a glimpse of an old foundation, a turbine pit, a canal raceway, a grinding stone, or other ephemera associated with the area's industrial past. In this book, David T. Gilbert does an admirable job of transforming these disconnected ruins into a vivid rendition of Harpers Ferry during its heyday as a focal point in early American industrial development.

Bruce J. Noble, Jr.
Chief, Interpretation & Cultural Resources Management
Harpers Ferry National Historical Park

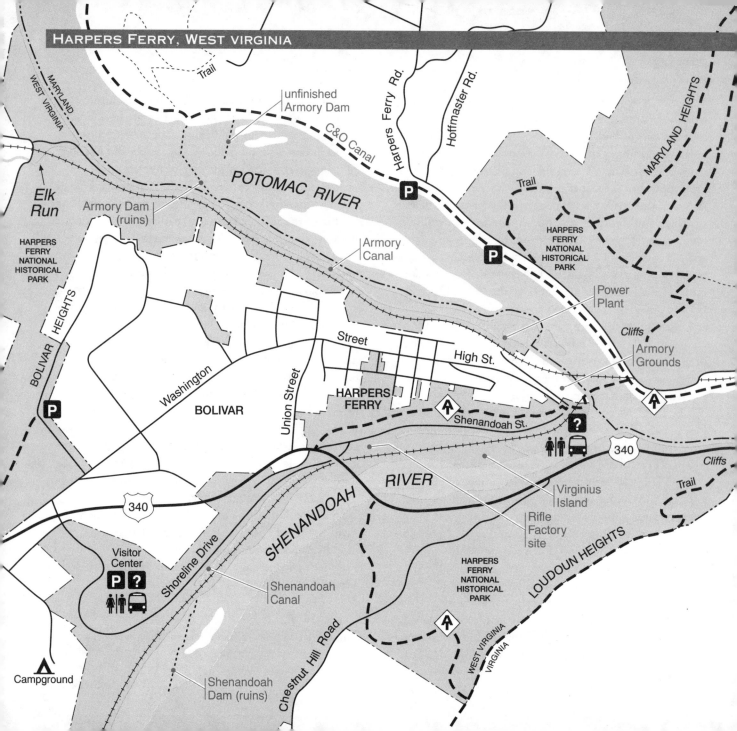

Trail

unfinished
Armory Dam

C&O Canal

Harpers Ferry Rd.

Hoffmaster Rd.

MARYLAND HEIGHTS

*Elk
Run*

MARYLAND
WEST VIRGINIA

POTOMAC RIVER

Trail

P

P

HARPERS
FERRY
NATIONAL
HISTORICAL
PARK

Armory Dam
(ruins)

Armory
Canal

Power
Plant

Cliffs

HARPERS
FERRY
NATIONAL
HISTORICAL
PARK

BOLIVAR HEIGHTS

Street

High St.

Armory
Grounds

P

Washington

Union Street

HARPERS
FERRY

BOLIVAR

Shenandoah St.

?

340

Cliffs

SHENANDOAH   RIVER

Virginius
Island

Trail

Rifle
Factory
site

340

Visitor
Center

P   ?

Shoreline Drive

Shenandoah
Canal

Chestnut Hill Road

HARPERS
FERRY
NATIONAL
HISTORICAL
PARK

LOUDOUN HEIGHTS

WEST VIRGINIA
VIRGINIA

Campground

Shenandoah
Dam (ruins)

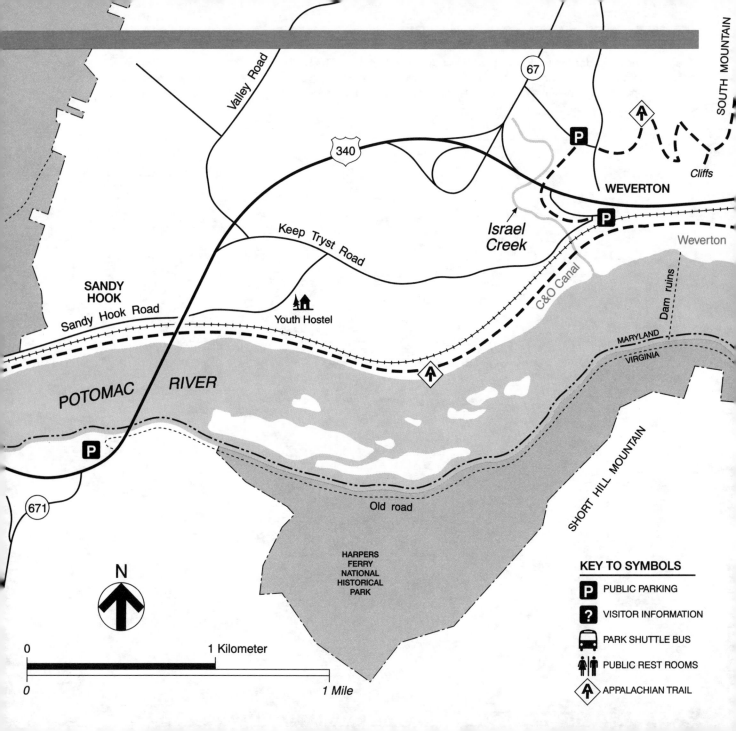

Aerial View of Harpers Ferry

The Potomac River descends 26¾ feet between Dam No. 3 and Lower Town Harpers Ferry over a series of rapids called "The Needles." The Shenandoah River drops 14 feet over "The Staircase" rapids adjacent to Virginius Island. The combined drainage area of both rivers above Harpers Ferry totals 9,180 square miles. (October 1994 photo courtesy Harpers Ferry NHP).

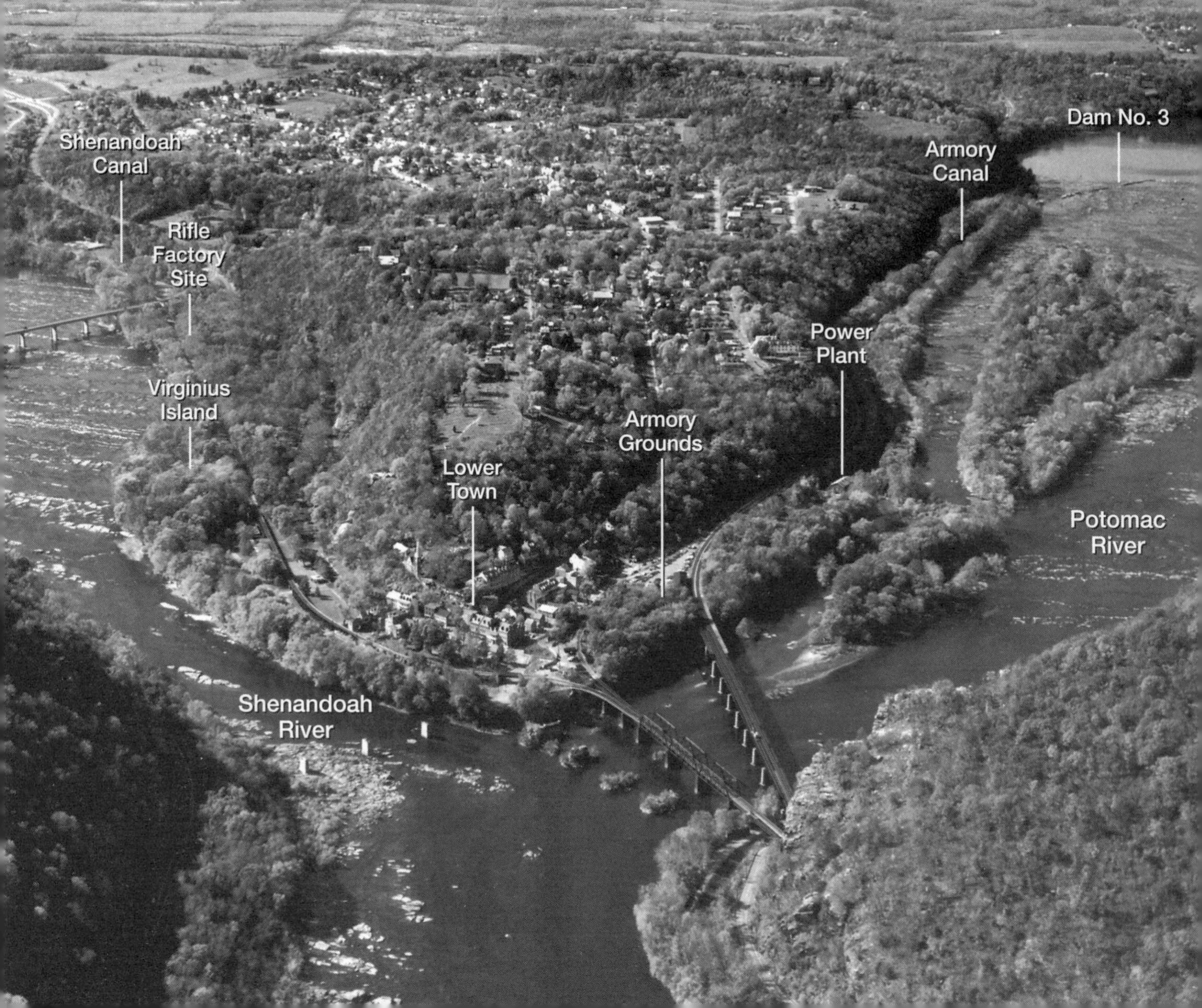

Shenandoah Canal
Rifle Factory Site
Virginius Island
Dam No. 3
Armory Canal
Power Plant
Armory Grounds
Lower Town
Potomac River
Shenandoah River

INTRODUCTION

The facilities for transportation are excellent, building materials are abundant, and there seems to be no reason why a large and fine power could not be utilized here. The site is probably the most favorable one on the river.

—Report of the Water Power of the United States, 1885

MANY VISITORS TO HARPERS FERRY TODAY are incredulous as they walk among the ruins of Virginius Island along the Shenandoah River. They cannot imagine what would induce a person to erect a home or factory here. "What were they thinking?" is a common question. Evidence of flooding is everywhere—debris wedged in tree branches high overhead, thick deposits of sand and silt, and the battered remnants of old ruined buildings.

The fact is, virtually every year some portion of Virginius Island in Harpers Ferry National Historical Park is inundated by spring run-off carried down the Shenandoah River. Along the adjacent Potomac River, high water often spills into the old Armory Canal, depositing considerable debris and further eroding already weak earthen berms.

Then there are those nasty "10-year" floods which periodically surge into the Lower Town Historic District. Since 1877, when official record-keeping began, there have been 20 floods at Harpers Ferry in which the flow of the combined rivers has reached or exceeded 18.5 feet

(*see* **Floods at Harpers Ferry,** *pages 164-165*). Of these floods, nine have reached or exceeded 27 feet, and four—1889, 1896, 1936, and 1942—have reached or exceeded 33 feet. To grasp the magnitude of these numbers, imagine you are standing in Park Building 45, the John G. Wilson Building (now the National Park Bookshop) along Shenandoah Street. When floodwaters reach 29 feet, the top of your head would be covered. At 34 feet, after you have climbed to the building's second floor, you would be standing in ankle-deep water. Now consider that Building 45 is several feet higher than those 19th century structures that once stood on Virginius Island!

Indeed, what *were* these people thinking when they erected their mills, factories, shops and homes alongside the Potomac and Shenandoah rivers?

Simply put, waterpower induced millwrights, engineers, and entrepreneurs to build industrial establishments along the rivers. With mills and factories came homes,

---

Footnotes for the Introduction begin on Page 175.

shops, and various other structures typical of an emerging American industrial community. As the primary, and virtually exclusive, power source for industry in the early decades of the 19th century, water was to millwrights and entrepreneurs what oil and gasoline are to Americans today.

These people were clearly aware of the risks they faced from the nearby rivers. Reports of flooding at Harpers Ferry went back as far as 1748, when Robert Harper first settled here, and some early observers seriously questioned the selection of Harpers Ferry as a waterpower site. Among them was Colonel Stephen Rochfontaine, a military engineer commissioned by the War Department to examine sites for a proposed national armory. In 1795, Rochfontaine remarked that "no water work would be safe" where the Potomac and Shenandoah rivers converged due to the potential for flooding.[1]

But the proponents of industry at Harpers Ferry far outnumbered—and their influence outweighed—the site's detractors. George Washington, the principal champion of locating a new federal armory at Harpers Ferry, wrote in 1798 that the site possessed an "inexhaustible supply of water."[2] In 1822, John H. Hall, the New England gunmaker who helped pioneer the manufacture of interchangeable firearm components at Harpers Ferry, wrote that the federal government possessed "an apparent command, at this place, of the waters of two rivers either of which alone, with the fall it has, ought to afford them sufficient [power] to drive all the machinery requisite for the fabrication of more than one hundred thousand stands of arms per year . . . ."[3] And when Fontaine Beckham, proprietor of the Island Mill on Virginius Island, advertised his property for sale in 1832, he wrote:

> The water power is not surpassed by any situation in the country, and a sufficiency may be obtained for almost any eligible purpose. The advantages of this concern, will so completely strike any intelligent observer, that it is needless to enlarge upon them. A man of enterprise cannot fail to turn them to good account.[4]

Indeed, men of enterprise flocked to Harpers Ferry. Lewis Wernwag, Hugh Gilleece, James Giddings, Abraham H. Herr, Jonathan C. Child, John McCreight, Thomas Savery, and many others invested considerable capital and labor to erect and operate waterpowered establishments of all shapes and sizes. At one time or another, there stood on Virginius Island a flour mill, iron foundry, machine shop, sawmill, carriage manufactory, blacksmith shop, cooper shop, and two cotton mills. Along both the Potomac and Shenandoah rivers, the federal government spent tens of thousands of dollars to erect, repair or rebuild Armory workshops, milldams, and power canals. After the Civil War, private entrepreneurs and government engineers continued to champion the use of waterpower at Harpers Ferry.

⌒

In 1880, for the Tenth Census, government engineers conducted a comprehensive survey of waterpower in the eastern United States. Their exhaustive report, published in 1885, documented the topography, geology, stream gradients, and streamflow characteristics at hundreds of millseats where falling water provided a "head" of pressure necessary to place water wheels in motion. One site the report paid particular attention to was Harpers Ferry, describing it as "probably the most favorable one on the [Potomac] river" for the development of water-power.[5]

Situated at the confluence of the Potomac and Shenandoah rivers, Harpers Ferry could tap the flow of two rivers. According to the Census Bureau report, the Potomac River drainage area above Harpers Ferry comprised 6,380 square miles, supplying a streamflow ranging from 575 to 5,740 cubic feet per second, and furnishing from 1,430 to 14,350 potential gross horse-power. Although the Shenandoah River drainage area was considerably smaller—only 2,800 square miles—it nonetheless provided significant streamflow, ranging from 280 to 2,520 cubic feet per second and supplying from 450 to 4,000 potential gross horsepower.

Streamflow numbers told only part of the water-power story at Harpers Ferry, however. More significant for 19th century millwrights, engineers, and entrepreneurs was the "fall" in both rivers occasioned by rapids. The difference in height between supply water in a headrace and waste water leaving a mill's tailrace provided the "head" necessary to put water wheels into motion. On the Potomac immediately upstream from Harpers Ferry, the river descended 22 feet over a distance of about one and a half miles. Along the Shenandoah River, the descent was equally abrupt, dropping 17½ feet per mile over its last two and a half miles from Bull Falls to Harpers Ferry. The fall at Virginius Island alone was 14 feet.

While the Census Bureau report noted the destructive floods of 1870 and 1877, it remarked that flooding along the rivers was not, on average, overly severe. It did, however, caution that "as a water-power stream the principal disadvantage of the Potomac is the great variability of its flow."[6] This "great variability" and consequent unreliability of streamflow was a major factor in the demise of waterpower not only at Harpers Ferry, but all across America during the late 19th and early 20th centuries.

∾

This book explores the legacy of waterpower at Harpers Ferry. From about 1762, when millwright Robert Harper first harnessed the Shenandoah River to power a gristmill and sawmill, to 1991, when the Potomac Power Plant ceased operation, Harpers Ferry witnessed successive applications of mechanical ingenuity for extracting optimum power from falling water. Significantly, the evolution of hydraulic technology at Harpers Ferry mirrored key stages in the development, use, and ultimate decline of waterpower throughout America.

With the establishment of the Harpers Ferry Armory in 1800, five breast-type water wheels were put into operation along the Potomac River. In succeeding decades overshot, undershot, backshot, and tub wheels—virtually every known type of conventional water wheel—were employed at Harpers Ferry. When such well-known 19th century inventors as Uriah A. Boyden, James Leffel, and others introduced innovative turbine designs, local millwrights, plant managers, and entrepreneurs quickly adopted them. The Harpers Ferry Armory was a forerunner in adopting new hydraulic

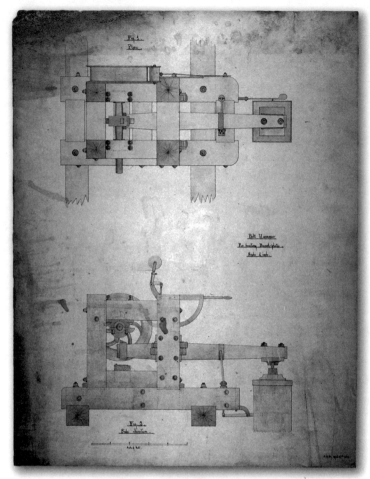

"Belt hammer for bending barrel plates, April 17, 1852." This drawing, signed by James H. Burton, Acting Master Armorer of the Harpers Ferry Armory from 1849-1854, illustrates a trip hammer run off a water-powered belt. On the upper part of the machine is a wheel and a handle or lever to engage and disengage the belt drive. Cogs on the machine gradually raised the hammer and then released it, causing the hammer to drop quickly and with considerable impact into a recessed groove (lower right). Burton Drawings, Harpers Ferry NHP (Catalog No. 13637).

technologies, installing a "Turbine reaction Water Wheel, with Penstock and Cast iron gates" as early as 1845.[7]

Technical innovation and mechanical ingenuity also characterized the local adoption of labor-saving machinery. Thomas Blanchard's "Lathe to Manufacture Gunstocks," Sylvester Nash's lathe for turning musket barrels, John H. Hall's "great" and "small" forging machines, Pearson Crosby's "Sawmill for Resawing Boards and Other Timber," and Charles Danforth's "Cap Spinner" were just a few of the innovative patent machines powered by water at Harpers Ferry.

Technology and innovation were certainly key components of the legacy of waterpower. Also prominent were the myriad problems associated with harnessing rivers for power. Seasonal variations in streamflow interrupted operations, taxing the patience of millwrights and entrepreneurs throughout the age of waterpower. At Harpers Ferry, Armory superintendent James Stubblefield brought the extent of these problems to the attention of his superiors on several occasions. In 1820, for instance, he wrote that the government works had "lost the finishing of at least one thousand Muskets in consequence of the water being so low in the last summer & fall." Just a year later, Stubblefield reported that "the month of January was so extremely cold that our water wheels were frozen-up nearly all the month which prevented our finishing as many Guns as we ought to have done . . . ."[8]

Armory records are also replete with references to poorly-constructed power canals and to mill dams that

Early 20th century view of the Armory Canal (left), Bollman railroad truss, and footbridge to Island Park—a small amusement park and picnic area operated by the Baltimore and Ohio Railroad. The Armory Dam or Potomac Dam is visible upstream from Island Park. Harpers Ferry NHP (HF-76).

leaked badly. Colonel Decius Wadsworth, for instance, informed the Secretary of War in 1817:

> The deficiency of water at Harper's Ferry may be remedied by the building of a new dam across the Potowmac. The present dam was defectively built at first and a considerable annual expense is now incurred to keep it in order.[9]

This book will show, in fact, that deficient waterworks and inadequate streamflow proved to be significant factors in slowing the introduction of water-powered machinery at the Harpers Ferry Armory.

Contentious disputes over riparian rights proved another obstacle to the productive use of waterpower. Such disputes, and the considerable litigation they spawned, were a product of English common-law doctrine which specified that ownership of a water privilege went with the land bordering *both* sides of a stream or river. Ownership did not extend to the river itself, but only conveyed rights of usage, called riparian rights. This usage was subject to the rights and claims of other users both upstream and downstream of a particular "mill-seat" or "water privilege."[10]

At Harpers Ferry, riparian disputes often resulted from conflicting deeds, bureaucratic oversight or from the simple fact that, during periods of drought, there just wasn't enough water to go around. In 1832, for instance, an Armory clerk informed John H. Hall that he could not "discover any record of any conveyance of a right to the United States, to use the water power of the Shenandoah river among the record of this county."[11] Since mechanical innovations being developed at Hall's Rifle Works depended to a large degree upon efficient application of waterpower, the matter consumed the attention of Hall, Ordnance Department officers, and government lawyers for eight months, until proper water privileges were finally acquired for a sum of $2,600. Legal fees incurred both by the federal government and private entrepreneurs just to establish clear title to riparian land at Harpers Ferry consumed considerable capital during both the 19th and 20th centuries.

∾

The Census Bureau's 1885 waterpower report was significant in the context of the changing industrial landscape. By the 1870 Census—the first federal census to enumerate power used in manufacturing by kind and amount—steam power had surpassed waterpower, accounting for slightly more than 50 percent of the total power used in manufacturing. Nationally, waterpower usage declined to just 21 percent in 1889, 15 percent in 1899, and 11 percent by 1909.[12]

However, the very size and scope of the 1885 waterpower report, and the expense and manpower evidenced in its production, indicate the important role waterpower continued to play in American industrial thinking. Even as steam power was rapidly surpassing waterpower as the prime mover of American industry, "the deeply rooted belief that manufactures and water-power were inseparable companions was slow to yield."[13] All across America considerable interest, attention, and entrepreneurial capital remained devoted to the contin-ued application and improvement of hydraulic technol-ogy. Nowhere was this clearer than at Harpers Ferry, where the community's deep-rooted relationship with the rivers kept attention squarely focused on waterpower well into the 20th century.

With the burgeoning of America's steam age in the second half of the 19th century, industry's dependence upon waterpower quickly diminished. While the inherent limitations of waterpower had always been apparent, they became far less tolerable as manufacturing took on a larger and increasingly commercial complexion. The growing interdependence of America's market economy, spurred earlier in the century by the advent of the transportation revolution, had raised the competitive stakes enormously. With the arrival of canal and rail-road, industrial production for local consumption had given way to manufacturing for sale in regional and national markets. Steam-powered factories adhered to a predictable schedule of mechanical operations, and could increase horsepower output simply by adding more engines and boilers or burning more fossil fuel. Because waterpower provided no such benefits, steam engines ultimately revealed the fatal flaws of streamflow dependency for industrial production.[14]

The persistent reliance on waterpower at Harpers Ferry, and the community's reluctance to depart from decades of industrial tradition, began to take a toll. While the power demands of larger and more complex machines continued to grow, the flow of the Potomac and Shenandoah rivers became even more erratic in the decades following the Civil War. That workers were idled by extended periods of drought was nothing new—but the impact periodic shutdowns had on a company's ability to compete in the new commercial marketplace was devastating.

At the other extreme, the pattern and severity of flooding clearly changed for the worse with the precipitous reduction in forest cover across the Potomac and Shenandoah watersheds during the middle of the 19th century. Land cleared for agriculture and trees cut to fuel iron furnaces and blacksmith forges were the principal culprits. By about 1870, forest cover across the region had been reduced to just 40 percent, compared to an estimated 85 percent forest cover in 1750.[15]

Harpers Ferry resident and chronicler Joseph Barry recognized this in 1903, when he wrote:

> Since the [Civil] war these inundations are more frequent and far more injurious . . . because of the wholesale destruction of the forests for the use of the armies . . . and for mercantile purposes.[16]

Although the watersheds have recovered in the present century to approximately 60 percent forest cover, flooding still poses a considerable threat to historic

Virginius Island is inundated by the record Flood of 1889. The rooftop of the Shenandoah Pulp Company is just barely visible in the upper right corner of the photograph. Harpers Ferry NHP (HF-0611).

ruins and 19th century buildings in Harpers Ferry National Historical Park.

❧

Harpers Ferry provides an important connection to America's waterpower past. For more than two centuries the pace of industry, accumulation of capital, and vitality of this community were bound to, and determined by, the flow of the Potomac and Shenandoah rivers. Perhaps nowhere else in America is the historical relationship between man, machine, and river quite so apparent. The pages that follow will document the evolution of hydraulic technology at Harpers Ferry, and explain how local events mirrored the development, use, and ultimate decline of waterpower throughout America.

Flood-battered mill dam ruins, rusting iron, abandoned power canals, and crumbling stone foundations now preserved within Harpers Ferry National Historical Park illuminate the connection between past and present. But the waters of the Potomac and Shenandoah rivers, never more distant than a few hundred feet and still as unpredictable as ever, provide the strongest link to the past. For those who make this connection, there comes a better understanding of the millwrights and entrepreneurs who came before us, of the innovative technologies they developed and embraced, and of the powerful role the rivers played in their everyday lives. ❧

Trash rack remains at the Potomac Power Plant. Racks like this helped catch sticks, branches, and other floating debris before they could reach a turbine and damage its runner vanes. They did not always work, however. According to a General Manager's Report of the Harpers Ferry Paper Company dated Dec. 28, 1921, a small stick of pulp wood found its way into #3 Flume, wedged into the upstream runner, and tore out several buckets. April 1995 photo by the author.

CHAPTER 1
COMMUNITY ENTERPRISE IN RURAL AMERICA
1762-1800

To the farmers in Maryland and over the Blue Ridge in Loudoun County. This is to certify that all persons bringing grist to my mill, under the charge of William Griffith, will be ferried over the Potomac and Shenandoah rivers free of expense.

—public notice attributed to Robert Harper

TWO OF THE MORE NOTABLE VISITORS TO HARPERS FERRY in the 18th century were Thomas Jefferson and George Washington. Jefferson's visit is best remembered for the eloquent words in his *Notes on the State of Virginia*, in which he declared that "the passage of the Patowmac through the Blue Ridge is perhaps one of the most stupendous scenes in Nature." Jefferson had long championed pastoral ideals as the foundation for the economic and political institutions of Colonial America. He traveled widely across the Virginia countryside, filling his notebooks with idyllic descriptions of the land's rustic beauty, often espousing agrarian values over the "depravity" of industrial civilization.[1] High above Lower Town, a rock where Jefferson obtained his celebrated view of Harpers Ferry on October 25, 1783, still bears his name.

Washington had more pressing business during his visit of August 7 and 8, 1785. As president of the newly formed Patowmack Company, he was conducting a tour "to inspect minutely the course of the Potomac from Georgetown to Harper's Ferry, and ascertain in what places and to what extent it was necessary to construct canals and remove obstructions in the river."[2] Although their motives differed, the words and actions of both men clearly show that the rivers dominated the landscape at Harpers Ferry from a very early date.

While Washington and Jefferson were perhaps its most celebrated visitors, decades earlier Robert Harper quite literally put Harpers Ferry on the map. Harper, an accomplished builder and millwright, was born in Oxford Township near Philadelphia in 1718. Among his many successful projects was Burly's Mill in Frankfort, Pennsylvania. But when he attempted to build the New Oxford Church "on his own account," he became financially overextended. Embarrassed and evidently bankrupt, Harper was making plans to leave for the Carolinas in 1747 when he met several members of the Society of Friends who were attending a meeting in Philadelphia. Learning of his skills as a builder and millwright, the group engaged Harper to erect a meeting house on Opequon Creek near the present site of Winchester, Virginia.[3]

Footnotes for Chapter 1 begin on Page 175.

Traveling to the Shenandoah Valley through Maryland, Harper was persuaded by a German trader to forego the wagon road which crossed the Potomac River at Pack Horse Ford near present-day Shepherdstown, and instead take a more direct route through "The Hole" where the Potomac and Shenandoah rivers converged. Here, Harper met Peter Stephens, a trapper and trader who had been living at the place for 13 years. Harper "was so astonished at the grand scenery and the unsurpassed water power that he decided to make it his future home."[4]

The natural beauty of the place was surely as impressive to Robert Harper in 1747 as it would be to Jefferson in 1783. But first and foremost, Harper was a practical man whose entrepreneurial skills had been sorely tested during his years in Philadelphia. Already a seasoned builder and millwright at age 29, Harper recognized the power he could tap from the falling waters of the Potomac and Shenandoah rivers. He also found nearby stone and mature timber for building material.

Harper purchased Stephens' log cabin, corn patch, and ferry equipment in 1747 for a reported sum of 50 British guineas. As for the land, Stephens had enjoyed only the precarious tenure of squatter's rights. Ownership was vested in Lord Fairfax, Proprietor of Virginia's "Northern Neck." This vast holding, "bounded by and within the heads" of the Potomac and Rappahannock rivers, comprised more than five million acres of land. The grant had originally been set aside by Charles I of England in 1649. In 1688, Lord Culpeper obtained title to the land and in 1736, his grandson Thomas, the sixth Lord Fairfax, came to America to claim the property.

Harper obtained a patent from Fairfax in 1751 for 125 acres of "waste and ungranted land" at the junction of the Potomac and Shenandoah rivers. Eleven years later, in 1762, Harper acquired 92 additional acres adjoining his previous patent. An act of the Virginia General Assembly established "Shenandoah Falls at Mr. Harper's Ferry" the following year. During this period, Harper also completed the structure he had promised the Quakers, obtained exclusive rights to establish and maintain a ferry across the Potomac River, and began erecting mills of his own along the Shenandoah River.[5]

❧

Harpers Ferry in 1763 was considered a "mill-seat" or "water privilege"—a site alongside a river "where an abrupt descent in the streambed, a succession of lesser falls, or an extended rapids offered a concentration of fall favorable to power development."[6] The irregularities in geological formation that created the rapids of the Potomac and Shenandoah rivers here resulted from natural processes acting over millions of years.

At the dawn of the Paleozoic Era, 600 million years ago, a great depression in the earth's crust—the Appalachian geosyncline—extended from Alabama north to Newfoundland. A broad, shallow sea spread across this trough. Here erosional debris from ancient land masses slowly gathered; sediments accumulated in layers several thousand feet deep, and were compacted and cemented into sedimentary rocks. Sand particles became sandstone, clay and silt combined to form shale, and the decaying remains of plants and animals—corals, sponges, trilobites, and brachiopods—lithified into limestone.

Ledges of Harpers shale *cut across the Potomac River just upstream from Harpers Ferry. George Washington called these rapids the "Shannandoah Falls" in August 1785. Today they are commonly called "The Needles." October 1978 photo by the author.*

Toward the close of the Paleozoic Era, about 230 million years ago, tremendous pressure exerted from the southeast drove the earth's crust westward, compressing the strata of the Appalachian geosyncline into parallel faults and folds. Along the eastern edge of the geosyncline, in an area extending north-south from Pennsylvania to Virginia, this "Appalachian Revolution" forced up an immense fold in the earth's crust called the South Mountain anticlinorium. South Mountain, Short Hill Mountain, Maryland Heights, Loudoun Heights, and Bolivar Heights are all second-order folds within this massive formation (*see map on pages 6-7*).

The tremendous forces that created the South Mountain anticlinorium also subjected the rock strata to intense heat and pressure. Sedimentary rocks were metamorphosed, their internal structure being altered or altogether changed. In the Harpers Ferry area, sandstone became quartzite (*Weverton quartzite*) and shale became a schist, slate or phyllite (*Harpers shale*). These two formations, which have been tilted up on end and dip steeply to the east, meet at the confluence of the Potomac and Shenandoah rivers. The belt of *Weverton quartzite*, which extends downstream from Harpers Ferry, varies from 200-300 feet thick. The belt of *Harpers shale* is about 2,000 feet thick and extends westward up the Potomac and Shenandoah rivers.

The actual formation of the present-day streambeds and rapids didn't begin until about 70 million years ago, when cycles of uplift and erosion commenced. River valleys were now cut into the mountain ridges, and the rapids in and around Harpers Ferry began to form as the Potomac and Shenandoah rivers slowly cut a path through the thick beds of *Weverton quartzite* and *Harpers shale.* Thomas Jefferson recognized this long process when he wrote in his *Notes on the State of Virginia:*

> The passage of the Patowmac through the Blue Ridge is perhaps one of the most stupendous scenes in Nature. You stand on a very high point of land. On your right comes up the Shenandoah, having ranged along the foot of the mountain a hundred miles to seek a vent. On your left approaches the Patowmac in quest of a passage also. In the moment of their junction they rush together against the mountain, rend it asunder and pass off to the sea. The first glance of this scene hurries our senses into the opinion that this earth has been created in time, that the mountains were formed first, that the rivers began to flow afterwards . . .[7]

Geology and streamflow, however, were only part of the waterpower equation. While the concentration of fall produced by geological irregularities greatly simplified

---

These steeply tilted layers of Harpers shale *are exposed along the banks of the Potomac River near Harpers Ferry. May 1978 photo by the author.*

the capture and diversion of streamflow, skill and ingenuity were required to harness the available power. It was a millwright's job to calculate the average volume of streamflow and working "head" occasioned by the breaks or rapids in the riverbed, then match these calculations to an appropriately sized water wheel. Wheel type, width, diameter, and rotating speeds largely determined the effectiveness and economy of a particular water mill. Also important was the design and construction of mill dams and power canals used to divert and deliver water to the wheel. In addressing these concerns, millwrights applied knowledge acquired from experience or consulted millwright handbooks such as *The Young Mill-wright and Miller's Guide* by Oliver Evans, first published in 1795.[8]

No physical remains and few written details of Robert Harper's first mills have survived. Typical of early settlements in America's expanding frontier, Harper erected a sawmill to convert logs into lumber and a gristmill to grind wheat into flour. These mills were small, serving the needs of the local community on a toll-exchange or limited commercial basis. "Toll" might vary from 15-20 percent of the wheat, corn or rye ground at the gristmill. For lumber the operator might keep every third log brought to the sawmill.

Timber was particularly important in frontier America. Into the early 19th century, "wood was not only the basic material of frame dwellings but the most important of all fabricating materials for domestic, agricultural, and industrial purposes."[9] Although building stone was available near Harpers Ferry, the cost to quarry and transport this material was very high, and

Over a series of ledges once known as Sawmill Falls, and now called The Staircase, the Shenandoah River drops 14 feet in just under a mile. These rapids powered mills and factories on Virginius Island (left shore) for almost two centuries. October 1980 photo by the author.

there were few experienced stone masons. Harper's sawmill, and probably his gristmill as well, were constructed of wood.[10]

Harper's two mills were situated on land he acquired from Lord Fairfax in 1762 along the Shenandoah River; both structures were probably built a short time later. The sawmill stood on the present site of the Shenandoah Pulp Company ruins (*see **Virginius Island, 1861** map on pages 110-111*). Here Harper was able to develop a head of about 10 feet by constructing a headrace from "Sawmill Falls" on the Shenandoah River. There is no evidence that a milldam was ever built or that Harper ever obtained riparian rights to this site.[11]

Harper died on October 21, 1782. He bequeathed both mills to his nephew, Robert Griffith. He also left instructions for his niece, Sarah Harper (to whom he had bequeathed his Ferry and much of his land) to provide free passage for "every person or persons who shall bring with them grist of any kind to the Mills on the lands now belonging to me."[12]

The sawmill was subsequently sold to the federal government on February 20, 1797, as part of the land purchased for the United States Armory. This mill probably produced lumber used in the construction of the new armory workshops along the Potomac River. Between 1806-1807, the sawmill was dismantled when the lower locks of the Patowmack Company's Shenandoah River bypass canal were erected. The fate of Harper's gristmill is not known.[13]

There is no evidence of any commercial milling operations at Harpers Ferry for two decades following the government's 1797 land purchases. Rather, neighboring mills appear to have served the local community. One was Shepherd's Mill, erected between 1734 and 1739 at the present site of

George Washington. Harpers Ferry NHP (HF-1388).

Shepherdstown, ten miles upstream from Harpers Ferry. Another was a gristmill at the mouth of Israel Creek, established in 1774 about three miles downstream from Harpers Ferry at the present site of Weverton. Dozens of smaller mills sprang up along the many nearby tributaries of the Potomac River, including the Shenandoah River, Antietam Creek, Opequon Creek, and Elk Run. Although small in scale and oriented primarily to milling for local needs, improved transportation along the Potomac River extended the range of these community mills.

Increased commerce along the Potomac River was a product of improvements completed by the Patowmack Company in the late 18th and early 19th centuries. Chartered by the state legislatures of Maryland and Virginia in 1784, the Patowmack Company was formed to improve navigation on the Potomac River and its principal tributaries. Engineers were authorized to deepen existing river channels and to construct short bypass canals around impassable river rapids in order to permit boats drawing 12 inches of water and carrying 50 barrels of flour to pass on a year-round basis.

Most of the river improvements in the Harpers Ferry area resulted directly from George Washington's personal inspection of the rapids here on August 7-8, 1785. On Sunday, August 7th, Washington wrote in his diary:

About Sunrising, the Directors & myself rid up to Keeptrieste, where Canoes were provided, in which we crossed to the Maryland side of the river and examined a Gut, or swash through which it is supposed the Navigation must be conducted. This Swash is shallow at the entrance, but having sufficient fall, may easily (by removing some of the rocks) admit any quantity of water required. From the entrance to the foot, may be about 300 yards in a semicircular direction with many loose, & some fixed rocks to remove. Having examined this passage, I returned to the head of the Falls, and in one of the Canoes with two skilful hands descended them with the common Currt. In its Natural bed—which I found greatly incommoded with rocks, shallows and a crooked Channel which left no doubt of the propriety of preferring a passage through the Swash.[14]

Washington and his party, joined at Harpers Ferry by James Rumsey (the Patowmack Company's first superintendent), continued down the river to the present site of Knoxville Falls, a distance of about three miles. Here Washington and the Directors

held a meeting—At which it was determined, as we conceived the Navigation could be made through these (commonly called the Shannan-

doah) Falls without the aid of Locks, and by opening them would give eclat to the undertaking and great ease to the upper Inhabitants as Water transportation would be immediately had to the Great Falls from Fort Cumberland . . .[15]

Following Washington's tour, the Patowmack Company kept crews at work for the next several years excavating the "Long Canal"—a 1,760-yard bypass canal around Shenandoah Falls. A shorter passage of about 50 yards was cleared through House's Falls just downstream. About a half mile below Harpers Ferry, obstructions were cleared from two short canals at Payne's Falls. Work on these projects was finally completed in about 1792. None of these improvements originally possessed either lift locks or lock gates.

An 1803 report to Patowmack Company stockholders described the principal river improvements at Harpers Ferry:

The navigation is then good to the head of the long canal at the beginning of the Shenandoah Falls; the entrance to this canal is somewhat difficult in high water, it may be rendered safer by extending an abutment into the river on the lower side to prevent the strong draft of water just without the present entrance. The current is very strong through the canal, but with care safe to descend. The ascent is very laborious, but is much facilitated by a substantial wall and tracking way when ropes can be used to great advantage. About half a mile below the Ferry are two short canals (called by the boatmen—The Bull ring falls) taken together with a short sheet of smooth water between them, the distance may be one quarter of a mile, the fall is 6.6 feet . . . . The fall from the head of Shenandoah Falls to the landing at Harper's Ferry is 26.75 feet.[16]

The boats then common on the Potomac River were variously called "batteaux," "gondolas," or "sharpers." They were described as being approximately 50-75 feet long, 5-10 feet wide, and capable of carrying from 70-120 barrels of flour. Other commercial cargoes included grain, lumber, pig iron, whiskey, and occasionally even livestock. While limited in use by the seasonal fluctuations in water level, these river craft nonetheless began to open up new markets to rural entrepreneurs.

In the coming decades small rural mills up and down the Potomac River, which had traditionally served the limited needs of their local communities on a custom-toll or barter-exchange basis, began to give way to larger commercial establishments which produced goods for a regional market. The added power requirements and concentration of transportation facilities made necessary by this emerging market economy forced entrepreneurs to pick their millsites carefully.

In the early 19th century, several entrepreneurs focused their attention on Harpers Ferry. Not only did this site apparently possess an "inexhaustible supply of water," nearby stone for building material, and convenient access to river transport, but the place now hosted a United States Armory—creating almost overnight considerable demand for commercial goods. ◈

CHAPTER 2
FOUNDATIONS OF INDUSTRY
1800-1840

This manufactory has been carried to a greater degree of perfection, as regards the quality of work and uniformity of parts than is to be found elsewhere—almost everything is performed by machinery, leaving very little dependent on manual labor.

—Col. George Talcott on Hall's Rifle Works, December 15, 1832

THE INDUSTRIAL AGE DAWNED AT HARPERS FERRY with the establishment of the Armory. The manufacture of firearms spawned technological innovations which would transform the United States from an infant democracy into a worldwide industrial leader.

During the early decades of the 19th century, the American firearms industry experienced a gradual but remarkable transition from a craft-based to factory-based production system. The traditional skills of an individual craftsman, who was able to fashion a complete gunstock or forge and assemble all the components of a single musket lock, were less and less suited to the economic and technical requirements of large-scale firearms production. Discrepancies in fit, finish, and quality between different firearm manufactories, and even between firearms produced at the same manufactory, created considerable problems for field commanders who needed replacement parts for broken or damaged weapons. Equally unacceptable were the staggering costs associated with producing large numbers of weapons solely by traditional hand-tool methods.

The War Department became a strong advocate of the "uniformity principle" of manufacturing, and the national armories at both Harpers Ferry and Springfield became instrumental in developing what the British later called "the American system of manufactures." This "system" made use of special-purpose machines to produce parts so accurately sized that they were interchangeable. By integrating skilled labor and precision machinery into a series of sequential operations, these manufactories were able to attain a level of mechanization and uniform production that would become the core of America's emerging factory system.

At the Harpers Ferry Armory, the dexterous use of hand tools gradually gave way to the adoption of precision machines powered by water. The barrel lathe of Sylvester Nash, the stocking machines of Thomas Blanchard, and the special-purpose stocking, forging, and cutting machines of John H. Hall were key components of this transformation. Also critical was the application of waterpower to the manufacturing process.

Footnotes for Chapter 2 begin on Page 177.

THE HARPERS FERRY ARMORY

In May 1799, construction commenced on the "United States Armory & Arsenal at Harpers Ferry." This new government manufactory was the result of a bill approved by Congress in 1794 "for the erecting and repairing of Arsenals and Magazines." Springfield, Mass., was selected as the site for the first national armory. President George Washington, who was given wide discretionary powers in executing the legislation, then chose Harpers Ferry as the site for a second national armory.

In championing the Harpers Ferry location, Washington was drawing upon first-hand knowledge he had obtained during his personal inspection of the Potomac River on August 7-8, 1785. On September 28, 1795, he wrote Secretary of War James McHenry that the site "affords every advantage that could be wished for water works to any extent."[1] Over the objections of the War Department, which favored expanding existing establishments rather that constructing a single new one, and Colonel Stephen Rochfontaine, a military engineer who claimed that "no water work would be safe" from exposure to floods, Washington's view prevailed. On June 15, 1796, the government acquired 118 acres from John Wager, Sr. and his late wife, Sarah Harper Wager—heirs to the estate of Robert Harper—which included much of the land along the Potomac River. The following year, on February 20, 1797, the government purchased another 310 acres which included Harper's old sawmill site along the Shenandoah River.

On August 6, 1798, Secretary of War McHenry instructed Joseph Perkin, the Armory's first superintendent, to conduct a preliminary survey of the "Waters and grounds for erecting the necessary buildings and works for the establishment of an Armoury."[2] Perkin, with the able assistance of James Brindley, a noted engineer who had visited Harpers Ferry in 1786 as a consultant to the Patowmack Company, concluded that the most promising spot for waterworks lay along the Potomac shoreline. The fall of the Potomac River from the head of Shenandoah Falls to the boat landing at Harpers Ferry, as measured by Patowmack Company engineers, was 26.75 feet. This compared favorably with the fall of the Shenandoah River from the head of Sawmill Falls, which totaled just 14 feet. The average flow of the Potomac was also about twice that of the Shenandoah at Harpers Ferry.[3]

These rapids below Bull Falls on the Shenandoah River were the site of Strider's Mill Dam, one of several 19th century dams built near Harpers Ferry to divert streamflow into millraces for the development of waterpower. October 1994 photo by the author.

"Junction of the Potomac and Shenandoah, Virginia." This 1803 print shows the new government arsenal, Potomac Ferry, and a gundalow descending the Shenandoah River (far right). Twenty years earlier, in 1783, Thomas Jefferson had declared that this scene was "worth a voyage across the Atlantic." Harpers Ferry NHP (HF-21).

On December 26, 1799, the first Armory workshops were completed. The Smith Shop, which measured 80 feet by 26 feet, contained ten forges on the first floor, each with its own chimney, and a workshop for filers on the second floor. The Factory, measuring 120 feet by 26 feet, served as a finishing shop with boring, grinding, and polishing machines on the first floor. Benches for lock filers and stockers were located on the second floor. A Mill for heavy forging was completed a year later. This workshop contained a tilt-hammer for working iron and three or four forges for welding gun barrels by hand. This tilt-hammer, and the boring, grinding, and polishing machines in the Factory, were powered by five breast-type water wheels:

I Tilt-Hammer Wheel (8-foot-wide)
I Bellow Wheel for Tilt-Hammer (2-foot wide)
I Boring Wheel (3-foot-wide)
I Grinding Polish Wheel (6-foot-wide)
I Smith Forge Wheel (2-foot-wide)

Total wheel width available to convey power to these various arms-making machines was 21 feet, with a fall of 12 feet "clear of Floods."[4]

Breast wheels were a widely used adaptation of the conventional overshot water wheel (*see illustrations on opposite page*). While construction of the two wheels was virtually the same, the position of the buckets on the breast wheel and the direction of rotation were reversed. Another important difference was that headwater was admitted to the breast wheel's upstream side. The wheel, which possessed deep bucket or troughs, was turned both by the weight of the water carried in the buckets and the impulse of the water striking the wheel. A tight-fitting apron, or "breast," helped prevent water from leaving the buckets prematurely, thus increasing the effect of gravity upon the wheel. Since water passing under the breast wheel traveled a shorter distance than water traveling over an overshot wheel, millwrights also learned that more power could be obtained by making breast wheels wider than overshot wheels in proportion to their diameter.

In addition to wheel diameter and width, an important design consideration in a breast wheel was the "tangential direction" in which headwater was admitted into the buckets. *The Young Mill-wright and Miller's Guide*, one of the 19th century's most popular millwright handbooks, stressed the importance of properly attending to this arrangement, stating:

> if the buckets and the direction of the shute be right, the wheel will receive the water well, and move to the best advantage, keeping a steady, regular motion when at work . . . .[5]

Depending upon the physical characteristics and operating circumstances of a particular millseat, millwrights could admit water onto a breast wheel at various heights, from a level slightly below the wheel shaft (*low breast wheel*) to a level near the top (*high breast wheel*)—and anywhere in between (*middling breast wheel*).

For Armory managers at Harpers Ferry, breast wheels possessed several operating advantages lacking in overshot wheels. First, since headwater did not have to be carried over the wheel's top, breast wheel diameters much greater that the height of the fall were possible. This permitted higher operating speeds: for a head and fall of 12 feet, a breast wheel 15 feet in diameter made almost 18 revolutions per minute; by comparison, an overshot wheel 10 feet in diameter operating under the same head and fall made just 13 revolutions per minute. Since the Armory's forge hammers, grinding wheels, and other arms-making equipment exerted widely varying loads as workmen either engaged or disengaged them, high wheel speeds helped maintain steady, regular motion.[6]

A second advantage of the breast wheel was its adaptability to changes in water level resulting from seasonal and short-term variations in streamflow. Whereas overshot wheels accepted headwater only at their very top, the height at which headwater was admitted onto breast wheels could be adjusted up or down. While low water often impaired a breast wheel's efficiency, it was not necessary to shut the wheel down. As we shall shortly see, wide variations in streamflow characterized the Potomac River.

A third advantage of the breast wheel was its ability to operate in backwater—a common occurrence caused by river water backing up into the tailrace. Since the lower half of the breast wheel rotated with, rather than against, the current in the tailrace, the wheel was still able to operate, albeit again at reduced efficiency. Overshot wheels proved useless under similar circumstances.

Before the common use of iron in construction, all water wheels shared an important disadvantage—

Illustration, from top to bottom, of a low, middle, and high breast wheel, from The Young Mill-wright and Miller's Guide, *by Oliver Evans (eighth edition, 1834). Courtesy National Park Service, National Capital Parks, Washington, D.C.*

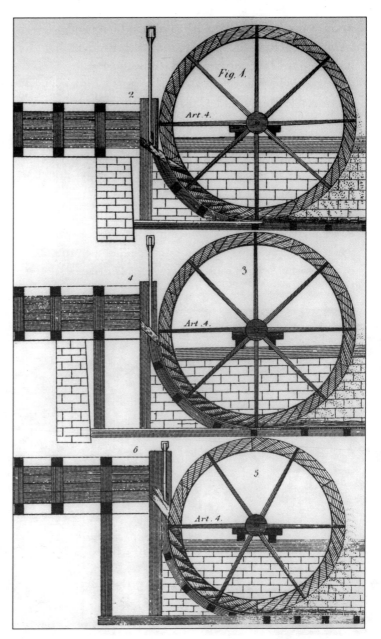

wooden water wheel components required frequent repair or replacement. In 1825, the superintendent of the Springfield Armory reported that wooden water wheels would not last more than eight years without considerable repairs, adding that "with constant expense they may be kept along with frequent interruptions two or three years longer."[7]

Problems with the water wheels at Harpers Ferry were typical of the problems faced by 19th century millwrights everywhere. On October 20, 1820, Armory superintendent James Stubblefield informed the Ordnance Department that in "the month of Sept our water wheel in the polishing Mill gave way & I had then to put in a new wheel which caused a considerable delay . . . ."

Nine years later, in 1829, Gen. John E. Wool reported that the Armory's "water wheels and fixtures are in a state of decay, and new ones should be substituted as soon as practicable."[8]

When Chief of Ordnance George Bomford requested funds from Congress for three new water wheels in 1833, he wrote:

> The water-wheels and machinery (generally) are so much worn and decayed as to require very frequent repairs . . . the loss of time sustained by the workmen for the want of the necessary power to propel the machinery causes the cost in fabricating some of the component parts of the musket to be much greater than it would be were the machinery improved and sufficient power acquired to drive all the requisite machinery at the lowest stage of the waters.[9]

Freezing weather also posed operational problems for millwrights. Because water wheels generated so much dampness, they were often located outside of the mills and factories they served. At the Harpers Ferry Armory, all of the original breast wheels were placed outdoors, with some predictable consequences. On February 13, 1817, Stubblefield advised the

A discarded oak wheel shaft slowly rots away at the Burwell-Morgan Gristmill in Millwood, Virginia. Wooden water wheel components like this required constant care and attention from 19th century millwrights. September 1981 photo by the author.

Ordnance Department that, "Owing to extreme cold weather which has stopped our water works for the last four weeks, we have not been able to complete the Rifle & Musket." The story was the same in 1821, when Stubblefield wrote that the "month of January was so extremely cold that our water wheels were frozen-up nearly all the month which prevented our finishing as many Guns as we ought to have done . . . ." These problems were rectified in 1822, when three sheds were erected over the principal water wheels and furnished with stoves for heat.[10]

Shaft and spokes of a typical 19th century wooden water wheel. This particular wheel still operates at the Colvin Run Mill near Dranesville, Virginia. May 1982 photo by the author.

Construction of the Armory dam and canal did not fare nearly as well as work on the Armory workshops. James Brindley had commenced construction on the Potomac Dam on August 9, 1799. But only a portion of the masonry structure was completed when Brindley left Harpers Ferry on October 22—the terms of his service to the War Department having apparently been fulfilled. By December 1799, John Mackey, the Armory paymaster, reported that only a third of the dam was complete. Progress on the Armory Canal, for which Mackey had assumed personal responsibility, was even slower. Only a quarter of the 1½-mile-long millrace had been excavated. On April 22, 1800, Samuel Annin replaced Mackey as the new Armory paymaster. Construction resumed with vigor in May 1800, but canal and dam were still not finished until May 1801.

At last, the Armory's five breast wheels began to turn, and forging, grinding, boring, and polishing operations were able to commence. But the canal, it was found, leaked so badly that very little heavy work could be performed on gun barrels and other iron components. Just three months after the dam and canal were completed, the War Department wrote Armory paymaster Samuel Annin:

> I am directed by the acting Secretary to inform you, that it is represented, that the works at Harpers Ferry are much impeded in their progress by the leakings of the Canal, and that proper attention to a remedy is not paid.[11]

What immediate measures Annin took are not known, but eight years later, in 1809, he "was obliged to attend to the building of a very extensive dam on the Potomac to furnish a sufficient quantity of water to the works at all times, the old dam having failed!"[12]

Problems persisted even after extensive repair and reconstruction of both dam and canal. Writing to the Secretary of War in 1817, Col. Decius Wadsworth reported that the Harpers Ferry Armory labored under "a deficiency of water at some season of the year," and that the "present dam was defectively built at first and a considerable annual expense is now incurred to keep it in order."[13]

Insufficient streamflow on the Potomac River compounded problems with the dam and canal. During the summer and fall of 1819, the Armory "lost the finishing of at least one thousand Muskets in consequence of the water being so low." Idled workmen had to be assigned to other jobs that did not rely on waterpower, resulting in fewer arms produced for the same expense of labor. The following summer proved no better, and workmen were forced "to keep the Machinery running day and night" just to meet their allotted output.[14]

A new dam erected between 1820 and 1821, and described by Armory superintendent James Stubblefield as "the most substantial in the country and possibly even the whole world," did little to alleviate the Armory's water supply problems. A "scarcity of water" during the summer of 1822 and an "excessive drought" in August 1825 curtailed Armory production by as much as 50 percent.[15]

Remarkably, ever since the original Armory Dam was completed in 1801, water had been permitted to flow freely through the Patowmack Company's "Long Canal" along the Maryland shoreline. Stubblefield had "often been compelled during the summer season to make a temporary dam in this canal" just to secure enough water for the Armory workshops. This solution, however, proved ineffective as boatmen passing through the canal simply removed the temporary blockage. In 1826, Stubblefield finally sought permission to fix a permanent "lock gate in the Canal on the opposite side of the river." By a resolution of the Patowmack Company's Board of Directors, permission for the lock gate was granted on June 22, 1826.[16]

The scarcity of water in the Potomac River, however, apparently continued. So, too, did criticism from the War Department. In a confidential report on the Harpers Ferry Armory submitted on November 16, 1827, Gen. John E. Wool wrote:

> The Canal through which the water is conveyed to the shops, is too small for its length, consequently, when the water is low the works are suspended at intervals for the want of a supply of water to propel the Machinery. This deficiency ought to be remedied, but it will cost some thousands of dollars.[17]

Armory managers responded by spending over $10,000 between 1828-1829 to rebuild the Armory Dam and thoroughly repair the Armory Canal. The new dam, erected by Lewis Wernwag, was comprised of a timber framework fastened together with iron and "filled in with stone in such a manner as to render it tight and permanent." Freshets in 1831, however, washed away "a considerable portion of the dam," and by July 1832 more funds were being sought to repair the structure.[18]

Also in 1832, the Chesapeake & Ohio Canal Company obtained temporary permission from the

A canal boat passes through Inlet Lock No. 3 on the Chesapeake & Ohio Canal in this circa 1900 photo. The mule crossover bridge in the distance was located along the main channel of the canal. Boats passed through this lock into the Potomac River immediately upstream from the Armory Dam to make deliveries of coal, lumber, and other supplies to the Harpers Ferry Armory. Chesapeake & Ohio NHP (EODC 116-27).

government to use water from the Armory Dam, and a head gate or inlet lock was constructed on the Maryland side of the dam. The C&O Canal, unlike the Patowmack Canal which it replaced, was an artificial waterway situated within a man-made canal bed. Construction had begun on July 4, 1828, near Washington, D.C. In November 1833, the canal reached the Maryland shore just across the Potomac River from Harpers Ferry. An inlet lock opposite the mouth of the Shenandoah River, commonly called the Shenandoah River Lock, permitted boats taking on goods at Harpers Ferry or traveling down the Shenandoah River navigation system to enter the C&O Canal and continue downstream to the nation's capital.

The inlet lock adjacent to the Armory Dam, about 1½ miles upstream from the Shenandoah River Lock, furnished the C&O Canal with water downstream to Seneca, Maryland, a distance of 42 miles. Although further diminishing the water supply available to the Harpers Ferry Armory, the government favored this arrangement over the Canal Company's plan to build their own dam immediately downstream from Harpers Ferry. Such a dam, John H. Hall declared in July 1832, would impede manufacturing operations with backwater, putting the Armory grinding mill "out of business" with a rise in the river of just two feet.[19]

George Rust, Jr., also feared that, should the proposed dam be built, the Canal Company would abandon the common practice by which boats and rafts made deliveries to the Armory via the Armory Canal:

> At present the coal and lumber brought down the Potomac for this Armory passes into the canal that supplies the works with water, from the banks of which they are removed, with but little expense into the coal house & lumber yard.[20]

According to Rust, having supplies unloaded at the downstream end of the Armory grounds would add "considerable expense" in labor required to move deliveries to the coal house and lumber yard.

Due to a lack of funds, plans for the Canal Company's dam were eventually dropped. In 1833, the government spent $5,000 to make the Armory Dam "higher, more extended, and more perfect in all respects than it has hitherto been." Despite joint use of the dam by both the U.S. Government and the C&O Canal Company, however, no record exists of a permanent arrangement between the two parties.[21]

The Armory Canal too received a thorough upgrade between 1833 and 1835. Claiming that "the present canal has never been sufficiently wide to admit an abundant supply of water for the works," the Ordnance Department obtained more than $13,000 to enlarge the raceway and erect a new wall and embankment along most of its length. When completed, the new canal was 20 feet wide and paved with a one-foot-thick stone lining.[22]

Yet as fast as these Armory waterworks were repaired or rebuilt, ice and springtime floodwaters continued to take their toll. Even more challenging for government engineers was how to meet the increasing power demands of the rapidly expanding Armory.

∽

In the early 1800s, musket manufacture at the Harpers Ferry Armory was divided into four basic categories: lock, mounting, stock, and barrel.

The lock, or firing mechanism, was the most fragile and complicated part of the musket. Lock components—lock plate, tumbler, bridle, sear, hammer, pins and screws—were carefully machined with forging, drilling, and filing tools. The mounting, which was comprised of trigger guards, bands, and heel plates, was machined in stages very similar to the parts of the lock.

The shaping of the gun stock was basically a hand operation in the early 1800s, requiring a single craftsman to whittle, bore, and chisel each stock. One skilled worker could make one or two stocks in a day, much of the work being in the fitting of the metal weapon parts.

Blanchard's Lathe to Manufacture Gunstocks, built in 1822 by Thomas Blanchard for the Springfield Armory. This machine traced a master pattern to allow the rapid production of gunstocks from sawn lumber. Blanchard subsequently developed a series of 14 machines that largely mechanized the entire process of gunstock production. Harpers Ferry NHP (HF-1393).

In 1819, New England inventor Thomas Blanchard installed his "Engine for turning or cutting irregular forms" at the Harpers Ferry Armory (*see photograph above*).

Blanchard's lathe used a standard gun stock as a template from which to cut identical copies. Armory superintendent James Stubblefield had considerable praise for the new machine:

> It shews that Stocks can be turned in a Lathe, and I think it will be a great improvement in the Stocking of Muskets, and will also save expence, and insure uniformity in the stocks.[23]

Between 1827 and 1828, Blanchard built and installed a set of nine new special-purpose stocking machines at Harpers Ferry. Powered by water, these devices carried out additional operations on the stocks such as cutting in recesses for the barrel, lock, and trigger mechanism. Combined with the "lathe," these machines formed a mechanized production process sequentially linked, virtually eliminating the use of skilled labor in stock-making at Harpers Ferry.

Producing the gun barrel was the most expensive and physically demanding part of arms manufacture. First a piece of bar iron was rolled into a long, narrow *skelp*. At the barrel forging shop this *skelp* was welded into a barrel. Two men working in tandem, called "strikers," could hand weld about six barrels a day. But waterpowered trip hammers, adopted by the Springfield Armory in 1815, were capable of producing a sounder seam in about half the time. Operated by just one "striker," a trip hammer could weld 14 to 16 barrels in a single day. Barrel welding by trip hammers was not introduced at Harpers Ferry, however, until 1836, and it would be another four years before trip hammers completely replaced manual methods for welding barrels at the Potomac site.[24]

Nash's lathe for turning musket barrels, patented April 11, 1818. National Archives (Records of the Patent and Trademark Office, Record Group 241).

Annealing was the next step, restoring malleability to the gun barrel which was rendered brittle by several heatings during welding. The barrel was then straightened by hand and the bore was drilled. Commonly, the boring machine had a large wooden frame with a sliding carriage attached to a rack-and-pinion feed. The barrel was fastened to the carriage and then advanced against a rotary cutting bit powered by water. The barrel was reamed, rough-bored, and smooth-bored in succession.

Dents and imperfections on the outside of the barrel were removed in the grinding shop. In early days, grindstones turned by hand removed 2-3 pounds of metal, creating a rounded, more uniform surface. Then in 1817, a water-powered barrel turning lathe designed and built by Sylvester Nash was installed and tested at the Harpers Ferry Armory (*see drawing on facing page*). Nash's lathe comprised "a common turning Engine" which served to finish the outside surface of a welded gun barrel, replacing the slower and more tedious use of grindstones. A three-month trial of the new machine impressed Armory superintendent James Stubblefield, and on February 28, 1818, he requested permission "to erect two others." [25]

At the proof house the barrel was charged with powder and ball to test the strength of the weld. A barrel that withstood two charges was given a proof mark and sent back to the boring mill to be finish-bored and polished. Finally, the barrel went to the finishing shop for final assembly with the lock, mounting, and stock.

❧

Between 1801 and 1840, the Harpers Ferry Armory experienced considerable growth. In 1807, the establishment comprised six buildings and 67 workmen. Three years later, in 1810, there were 12 workshops and 197 armorers. By 1822,

the physical plant comprised 21 workshops and 234 armorers. In 1835, the Armory employed 255 workmen, and by 1840, the number had grown to 274.[26]

Expanding production and the introduction of new water-powered machinery forced government engineers to continually repair, rebuild or enlarge both Armory Dam and Armory Canal. At the same time, old water wheels were replaced and new water wheels added. In 1827, an "additional large water wheel" was erected to furnish power to one of Thomas Blanchard's new stocking machines. In 1834, three new water wheels were built by millwright Charles Starbuck to drive the

Harpers Ferry Armory workshops and dwelling houses along the banks of the Potomac River, circa 1824. Harpers Ferry NHP (HF-628).

machinery in the boring, turning, and stocking shops. The cost for just one of these new wheels was $2,908, including "the necessary shafts, drum, frames, supports, bearing, and fixtures complete." At the new Tilt-Hammer & Barrel Welding Shop, erected between 1834 and 1839, a separate water wheel and gearing was installed for each of the workshop's eight hammers. Six of the eight wheels were tub wheels.[27]

Tub wheels were comprised of wooden paddles or "floats" mortised tightly into the lower end of a vertical wheel shaft (*see adjacent illustration*). They were commonly between three and six feet in diameter, with an estimated efficiency of only about ten percent. As described in *The Young Mill-wright & Miller's Guide,* a "tub-mill has a horizontal water-wheel, that is acted upon by the percussion of the water altogether; the shaft is vertical; the water is shot on the upper side of the wheel, in the direction of a tangent with its circumference."[28]

Although not very efficient, they were nonetheless favored by Armory managers—both at Springfield and Harpers Ferry—for their cheapness, simplicity, ease of maintenance, and regularity of motion. Additionally, because of the severe shaking and sudden stresses attending the use of trip hammers, pairing each hammer with a single tub wheel proved operationally superior to providing power to all the trip hammers from less durable general purpose line shafting operated by a single water wheel. The only serious complaint Armory workmen had with the tub wheel, besides its relative lack of power, was the fact that it was "rendered useless by back-water rising only to the top of the floats."[29]

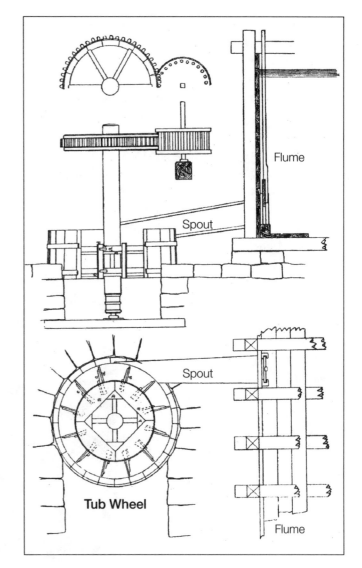

Flume

Spout

Spout

Tub Wheel

Flume

Despite new workshops, new water-powered machinery, an expanding workforce, and a considerable investment in waterworks, expected gains in productivity at the Harpers Ferry Armory did not materialize. Comparing the wages paid at Harpers Ferry to those paid at Springfield in March 1832, George Rust found that the total cost of labor in manufacturing a musket at the Springfield Armory was $5.54¼, compared to a cost of $6.40 at Harpers Ferry. He attributed much of the difference "to the superiority of the machinery at the Springfield Armory" and, in particular, to "welding of the barrels by waterpower." Rust then added:

> Another reason for the increased paid at Harpers Ferry arises from the want of regular applicable water power. The operation of the Armory being frequently suspended during the summer season, for the want of water, and impeded during the winter & spring by the ice and freshets.[30]

The long delay in the introduction of trip hammers for barrel welding at Harpers Ferry illustrates to what extent the Armory's deficient waterworks and inadequate water supply retarded the mechanization of arms manufacture here. In 1816, just one year after trip hammers were introduced at Springfield, James Stubblefield asked permission to introduce "four tilt hammers for the purpose of welding Musket Barrels by water" at Harpers Ferry, claiming the savings to the government in labor would pay for the new machinery in just one year. No action was taken, however, and twelve years later, in 1828, Stubblefield was still pressing his case, writing: "In regard to the contemplated Tilt hammer for welding Barrels - The advantage and saving to the Armory will be so great that it is very desirable to put it in operation as soon as practicable." General John E. Wool, in his 1829 report on the Harpers Ferry Armory, also urged that "Trip Hammers for welding Barrels, should be set in operation as soon as practicable, as by welding in that manner a considerable expense in labor would be saved to the Government."[31]

Roswell Lee, superintendent of the Springfield Armory, and acting superintendent at Harpers Ferry in 1829, shed some light on the long delay in the installation of trip hammers. Writing to the Ordnance Department from Harpers Ferry, he remarked that "it is very desireable to put the hammers into operation soon as practicable." But he acknowledged that "in the present state of funds" priority should be given to repairing "the flumes, Forebays and Water Gate" of the canal, and that "The finishing of the shop for welding barrels by trip hammers may be suspended."[32]

A month later, Major John Symington echoed Lee's concerns, reporting that without sufficient funds for enlarging the Armory Canal, "the supply of water will not be sufficient for the trip hammer establishment which is now ready completed." He added that failure to attend to the matter would "of course prevent the operations of the trip hammers until a much later period."[33]

Armory superintendent George Rust further explained the government's predicament in 1835, reporting to the Ordnance Department:

That periodically there has not been a sufficient supply of water to propel the machinery of the workshops situated on the Potomac river, to the full extent of its capacity; that when the new Tilt Hammers are put into operation, the consumption of water, will no doubt, be much greater, and consequently, it is apprehended, that the inconvenience arising from the insufficient supply, will be increased during the dry seasons, of the coming summers . . . .[34]

Clearly, the continued deficiency of the Armory Dam and Canal, coupled with a chronic shortage of streamflow on the Potomac River, served to retard both the mechanization of arms manufacture and the productivity of the workforce at the Harpers Ferry Armory. Until either additional appropriations from Congress were forthcoming, or more powerful and efficient water wheels could be obtained, there seemed little likelihood that the situation at Harpers Ferry would improve. To what extent John H. Hall and the entrepreneurs on Virginius Island, situated along the nearby Shenandoah River, suffered from the same problems will be seen in the following sections.

HALL'S RIFLE WORKS

On March 19, 1819, John H. Hall, a gunmaker from Portland, Maine, signed a contract with the War Department to produce 1,000 breech-loading rifles. The novel weapon, which Hall patented in 1811, had undergone rigorous testing by the War Department during the years leading up to the 1819 contract. Hall's rifle, it was found, took one-third the time to load as a conventional muzzle-loader, was lighter, and had greater accuracy with less recoil. Under the terms of the contract, Hall was assigned to the Harpers Ferry Armory, where he would "perform the Duty of an Assistant Armourer in instructing and directing the Workmen, to be employed in fabricating the Firearms above Specified."[35]

When Hall arrived at Harpers Ferry in April 1819, the War Department advised Armory superintendent James Stubblefield to make space available for the New England gunmaker in one of the existing government workshops along the Potomac River. Both Hall and Stubblefield, however, protested, replying "that the erection of proper buildings and machinery on the Shenandoah will be more compatible with the public interest." Stubblefield offered Hall the use of a small frame sawmill along the Shenandoah River dating from 1807. The structure, owned by the government but apparently abandoned, was approximately 16 feet by 50 feet and in much need of repair. Stubblefield obtained $600 for "Fitting up the old saw mill & a water wheel to the same," and the building was converted into a machine shop. Power was obtained from a new breast-type water wheel 12 feet in diameter erected by millwright Robert Painter. A new two-story stone blacksmith shop measuring 30 feet square was also erected, and Hall took possession of both buildings by Feb. 1820. This manufactory became known as Hall's Rifle Works, and the land on which it stood was called Lower Hall Island.[36]

The principal physical feature of Lower Hall Island, and the sole source of waterpower for the Rifle Works, was a bypass canal that separated the island from the riverbank. This canal had been excavated between 1806 and 1807 by the Patowmack Company, which just a few years earlier had completed the 1,750-yard "Long Canal" along the Potomac River above Harpers Ferry (*see pages 22-24*). Originally called the Patowmack Canal, by the time Hall took possession of his new workshops in 1820, it was commonly called the Shenandoah Canal. This waterway would play a critical role in the mechanical operations of the Rifle Works until the Civil War.

The original terms of the Patowmack Company's 1785 charter had stipulated that, in addition to rendering the Potomac River navigable for boats of shallow draft, all the river's major tributaries should be opened to commerce as well. In 1797, the Virginia legislature passed an act requiring the company to commence work "on the Potomac tributaries at once," and arrangements were made for "the business of clearing obstacles from the Shenandoah River." Little progress was made, however, and no further work was done for several more years.[37]

In 1802, attempting once again to stimulate action, the Virginia General Assembly passed another act explicitly authorizing the Patowmack Company to open the Shenandoah River to navigation from Harpers Ferry to Port Republic, a distance of 165 miles. The act further specified that the improvements be completed within seven years. Activity along the Shenandoah River

These stone courses are all that remain of Strider's Mill lock, part of the old Shenandoah navigation system about 1½ mile upstream from Harpers Ferry. October 1982 photo by the author.

resumed in February 1803, when Leonard Harbaugh and Nicholas King drafted detailed plans for "a Canal at the Lower Falls of the Shenandoah." But because the Patowmack Company lacked sufficient funds, and because the government was reluctant to grant a right-of-way through their land at Harpers Ferry, work on the proposed Shenandoah improvements failed to materialize.[38]

Finally, between 1805 and 1806, the company was able to raise over $15,000 from stock subscriptions, and work was pushed forward on the Shenandoah River from

Little's Falls downstream to Harpers Ferry, a distance of 6½ miles. Locks and short bypass canals at Little's Falls (Hopewell Mills), Wilson's Upper Falls, and Wilson's Lower Falls (Strider's Mill) were built, and the Bull's Falls Sluice—112 feet long and 25-30 feet wide—was completed.

At Harpers Ferry, on March 3, 1806, an agreement was finally reached with the government to build a canal across the public land along the Shenandoah River:

Witneseth that whereas the said Company are anxious to improve the navigation of the River Shenandoah, by means of a Canal to be taken out of said River upon the ground belonging to the U.S. and continued down to a point at or near the old Saw Mill upon the said ground, where it is proposed to descend by means of Locks into the bed of the river. In consideration whereof they agree that the United States may have the full use and benefit of the Surplus water in said canal.

The said Thomas Jefferson President as aforesaid <u>Saith</u> and <u>Doth</u> hereby grant to the said Company the right and privelege of cutting making and keeping in repair at their own proper and exclusive expense a Canal through the said land belonging to the United States, and in such a manner and direction as will take the water out of the Shenandoah River and convey the same to a point at or near the old Saw Mill where their Lock may be inserted to descend again into the bed of the River . . . .

And the said President and Directors [of the Patowmack Company] . . . do hereby grant unto

the United States as aforesd. for ever hereafter the right and privelege of drawing waters from any part or parts of said Canal for the use of any water works which may hereafter be erected on any part of the Public Lands in so far as may consist with the free complete and uninterrupted use of the said Canal by the said Company . . . .[39]

What constituted "Surplus water," and to what extent its use by the government might actually impair the "free complete and uninterrupted use" of the canal were hazy concepts at best. In time, these provisions caused considerable trouble for the government.

Excavation of the new canal soon commenced, and work was completed in 1807. The canal ditch was 580 yards long and served to connect natural channels of the Shenandoah River above and below the site, creating a waterway 9,200 feet long. A double lock with a fall of about 17 feet was built at the downstream end of the ditch. Thomas Harbaugh, who served as "Toll Geatherer" for the Patowmack Company at Harpers Ferry from 1807-1812, recorded that:

the Locks are 10 feet wide and 90 feet in length - all are built of fine slate stone, except at the gate recesses which are of yellow sand stone . . . . The Lock gates and Lock gate sills are all on this river made of Best yellow Locust timber . . . .[40]

Robert Harper's old sawmill, acquired by the government in 1797, apparently sat in the path of construction. The building was dismantled and a new one built at the expense of the Patowmack Company in

1807. The rebuilt sawmill, which Hall took possession of in February 1820, sat right next to these double locks (*see Hall's Rifle Works, 1835 map on page 49*). With a convenient supply of waterpower now available from the canal, the government also erected two new Armory workshops nearby. A brick Grinding Mill measuring 45 feet by 85 feet and a brick Tilt-Hammer Shop 45 feet square were erected between 1808-1809. Each shop had its own water wheel.[41]

With completion of the various locks, sluices, and canals along the lower Shenandoah River, the Patowmack Company had exhausted its financial resources. An exasperated Virginia General Assembly, after granting the company three separate extensions to complete the authorized improvements upstream to Port Republic, finally turned the job over to a new company. In 1815, "the canals, cuts, locks and all and every of the rights, claims and interests of the Potowmack Company on the Shenandoah" were conveyed to the New Shenandoah Company for a sum of $15,000. By 1817, work was again underway to render the Shenandoah River navigable from Harpers Ferry to Port Republic. Although additional improvements were made to the river during the next several years, surviving accounts indicate that navigation along the waterway was never satisfactory. Nonetheless, beginning about March 23, 1807, Thomas Harbaugh commenced collecting tolls "on produce descending the Shenandoah."[42]

Lock gate recess at Little's Falls Lock on the Shenandoah River, about 6½ miles upstream from Harpers Ferry. Completed by the Patowmack Company in 1806, this is the best-preserved lock from the old Shenandoah navigation system. May 1994 photo by the author.

Boats that traveled down the Shenandoah River were called gundalows—narrow flatbottom barges about nine feet wide and from 76 to 90 feet long. Principal cargoes were iron, flour, and lumber. Also common were loads of tan-bark, posts, shingles, apples, potatoes, corn, and brandy. One hundred and ten barrels of flour, weighing about ten tons, usually made a single load. At Harpers Ferry, iron brought $60 a ton; lumber, $1.80 to $2.25 for 100 feet; and flour, $8 a barrel. Six men usually crewed a gundalow—four polemen and a man each at front and rear rudders. It generally took three to four days to take the boat downstream from Port Republic to Harpers Ferry, and two to three days to walk back upriver. Each crew member received from $14 to $18 for the 165-mile trip. Boats that unloaded at Harpers Ferry were usually broken up and sold for lumber, a return trip upstream (against the current) being impractical.

An interesting first-person account of navigation on the Shenandoah River was published in the *Page Courier* of Luray, Virginia, in 1900:

> [M]y grand-mother took me to the High Rock to see the boats come through the shoot. We got in sight just in time to see the first boat go thro, strike a great rock, split in twain, and the whole cargo of pigiron went to the bottom. Each boat was manned by six men, and when the boat broke those on it were carried to such deep water that they had to swim. There were 18 boats in this fleet, and soon the men began to wade in and gather the iron together in a pile. The broken boat was then taken to the bank and repaired, reloaded and started on its way again. This was in March, I think, so you can see that a River sailor had his perils and hardships.[43]

◌

In 1820, Armory superintendent James Stubblefield transferred a rack-and-pinion rifling machine to Hall's Rifle Works. This machine, patented by James Ruple and William Parkinson of Washington, Pa., was comprised of a sliding carriage, revolving axle, and long cutting rod, all resting on a massive wooden frame nearly 18 feet long

by 19 inches wide. Actuated by a water-powered pulley, the mechanism drew a rifle barrel against the cutting rod, producing a spiral groove of one-third a turn per barrel. This would become just one of a battery of special-purpose machines either built or used by John H. Hall for the manufacture of his patent rifles on Lower Hall Island.

By 1826, Hall had introduced several machines of his own design. A "gang of circular saws set together on a spindle" was the principal stocking machine used at the Rifle Works. This "saw-gang" brought a stock to a square-edged profile, top, bottom, and sides, leaving the final work of shaving, cutting, and shaping to be done by hand. Although gradually replaced by Thomas Blanchard's stocking machines, stocking by Hall's "saw-gang" method continued at the Rifle Works until 1844.[44]

Hall's die-forging machines, which completely eliminated hand forging at the Rifle Works, were drop-hammers attached to chain drops:

> An endless chain, passing over toothed pulleys above and below, was actuated by a crank on the lower pulley. A hook upon the drop (the drop moving in ways) engaged with the chain, and the weight was thus lifted to the desired height, when it was disengaged by the action of a lever and cord.[45]

Once released, the weight of the drop fell downward, compressing the iron workpiece in the die with tremendous impact, thereby producing the desired form. By

1830, Hall had these machines operating by water-power.

Iron-cutting machines formed the largest portion of the production equipment used at the Rifle Works. Patented by Hall in 1827, these mechanisms were identified as "Straight cutting, Curved cutting & Lever cutting Machines." Operated by waterpower, these "excessively solid and heavy" machines combined great stability and accurate performance.[46]

Also significant were Hall's modifications to the millwork that transferred motion from his water wheels to machines. Traditionally, these power transmission systems were comprised of heavy oak shafting and wooden gear wheels, materials readily accessible and easily shaped in frontier America. But wood was subject to rapid wear and decay under conditions of high moisture and intermittent stress that characterized the operation of arms-making machinery. And to obtain the strength necessary to drive this cumbersome machinery, heavy shafting was required, resulting in slow operating speeds and considerable friction that could consume up to one-fourth of the power available.

The drive pulleys or "drums" that transferred power from shaft to machine by belting also posed problems. Typically made of planking and boards, drums of large diameter were necessary to increase machine speeds relative to the slow, ponderous line shafting. These drums took up valuable mill space and caused additional

Products of the Harpers Ferry Armory: U.S. Model 1816 musket (top) and U.S. Model 1819 Hall rifle. Photo by the author.

friction and power waste. As mechanization of arms manufacture increased, workshops at the national armories were becoming increasingly crowded with bulky, inefficient, and even dangerous power transmission equipment.

These problems were particularly acute at Hall's Rifle Works, where shop space was extremely limited and where mechanization was being applied to more and more manufacturing operations. Hall responded by introducing leather belts and balanced pulleys of his own design as early as 1826. Hall's wrought iron pulleys were turned in a lathe and then balanced by *"loading the light side* with lead or any heavy substance till an *equilibrium* takes place, by which means there is no tendency in their revolutions, however rapid, to wear more on one side of their Journals or gudgeons, than on the other." Consequently, the belts revolved "without any of that *shaking & trembling* which frequently accompanies their motions & which often proves injurious, especially when the motions are very rapid." With these innovations, Hall was able to obtain operating speeds for his machines as high as 3,000 revolutions per minute without sacrificing steady accurate performance.[47]

Some of Hall's improvements in millwork were apparently transferred to the Springfield Armory, where new water shops were erected between 1831-1832. These shops were equipped with lathe-turned wrought-iron shafting designed by Nathaniel French, a mechanic who had worked at Hall's Rifle Works from 1821-1827.[48]

∽

In July 1824, even before John H. Hall completed his first parcel of 1,000 patent rifles, the War Department approved a contract extension for another 1,000 of Hall's breechloaders. At the same time, Hall found the workshop space assigned to him inadequate for the requirements of his mechanized production process, and he requested more space.

By the end of 1824, his machine shop (the old sawmill) was enlarged and a second water wheel, 10 feet in diameter by 12 feet wide, was added. A year later a small brick workshop and two annealing furnaces were erected for the manufacture of Hall's patent rifles. In 1827, Hall obtained the use of the Armory grinding shop on Lower Hall Island, dating from 1809. A new

stone wing was added to the building and new millwork installed. This included a water wheel ten feet in diameter by seven feet wide and a wheel shaft 18 feet long and 23 inches in diameter, built by Lewis Wernwag to furnish power to Hall's various metal-working machines. Also built was a new stone Smith's shop 35 feet square containing four chimneys and four forges. One year later a new one-story Trip-Hammer shop, 45 feet square, was added to the Rifle Works.

Still, Hall lacked adequate workshop space. The extent to which this situation hampered Hall's operations was documented by the "Carrington Committee," a board of three commissioners appointed to examine and report to Congress on Hall's arms-making machinery. On January 6, 1827, committee members James Bell, Luther Sage, and James Carrington reported that Hall lacked the room necessary to set up all his machinery, forcing him to constantly move one machine out of the way so that another could be set up in its place. This "inconvenience" severely restricted Hall's ability to fully implement continuous mechanized production of his patent rifles.[49]

On July 24, 1830, Hall asked Col. George Bomford, the Chief of Ordnance, for the "remaining water shop on the Shenandoah." This was the Armory Tilt-Hammer shop, erected by James Stubblefield on Lower Hall Island in 1809. Hall was given part of this building in June 1831 to house machinery for grinding bayonets.

∽

Hall's July 24, 1830, letter to Bomford also raised important new concerns: the water supply from the Shenandoah Canal had apparently become insufficient for the simultaneous operation of all his machinery. Specifically, Hall indicated his intention to apply waterpower to his stocking machinery, which "renders it necessary that the whole of the waterpower, in the Shenandoah canal, should be at my command."[50]

The extent to which the deficiency of water impacted the Rifle Works became increasingly apparent as Hall endeavored to apply waterpower to more and more manufacturing operations. On July 18, 1831, Hall made his concerns clear to the Ordnance Department, writing:

> my business has now become greatly exposed or will be soon, in consequence of needing a larger supply of water to carry additional machinery viz. grind stones & iron grinding apparatus – all the water that can now be obtained by the aid of the dams alluded to is barely sufficient for the works on the Shenandoah and when the grinding machinery becomes ready for operation, it is evident, will prove deficient in quantity to an injurious extent . . . .[51]

Hall requested funds for construction of a new dam across the Shenandoah River in August 1831, submitting an estimate of just over $3,000. The funds were approved, and construction commenced sometime during the following year. Still, by September 1832, the situation at the Rifle Works had not improved. Hall reported that "Our machines are, at times, almost entirely stopped for want of water, and our business is greatly retarded by it."[52]

Even more distressing were claims by John Strider— owner of Gulph Mills near the upstream entrance of the Shenandoah Canal—to the water rights of the Shenandoah River. In November 1832, Strider informed the Secretary of War that "the United States are using at their works on the Shenandoah about three feet of my fall" and admonished the government "for trespassing on my rights & using my property." Furthermore, he claimed that the new Shenandoah dam "throws back a standing sheet of water to the verge of my mill wheels," and he threatened to demolish the structure.[53]

Strider's claims were soon confirmed. An Armory clerk informed Hall that he could not "discover any record of any conveyance of a right to the United States, to use the water power of the Shenandoah river among the record of this county."[54] Nor could Thomas Griggs, Jr., a lawyer hired by the Ordnance Department to look into the matter. Griggs, in particular, examined the government's 1806 agreement with the Patowmack Company regarding "the use of the surplus water from the canal for their works":

> Strider complains that the United States for the purpose of supplying their works at Harpers Ferry with a sufficient water power (not necessary for the purpose of navigation) have erected a dam in the river & the effect of this is to throw the water back on his mill wheel thereby lessening its power to his injury.[55]

In Griggs' opinion, "a sufficiency of water for the purposes of navigation can be thrown into the canal without effecting the operation of Striders Mill," and the use of the *existing* surplus water in the canal was "the extent of the right and privilege of the United States."

Any attempt to secure *additional* streamflow to propel machinery by building a dam was simply not legitimate.[56]

Hall was incredulous. He had spent the past decade perfecting tools and machines for the mechanized production of interchangeable firearms. Limiting the quantity of water passing through the canal to an amount sufficient *only* for the purposes of boat navigation would never meet the needs of his increasingly mechanized production process.

"It appears incredible that the Government should have omitted to secure a right to the use of the water in the Shenandoah for such of their works as lie along the border of that river," Hall wrote on November 28, 1832. The Rifle Works, he went on, "shall continue to be at the mercy of Mr. Strider for all the water that we use—and the progress of the United States business here will be liable to being wholly arrested by him, whenever he pleases—unless some arrangement be made with him for the purpose of preventing it."[57]

On January 3, 1833, a jury awarded Strider $3,600 for damages caused "by the erection of a dam across the Shenandoah River near the Rifle Factory." According to government records, however, this judgment was never paid. Instead, an accommodation was apparently reached with Strider in May 1833, when the government agreed to purchase "the right of water power on the Shenandoah river between the mills of said Strider and the Rifle Factory" for a sum of $2,600. The final deed of conveyance was executed by Strider on June 27, 1833.[58]

With the acquisition of Strider's water rights, the government now had full command of the waterpower of the Shenandoah River. Still, a chronic lack of

streamflow during the summer months, a poorly constructed dam, and an inadequate canal continued to plague operations at the Rifle Works. In 1834, Congress appropriated $2,000 "for repairing dam and removing obstructions in way of supplying water to rifle factory on the Shenandoah River." The Shenandoah dam was rebuilt by Lewis Wernwag, and mud, silt, and other debris obstructing the flow of water in the canal were removed.[59]

Still, Hall was not satisfied. In a letter to the Ordnance Department regarding planned construction of the new Winchester & Potomac Railroad alongside the Shenandoah River, he wrote that

effectual provision should be made for preventing that Company - or any of its contractors, or other agents from diminishing the width of any part of the canal or water course through which the United States works on the Shenandoah are supplied with water & from impeding the free passage of the water through it in any way & in any degree—the whole of the water that now flows through it is barely sufficient - after expending the two thousand dollars appropriated, at the last session of Congress for removing obstructions & obtaining a larger supply of water for the works now in operation here . . . .[60]

∽

While waterpower was consuming much of Hall's attention in the early 1830s, expansion of the Rifle Works continued. In 1832, a one-story filing shop 17 feet square and a new fire house were erected. In October

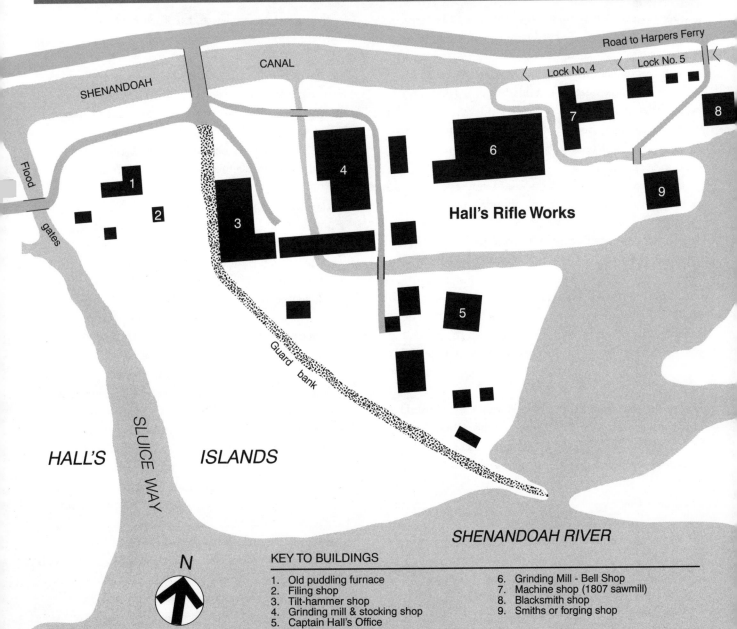

HALL'S RIFLE WORKS, 1835

Road to Harpers Ferry

CANAL

SHENANDOAH

Lock No. 4

Lock No. 5

Flood

gates

Hall's Rifle Works

HALL'S

SLUICE WAY

Guard bank

ISLANDS

SHENANDOAH RIVER

N

KEY TO BUILDINGS

1. Old puddling furnace
2. Filing shop
3. Tilt-hammer shop
4. Grinding mill & stocking shop
5. Captain Hall's Office
6. Grinding Mill - Bell Shop
7. Machine shop (1807 sawmill)
8. Blacksmith shop
9. Smiths or forging shop

Source: *Map of Harper's Ferry, Drawn by Lieuts. White, Allen, and R.S. Smith, U.S. Army, 1835.*

1835, Hall sought permission to raze the old sawmill shop, which he described as being "in such a state of decay as renders it disreputable in its appearance, and uncomfortable & unwholesome to the workmen."[61] Permission was evidently obtained, and in 1836 a one-story brick drill shop 17½ feet by 50 feet was erected in its place. A two-story browning shop and a filers work-shop were completed in 1837; a one-story stone tilt-hammer shop and a brick smith's & springmaker's shop was finished in 1838; and a new storehouse for iron, 25 feet by 75 feet and two stories tall, was completed in 1839.

In January 1840, due to deteriorating health, Hall was granted a leave of absence from Harpers Ferry. The following year, on February 26, 1841, John H. Hall died in Huntsville, Missouri, at the age of 60. Production of Hall's rifle was discontinued by the War Department, and the last parcel of breech-loaders manufactured at Harpers Ferry were put into storage in September 1843.

∾

From the outset, Hall sought to develop a system of firearms manufacture that combined mechanized pro-duction with the Ordnance Department's quest for weapons with interchangeable parts. He claimed for himself considerable success as early as December 20, 1822, writing:

> I have succeeded in establishing methods for fabricating arms exactly alike, & with economy, by the hands of common workmen, & in such manner as to ensure a perfect observance of any established model, & to furnish in the arms

themselves a complete test of their conformity to it.[62]

The extent to which Hall's production process had been mechanized was documented by the Carrington Com-mittee, three commissioners appointed by the Ordnance Department in December 1826 to examine the arms-making machinery at the Rifle Works. On January 6, 1827, the committee members reported that

> the machines, after the work is put into them, go thro' with the operation without any further aid from the boy, and when the operation is com-pleted, give notice to the boy, who had been employed during the operation, in putting in and taking out work from other machines.[63]

The Carrington Committee was astonished not only by the extent to which Hall had mechanized his operations, but by the actual results he had obtained: the production of the first fully interchangeable weapons in America.

Five years later, in 1832, Col. George Talcott, the inspector of arsenals and armories for the Ordnance Department, bestowed similar praise on Hall's Rifle Works. "This manufactory," he wrote, "has been carried to a greater degree of perfection, as regards the quality of work and uniformity of parts than is to be found elsewhere—almost everything is performed by machin-ery, leaving very little dependent on manual labor."[64]

Hall's Rifle Works witnessed the convergence of two critical elements in American manufacturing technology: uniformity or interchangeability of parts and the mechanization of production, aided to a large extent by the application of waterpower. By combining men, machines, and methods of precision measurement into a practical system of production, Hall accomplished at Harpers Ferry what no other arms maker had been able to do. In time, this production process became known alternately as the "uniformity principle of the armories" or the "American system of manufactures." Hall's work at Harpers Ferry laid a firm foundation for America's emerging factory system.

VIRGINIUS ISLAND

The trails that criss-cross Virginius Island are well-trod by today's visitors to Harpers Ferry National Historical Park. Unlike Hall's Rifle Works and the old Armory Grounds, which are virtually hidden from view by siltation, ground cover, and dirt fill, Virginius Island is readily accessible and its industrial ruins clearly visible. The site, formerly separated from the mainland by meandering channels of the Shenandoah River, is no longer an island. With the decline of waterpower in the late 19th century, the island's various millraces and river channels were left to fill in with sand and silt. Only a short stretch of the old Shenandoah Canal, now cut off from the river by the changing landscape, suggests the former separation between island and mainland. Island or not, the site's considerable industrial ruins continue to interest and intrigue park visitors.

While the town of Harpers Ferry was being settled and developed in the late 18th and early 19th centuries,

Virginius Island remained unoccupied. The property apparently was not included among the government's 1797 land purchases for the federal armory. The island remained unclaimed until June 25, 1803, when Daniel McPherson received a grant to "the lower-most Island in Shenandoah river" containing over eleven acres.[65]

With Virginius Island in private hands, entrepreneurs had a convenient and suitable location to establish commercial industries. However, it would be another two decades before the waterpower available at the site was

Virginius Island, circa 1889. Bordered on the left by the Shenandoah River and on the right by the Shenandoah Canal, the island offered a prime location for harnessing waterpower. The former Cotton Factory (lower left) and Shenandoah Pulp Co. (upper right) were the only mills still standing when this photograph was taken. Harpers Ferry NHP (HF-896).

developed. On May 18, 1817, John Peacher acquired the island for $1,000, and became the site's first resident entrepreneur. Peacher operated a boating business, and his purchase of Virginius Island coincided with the continued development of Shenandoah River navigation by the New Shenandoah Company. In January 1818, Peacher placed an advertisement in the *Farmers Repository*, announcing that he had moved his boating operation to the "island near Harper's Ferry, in the Shenandoah," and soliciting flour to boat to Georgetown and Alexandria. Peacher subsequently erected a small gristmill or chopping mill, completing the island's first industrial establishment sometime between 1822 and 1823.[66]

Peacher's mill marked the beginning of the island's rapid industrial development. With fourteen feet of head and fall available from the adjacent rapids of the Shenandoah River, Virginius Island soon attracted new entrepreneurs anxious to tap the site's waterpower. On August 30, 1823, Armory superintendent James Stubblefield acquired the island for himself from Peacher for a sum of $15,000—fifteen times the amount Peacher had paid for the property six years earlier. One day later, Stubblefield secured water privileges from the New Shenandoah Company, entitling him and future property owners to use all the water from the Shenandoah River that was not needed for navigation. The agreement included permission to build a permanent dam across "the main channel of said River" in order to enlarge the water flow into the island's channels, as well as permission to erect a small dam across one of the river channels separating his island from Lower Hall Island near the lower locks of the Shenandoah Canal. In return, Stubblefield was required to "make and keep a good and sufficient canal" from his small dam to the lower end of the island.[67]

With these water privileges secured, the waterpower on "Mr. Stubblefield's Island" was more fully developed. The small dam near the lower locks of the Shenandoah Canal was completed, and a new millrace and stone river wall were built. No sooner were these improvements completed than Stubblefield, in December 1824, sold the island in four sections to Fontaine Beckham, Townsend Beckham, Edward Wager, and Lewis Wernwag for a total sum of $28,500. A small scale building boom then took place, and just two years later the island contained an "extensive Saw-Mill, Merchant Mill, Oil Mill, Tannery, and about twelve dwelling houses."[68]

Believing that incorporating the island would hasten development of the site, the "landholders and residents of an Island in the Shenandoah River near Harpers Ferry" petitioned the Virginia General Assembly in December 1826 for the establishment of a town to be known as Virginius. On January 8, 1827, the General Assembly passed an act establishing the town of Virginius, and the island became known as Virginius Island.

∽

An "Oil Mill" which produced oil from flax seed already stood on Townsend Beckham's Tract 1 property at the upstream end of Virginius Island in December 1824. Beckham expanded this mill with the addition of a tannery and water-powered bark mill. The tannery possessed 31 vats and also included a number of shops and bark houses. Millstones in the bark mill reduced oak or chestnut bark—common tanning agents—into a coarse powder. The tannery profited from an "abundant

Park visitor surveys waterpower ruins on Virginius Island. These water supply tunnels were erected in 1848. February 1987 photo by the author.

It is situated at Harpers Ferry about one-fourth of a mile above the junction of the Shenandoah and Potomac Rivers. It is supplied with an inexhaustible fund of water from the Shenandoah, and may be enlarged to any extent with great advantage. The building, a substantial one of stone is 60 feet by 40; it has two water wheels, two pair of burrs, and room for another pair . . . .

The situation of this establishment is peculiarly advantageous. It is in an abundant wheat neighborhood, with a turnpike running within 60 yards of it. It is below the Shenandoah locks, and boats can be loaded almost at the mill door . . . .

The water power is not surpassed by any situation in the country, and a sufficiency may be obtained for almost any eligible purpose.[70]

supply of slaughtered hides afforded by Harpers-Ferry, and the vicinity, amounting to 1000 or upwards annually." The establishment also profited from Beckham's association with his brother-in-law, James Stubblefield, who as Armory superintendent allegedly allowed trees on government property to be cut down "for no other purpose than to procure bark" for the tannery.[69]

The "Merchant Mill" that stood on Fontaine Beckham's Tract 2 property apparently replaced the more modest structure John Peacher had erected on that site in 1822-1823. An August 1832 advertisement described the flour mill in considerable detail:

A cooper shop was also connected with the property. Subsequent advertisements in 1836 and 1838 stated that the Island Mill, as the establishment became commonly known, could produce from 150-200 barrels of flour per day.

In February 1839, the Island Mill was destroyed by fire; 12,000 bushels of wheat and 300 barrels of flour were also consumed by the blaze. The following year new owners replaced the structure with an even larger 3½ story stone flour mill measuring 96 by 48 feet.

Lewis Wernwag's Tract 4 property encompassed three acres at the eastern or downstream end of Virginius

Island. In about 1824, Wernwag erected a frame "Saw-Mill" here measuring 100 feet by 36 feet. Just as Townsend Beckham, owner of the island's tannery, allegedly benefited from his relationship with brother-in-law James Stubblefield, so too Wernwag may have profited from his association with the Armory superintendent. In 1826, an armory employee testified that when Stubblefield sold the Tract 4 property to Wernwag, "the Public Sawmill was dispensed with & all articles previously sawed there, bought of Wernwag—by which he was enabled to pay Mr. Stubblefield for his Island." Whether true or not, records show that the Armory did purchase lumber from Wernwag's saw-mill during 1825.[71]

Wernwag was a preeminent builder of long-span wooden truss bridges. His reputation was based on the *Colossus*, a single-span, arched wooden truss bridge that crossed the Schuylkill River in Philadelphia. Completed in 1812, the bridge was 340 feet long—the longest clear-span wooden bridge in the world when it was built. In October 1824, soon after Wernwag moved to Harpers Ferry from Philadelphia, he began erecting the town's first bridge across the Potomac River. Completed in 1829, "Wager's Bridge" was described as a "handsome double wooden highway bridge, 750 feet from one abutment to the other." Wernwag subsequently helped design the Baltimore & Ohio Railroad's Potomac Viaduct at Harpers Ferry in the fall of 1835, and began building the bridge's wooden superstructure the following year.[72]

A man of many skills, Wernwag also performed carpenter, mason, and millwright

This Virginius Island sawmill ledger, which dates from 1823, lists the accounts of John Picher [Peacher], James Stubblefield, Lewis Wernwag, the Harpers Ferry Armory, and many others. Harpers Ferry NHP (HAFE-283); photo by Eric Long.

work. In April 1827, John H. Hall hired Wernwag to erect a stone addition to the grinding mill at Hall's Rifle Works. Included in the contract was a "new water wheel, forebay, and necessary fixtures for [the] new mill shop."[73] In 1828, Wernwag rebuilt the Armory Dam across the Potomac River—an 1,800-foot-long timber and stone dam about 10 feet thick—for a reported sum of $3,512 in cash and timber. In August and September 1834, Hall again retained Wernwag to erect a new government dam across the Shenandoah. In hiring Wernwag, Hall wrote:

> The best services that I can obtain for directing those operations are those of Mr. Lewis Wernwag, a person of very superior ability and well known as a bridge builder, he is much better qualified for effecting the business alluded to than any person with whom I am acquainted.[74]

Sometime prior to 1827, Wernwag also erected a dam across the Shenandoah River at Virginius Island. This new structure apparently prompted a riparian dispute, and the government conducted an inquiry into the matter on April 28, 1827. John H. Hall testified that a "wall and embankment" previously erected to protect the Rifle Works from the river "became more necessary in consequence of the dam built across the Shenandoah to throw water on the Island." Lewis Wernwag in his turn testified:

> Mr. Stubblefield never did cause a dam to be erected in the vicinity of the Rifle establishment. I had it built myself for I had previously purchased the Island of Mr. S. The right to build the dam,

Remnant of a 19th century waterpower dam adjacent to Virginius Island. Timber cribwork and iron spikes like this were typical materials used in local dam construction. October 1994 photo by the author.

I obtained from the Shenandoah Company. The lines are so unsettled that I do not know whether my dam joins the Govt. land or the land of the Shenandoah Company.[75]

In consequence of the new Virginius Island dam, the government took immediate action to raise the wall and embankment at the Rifle Works "still higher."

From 1830-1832, the firm Wernwag & Sons operated Wernwag's saw-mill and a machine shop probably located in the same building. By the year 1832, however, a separate three-story stone machine shop measuring 50 feet by 30 feet was erected on the Tract 4 property. With the increasing use of iron in the tools, machines, gearing, and water wheels of American industry in the early decades of the 19th century, machine shops became essential additions to the industrial landscape. In these shops cast and forged iron was cut to size and the surfaces smoothed. A lathe—the most common machine tool of these early shops—spun a piece of iron while a sharpened steel cutter was applied to its edge to produce a perfectly cylindrical finished product. Most lathes were self-acting and were usually powered by water, with the cutting speed and depth of cut controlled by a drive screw or chain mechanism. Still, finishing a piece required much careful handwork by a skilled machinist.

From 1836-1844, the machine shop on Virginius Island was run by Wernwag's son John and Joseph P. Shannon. The establishment was equipped with water-powered turning lathes capable of turning wood, brass, iron, and steel. Hand tools included screw plates, taps and dies, bench screws, and mill screws. Products ranged from window sash fasteners to Farham's patent washing machines, and the shop could make or repair any kind of machinery. After 1840, the shop also furnished machine castings for the Harpers Ferry Armory.[76]

Sometime prior to 1835, the tannery on Tract I closed down, and the oil mill ceased operation due to a "scarcity of flaxseed." In 1835, the mill was converted into an iron foundry by Hugh Gilleece, who leased the Tract I property. This establishment "cast Machinery of every description," including McCormick and Loudoun Mould boards, Hillside Ploughs, branding irons, threshing machines, corn shellers, and straw cutters. In addition to stock items manufactured from patented patterns, the foundry also kept a "first rate Pattern Maker" on hand to perform custom casting work.[77]

Business was apparently good, and in December 1838, Gilleece purchased the Tract I property. Two years later, in June 1840, he announced that he had "completed his Chopping Mill, on the Island of Virginius, near the Foundry, where he is prepared to chop Rye and Corn . . . ."[78] But the iron foundry remained Gilleece's principal business and, based on newspaper accounts and advertisements which appeared in the early 1840s, demand for machine castings and mill gearing continued to grow. On September 29, 1842, the *Virginia Free Press* described an iron shaft weighing 3,600 pounds which the iron foundry had recently cast for the Harpers Ferry Armory. The following year Gilleece advertised:

> I am enabled to furnish patterns for Mill Gearing or Machinery at short notice . . . . I have made arrangements with Mr. John Wernwag, whose extensive machine shop is convenient to the Foundry, for the turning and fitting up of every description of Castings. His name as a Machinist, is a sufficient guarantee for the manner in which the work shall be done. Mill Spindles made and repaired.[79]

Iron had indeed become a significant component in the machines and hydraulic works of American industry.

A significant catalyst in the industrial development of Harpers Ferry was the arrival of canal and railroad in the mid-1830s. The Chesapeake & Ohio Canal was completed to the Maryland shore opposite the mouth of the Shenandoah River in November 1833. The

The B&O Railroad and C&O Canal advanced simultaneously up the Potomac River between 1828-1834. In this 1920 photograph, Capital Limited No. 5227 and Canal Boat No. 49 travel side by side just downstream from Harpers Ferry. Photo courtesy Chesapeake & Ohio Canal NHP.

Baltimore & Ohio Railroad followed one year later, reaching the same spot on December 1, 1834. And in March 1836, the Winchester & Potomac Railroad, which extended 32 miles from Harpers Ferry to Winchester, Virginia, began regular operations.

The convergence of railroad and canal at Harpers Ferry assured a steady supply of raw materials and furnished convenient access to lucrative new markets. Heavy machinery, previously transported by horse-drawn wagon over rough country roads at considerable expense, could now be shipped conveniently and economically from the machine shops of Baltimore, Philadelphia, New Jersey, and New England. Coal for the furnaces and forges of the Harpers Ferry Armory became more readily available from the mines of western Maryland. Building material for new Armory workshops also arrived by boat or rail. And the mills and factories of Virginius Island now had access to once-isolated communities of the Shenandoah Valley: wheat and corn were conveniently transported to the Island Mill, while farm

tools and household products from Gilleece's iron foundry found an increasingly wider market. In April 1835, for instance, Hugh Gilleece & Co. advertised that

> The Baltimore and Ohio Rail-Road, the Chesapeake and Ohio Canal, and the Rail-road to Winchester, all afford great facilities for forwarding any articles in our line to those who may favor us with calls through either of those channels . . .[80]

The Chesapeake & Ohio Canal was opened to Sandy Hook, Maryland, across the Potomac River from Harpers Ferry, in November 1833. In this 1876 photograph, a canal boat departs Lock 33 at the foot of Maryland Heights. Harpers Ferry NHP (HF-810).

The dawn of the canal era in the United States brought an end to the age of simple river improvements. Artificial waterways promised reliable transportation on a level, stillwater route. On July 4, 1828, construction of the Chesapeake & Ohio Canal began with great fanfare when President John Quincy Adams turned the first spadeful of dirt near Little Falls on the Potomac River. The following month, on August 15, 1828, the rights, improvements, and property of the Patowmack Company were conveyed by deed to the C&O Canal Company.

The Patowmack Company had never fulfilled the full terms of its charter, which specified that the company's improvements must permit the passage of boats carrying 50 barrels of flour in the driest season. Just as wide variations in the streamflow of the Potomac River created constant problems for the development of reliable waterpower, navigation too was entirely dependent upon the flow of water in the river. On ten different occasions between 1786 and 1820, the legislatures of both Maryland and Virginia had extended the time demanded by law for the completion of the Patowmack Company's river improvements. Yet by 1822, the terms of the charter had still not been met.

By contrast, the C&O Canal was a carefully engineered artificial waterway situated within a man-made canal bed. Inlet locks controlled the flow of water along the canal, and lift locks permitted canal barges measuring 92 feet long by 14½ feet wide to travel both upstream and downstream. John H. Hall, who traveled by canal boat many times between Harpers Ferry and the nation's capital, described the leisurely day-long trip in October 1837:

> The trip may be made by the Canal, from Georgetown in a packet boat that leaves there on Monday Morning—Wednesday morning—and Friday—each of these days a 4. o'clock A.M. The best course to pursue is, to proceed to a public house, near the place of departure, on the previous evening. You will arrive here, accident excepted, about four or five o'clock, through one of the best canals in the world—& through some of the wildest scenery of the noble Potomack—and here we can present to your notice some of the efforts of art.[81]

When finally completed in 1850, the C&O Canal extended 184½ miles from Georgetown to Cumberland, Maryland, along the north bank of the Potomac River.

Lock 33 today. Floodwaters have battered the old lock walls and swept the frame lockhouse and outbuildings away. Spring 1979 photo by the author.

In an interesting coincidence of American history, construction on the Baltimore & Ohio Railroad began the very same day that work commenced on the C&O Canal. Although the canal arrived at Harpers Ferry more than a year before the railroad, the railroad was completed to Cumberland, Maryland, in 1842—eight years before the canal was finished. Still, the B&O Railroad faced substantial obstacles at Harpers Ferry: a bridge was required to span the Potomac River, and a right-of-way was necessary through the Armory grounds.

In early 1837, contractor Lewis Wernwag completed the B&O Railroad's Potomac Viaduct, a seven-span timber structure that extended 830 feet across the Potomac River. The bridge included a toll road and a tracking path for mules to tow canal boats across the Potomac River between the Shenandoah River and C&O Canal. One year later, in 1838, the railroad company

This 1859 photograph shows the Baltimore & Ohio Railroad's Potomac Viaduct and, just beyond it, the Chesapeake & Ohio Canal. A short mule crossover bridge spans the canal's Shenandoah River Lock. Harpers Ferry NHP (HF-66).

received a ten foot right-of-way from the government through the Armory grounds. This right-of-way, however, required the construction of a costly 15-foot-high, 1,380-foot-long stone riverwall along the Potomac shoreline.

The final obstacle to completion of the B&O mainline through Harpers Ferry was how to connect the tracks along the Armory riverwall with the new bridge, which was built at a right angle to the Potomac shoreline. "Wager's Bridge" (erected by Lewis Wernwag between 1824 and 1829) ran parallel to and just upstream from the Potomac Viaduct, making a right turn off the railway bridge and up the Potomac shoreline impossible. The issue was finally resolved in December 1839, when the Wager family conveyed "all rights to take toll, including the rights incident to the original Ferry" which they had inherited from Robert Harper, to the B&O Railroad.[82] By this agreement, "Wager's Bridge" was torn down, and between 1840-1842 a curved or "Y" span was erected on the Harpers Ferry end of the Potomac Viaduct. The B&O Railroad mainline was finally opened through Harpers Ferry (*see map below*).

Completion of the Potomac Viaduct in January 1837 was actually a major boon to the new Winchester & Potomac Railroad, which had beaten the B&O Railroad into Harpers Ferry by several months. On

March 31, 1836, the 32-mile-long mainline of the Winchester & Potomac was officially opened between Harpers Ferry and Winchester, Virginia. The B&O

1837-1838 plan showing the proposed route of the B&O Railroad mainline through the Armory Grounds. The location of Wager's Bridge (shaded), the Winchester & Potomac Rail Road, and the proposed addition of a curved span or "Y" to the Potomac Viaduct are also depicted. Harpers Ferry NHP (Map 33B, Drawer 2, Item 240).

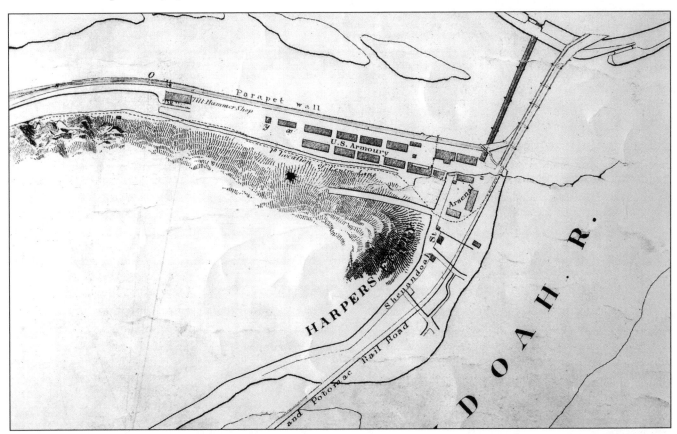

Railroad's new bridge established a direct connection with the tracks of the Winchester & Potomac, which traveled through Virginius Island and Lower Town Harpers Ferry along the Shenandoah River. Almost overnight, entrepreneurs on Virginius Island had access to new rural markets in the Shenandoah Valley and urban markets in and around Baltimore, Maryland.

Harpers Ferry was clearly emerging as one of the region's most important industrial and transportation centers. The advent of railroad and canal, coupled with growing popular and political support for Southern manufacturing, encouraged entrepreneurs on Virginius Island to further expand their manufacturing operations. An October 9, 1834 editorial in the *Virginia Free Press* echoed this sentiment:

> It has long been a matter of surprise to us, that the advantages of the Island of Virginius, near Harpers Ferry, for manufacturers, of all kinds, have been so long neglected by men of enterprise. It is decidedly one of the best situations in the United States for both cotton and woollen factories; the water-power is unsurpassed; and the facilities for getting supplies of raw material, and for transferring the manufactured articles to market are as great as could possibly be desired.[83]

The expansion of the United States Armory and Hall's Rifle Works also transformed the industrial landscape at Harpers Ferry. In 1836, Thomas Cather, a British traveler, wrote:

The scenery at Harpers Ferry is very grand. Jefferson, in his note on Virginia, says it is worth while to cross the Atlantic to visit it . . . . The view from the top of the rock on either side of Harper's Ferry is indeed glorious; but there is scarcely a pleasure in the world without an alloy of pain. No blessing without a curse close upon it; and this scenery is subject to the general rule. There is a most abominable little village just in the pass between the mountains. Here is the Government Manufactory of Firearms; and the smell of coal smoke and the clanking of hammers obtrude themselves on the senses and prevent one's enjoyment from being unmixed.[84]

For better or worse, Harpers Ferry had changed dramatically since 1800. No longer an isolated village on the frontier of rural America, Harpers Ferry was now poised to join the nation's industrial transformation. But ready access to raw materials, new industrial technologies, and new markets posed considerable new challenges. For the Harpers Ferry Armory to sustain the production requirements of the War Department and keep pace with her sister armory in Springfield, Mass., new production regimens and more labor-saving machines were necessary. For the industrial establishments of Virginius Island to keep pace with expanding markets and increasing competition, larger manufactories and further production economies were required. How the community responded to these challenges illustrates much about the history of waterpower in America. ❦

CHAPTER 3
EXPANSION OF MANUFACTURING
1840-1865

The great amount of water power on the Potomac and Shenandoah, bounding and running through Jefferson county, points out this location as equal, if not superior to, any in the U. States for Manufacturing purposes.

—*Spirit of Jefferson,* May 22, 1846

IN THE DECADES PRIOR TO THE CIVIL WAR, manufactories at Harpers Ferry profited from key economic and political developments in America. The Harpers Ferry Armory benefited from an improving national economy in the mid-1840s, which brought more revenues into the federal treasury. At the same time, war with Mexico seemed imminent. Appropriations from Congress for new workshops, waterworks, and machinery for interchangeable manufacture—so hard to come by during the preceding decades—were suddenly more forthcoming.

For entrepreneurs looking to expand their manufacturing operations on Virginius Island, the improving economy created more demand for their products. At the same time, sectional political issues were beginning to divide North and South, creating growing support for southern manufacturing. Many southern businessmen advocated greater economic independence from the North, where virtually all of the South's cotton was processed. One particularly outspoken individual was William Gregg, a South Carolina businessman and

mechanic who wrote a series of articles for the *Charleston Courier* in 1845 advocating a southern textile industry. Gregg's strong sectional sentiments were echoed at the cornerstone setting ceremony for a new cotton factory on Virginius Island on October 22, 1846. Richard Parker, a board member of the newly formed Harpers Ferry & Shenandoah Manufacturing Company, spoke at this event:

Gentleman, how often have we of the South been twitted by our Northern brethren for our indolence and want of enterprise. How often have we heard that Virginia was fast going to decay—that whilst the North, with her manufactures, and the West with its virgin soils, were making rapid strides towards greatness and improving in all the arts which adorn life, the people of Virginia were falling far behind—that for lack of energy our population was deserting for regions of greater enterprise, and that soon we should be but the poor shadow of what we once were.[1]

Footnotes for Chapter 3 begin on Page 180.

The call for southern manufacturing, a growing national economy, and imminent war with Mexico all gave considerable stimulus to the expansion of industry at Harpers Ferry. Also significant was the presence of railroad and canal, providing reliable "facilities for getting supplies of raw material, and for transferring the manufactured articles to market."[2]

The Potomac and Shenandoah rivers flowed on, however, heedless of economic and political developments. Water levels continued to rise and fall with the rains and the seasons, just as they always had. If millwrights, engineers, and entrepreneurs at Harpers Ferry were to meet the challenges presented by rapidly expanding economic opportunities, better methods for extracting power from falling water would be necessary. The innovative new technologies they developed and adopted to meet these demands both at Harpers Ferry and across America constitute a remarkable chapter in the history of waterpower.

TRANSFORMATION OF THE HARPERS FERRY ARMORY

In 1841, the War Department placed the national armories under direct military control, doing away with more than four decades of inconsistent and unsatisfactory civilian management. Criticism of the Harpers Ferry Armory had been particularly harsh, dating back to a report submitted to the Ordnance Department in 1827:

This establishment has, undoubtedly, been badly managed. Large sums of money have been expended without reference to permanency or utility. Every thing about it bears a temporary aspect.

Very few, if any, substantial buildings are to be found at the place. The shops are built of brick but in a state of dilapidation.[3]

Fourteen years later, conditions at the Potomac manufactory were still not satisfactory, prompting the Chief of Ordnance to report in November 1841 that "much yet remains to be done to place it on the footing required for a great National establishment." Another Ordnance inspector noted the Armory's total lack of architectural or functional unity, writing that the "whole establishment is cramped for room, not having been constructed upon a plan arranged beforehand, but put up building after building as appropriations were obtained."[4]

Consequently, when West Point engineer Major John Symington took command of the Harpers Ferry Armory in November 1844, he proceeded to draw up a master plan for the manufactory's complete renovation (see **U.S. Musket Factory, 1861** map on pages 72-73). Work began on the Potomac workshops in March 1845 with the construction of a new two-story Boring Shop. Here the "various operations upon the barrel, from the forged to the finished state" were performed.[5]

In 1846, a one-story Forging Shop and an adjacent two-story building "for Inspector's offices and model and pattern rooms" were completed. A large furnace stack, 90 feet high and 10 feet square at the base, was attached to the back of this two-story building. Two horizontal flues connected the chimney to a line of double forges in the adjacent Forging Shop. A new three-story Stock House or "Store-House for Stocks" was also completed in 1846.[6]

"The United States Armory or Musket Factory at Harpers Ferry, Virginia, from Magazine Hill," from Edward Beyer's Album on Virginia, *1857.* Harpers Ferry NHP (HF-959).

A one-story Smiths Shop completed in 1848 was connected to the Forging Shop by the small two-story building containing the furnace stack. The next workshop erected was a Stocking and Machine Shop. The south wing of this new shop, completed in 1849, housed the Armory's stocking machinery. The center and north wings were completed the following year. The center building housed offices, while the north wing contained the new machine shop. Each wing was two stories tall.

The "Bell" or Finishing Shop, erected in about 1810, was renovated in 1850. A new Polishing Shop was also erected, connecting the "Bell" Shop with the adjacent Boring Shop. According to Symington, the Polishing Shop was "40 by 22 feet, two stories high, of brick on stone foundations, and covered with slate."[7]

1851 saw completion of a new Grinding & Saw Mill & Carpenter's Shop, comprised of a two-story center building and two one-story wings. One wing housed grinding operations while the other wing and center building contained "saws, planing machine, wood turning lathes, and other machinery, necessary for making arms chests, &c." Also completed in 1851 was a large new one-story Tilt-Hammer & Barrel-Welding Shop. Of the $43,370 expended on this new workshop, $25,470 was for machinery alone, including "the whole of the main line of Shafting, four Trip Hammers (belt) and one Fan Blast and pipe."[8]

A single story Annealing Shop & Brass Foundry was completed in 1852. According to Symington, this new workshop was "109½ by 35 feet, divided by partition walls into three compartments, and of the same style of finish as the other new shops."[9]

The final workshop included in Symington's plan for the renovation of the Armory was a Rolling Mill. This workshop was needed:

> To work up scrap iron into bars of suitable sizes for use in the shops. For want of a rolling mill, the large amount of scrap iron, annually made at the Armory, has to be sold for whatever it will bring. This iron is of the best quality and the working of it into bars fit for use would make an annual saving of $1,000 or more.[10]

The Rolling Mill was completed in 1855 by Col. Benjamin Huger, Symington's successor, at the western end of the Armory yard (the former site of the Barrel Welding & Tilt Hammer Shop). Major William Bell described this new structure:

> New Rolling Mill: 146 by 45 feet, one story of 16½ feet, built of brick, on Stone foundation, covered with slate—paved with Stone and having 2 Reverbertory Furnaces, with Stacks 45 and 40 feet high—two tilt Hammers, one forge, one large

This circa 1862 photograph shows the main entrance to the U.S. Musket Factory. The "fire engine and guard house" (John Brown's Fort) is the first building on the left. The Smith & Forging Shop, with its 90-foot furnace stack, is the second building on the right. Harpers Ferry NHP (HF-27).

lathe for Rolls, two train of Rolls 13 and 8 inches, large shears, Fan blower, Water Wheel 15 Cube, Master Wheel and Gearing, pullies and other Machinery, one large cast iron flume from Canal to Forebay, is now completed . . .[11]

During this same period Hall's Rifle Works along the Shenandoah River was also completely renovated (*see* **U.S. Rifle Factory, 1861** *map on page 74*). A new two-story Finishing & Machine Shop with two small one-story wings was completed in 1848. This workshop housed polishing wheels; cutting machines for components; barrel-boring, turning, and rifling machines; and stocking machines. In 1851, a one-story Tilt-hammer & Forging Shop was completed, followed by a one-story Annealing Furnace & Proof House in 1852, and a two-story Machine Shop in 1853. The machinery in this last building included a lathe for turning gunstocks and a circular saw for cutting the stocks to length.

All the new buildings erected at the Harpers Ferry Armory consisted of brick superstructures with cast-iron framing, sheet-iron or slated roofs, copper gutters and downspouts, and large arched portals and windows, all erected upon heavy stone foundations. Considerable filling and grading of the workshop grounds, including the construction of stone culverts over the waterwheel tailraces, was also done in an effort to raise the buildings above the usual high water levels and to create a well-groomed appearance. The extensive reconstruction

Sketch of the Rifle Factory by Col. James G. Benton, Chief of Ordnance, on April 27, 1855. The large building in the foreground is the Finishing Shop, erected in 1848. An empty gundalow sits along the banks of the Shenandoah Canal in the foreground. Harpers Ferry NHP, courtesy U.S. Military Academy Library, West Point, New York (HF-794).

created a more integrated physical plant, whereby the flow of work from one stage or arms production to another was greatly facilitated. During this period, the workshops along the Potomac became known collectively as the "U.S. Musket Factory," while Hall's Rifle Works now became known as the "U.S. Rifle Factory."

Another new structure built by Symington was an "engine and guard-house, 35½ by 24 feet, one story brick, covered with slate, and having copper gutters and down spouts."[12] This relatively minor structure, completed in 1848, gained world-wide notoriety a decade later. It was in this building that John Brown and several of his followers barricaded themselves during the final hours of their ill-fated raid of October 16, 17, and 18, 1859. "John Brown's Fort," as the structure became known, would be the only Armory building to escape serious damage during the Civil War.

∽

The government's extensive renewal program for the Harpers Ferry Armory between 1845-1854 included the complete mechanical renovation of the workshops. Under the competent supervision of Master Armorer Benjamin Moor and his successor, Acting Master Armorer James H. Burton, a total of 121 new machines were installed in the Musket Factory. At the Rifle Factory, where many of John H. Hall's machines were adapted to the manufacture of muzzle-loading rifles, 33 new machines were installed.[13]

Benjamin Moor was appointed Master Armorer at Harpers Ferry in May 1830. Widely traveled, he had served at firearm manufactories in Springfield, Massachusetts; Philadelphia, and Pittsburgh, and was described as "an ingenious mechanik, compleat workman & judge of every part of a fire arm."[14] In April 1844, Moor received a capable new assistant, James H. Burton, who took employment as a "Machinist & Toolmaker" at the Rifle Factory. Burton,

just 20 years old, was a gifted machinist and, along with Moor, an ardent proponent of mechanized production. Burton also shared Moor's penchant for travel. During trips to the Springfield Armory, the nearby Ames Manufacturing Company in Chicopee, Massachusetts, and other New England manufactories, Burton took copious notes and made detailed sketches of the latest arms-making machinery. In 1845, Burton was promoted to Foreman of the Rifle Factory's Machine Shop. According to Major John Symington:

> In this situation, [Burton's] management was so satisfactory, and his ingenuity in devising, draughting and perfecting tools and machines so marked, as to cause me at once to select him as a fit person to fill the position of Master Armorer on the occurrence of a vacancy to that office . . .[15]

Burton's promotion to Acting Master Armorer came in November 1849, when Moor was forced to take an extended leave of absence owing to poor health.

Using furnished patterns and drawings, and their own notes and sketches, Moor and Burton were able to construct almost half of the

James H. Burton at age 37 in 1860. James Henry Burton Papers, Manuscripts and Archives, Yale University Library (Manuscript Group 117, Box 6, Folder 72, Copy negative no. 1356).

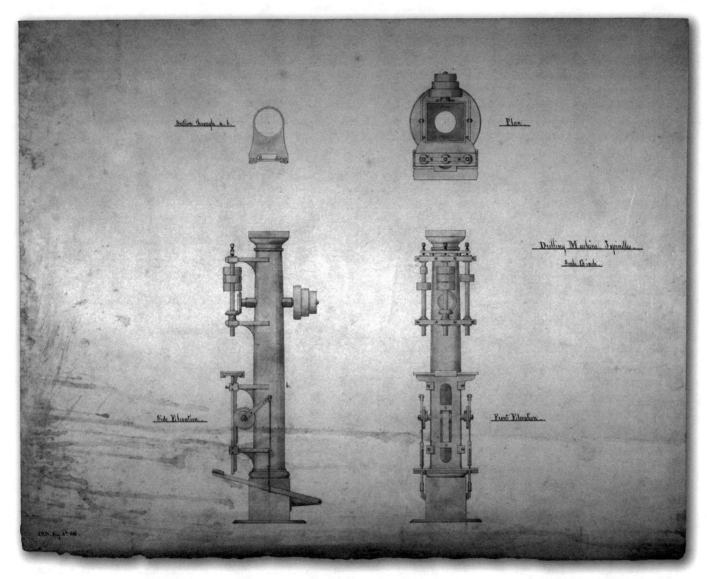

"Drilling machine, three spindles." The drawing, signed by James H. Burton on August 16, 1852, illustrates a vertical machine probably used for drilling locks, lock plates, and other small firearm components. A foot clutch mechanism raised and lowered a table beneath stationary spindles. Burton Drawings, Harpers Ferry NHP (Cat. No. 13655).

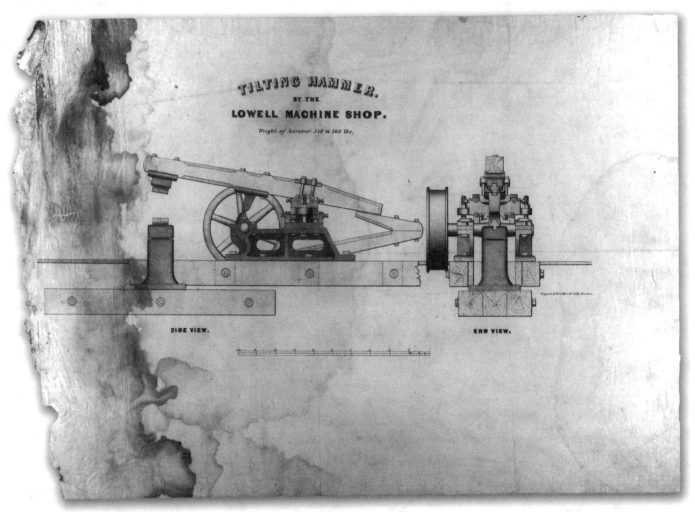

TILTING HAMMER,
BY THE
LOWELL MACHINE SHOP.

Weight of hammer 250 to 500 lbs.

SIDE VIEW.

END VIEW.

"Tilting Hammer by the Lowell Machine Shop. Weight of hammer 250-500 pounds." This drawing was probably obtained by James H. Burton or one of his Armory machinists during a visit to Lowell, Mass. Burton Drawings, Harpers Ferry NHP (Cat. No. 13724).

new machines for the Musket Factory and Rifle Factory in the Armory's own machine shops. Since the Armory lacked its own foundry facilities, however, castings for many of these machines were obtained from private firms, including Hugh Gilleece's Iron Foundry and John Wernwag's Machine Shop, both located on Virginius Island. Upon delivery to the Armory, these castings were fitted, filed, and assembled into finished units.

Buckland's improved versions of Thomas Blanchard's original stocking machinery. Ten of Buckland's new machines, featuring durable, compact all-metal construction, were purchased by the Harpers Ferry Armory. Separate units were furnished for turning, spotting, facing, double-profiling, and recessing the stocks of both muskets and rifles. Another 26 plain milling machines for the Musket Factory were also purchased from Ames. From the American Machine Works, the Harpers Ferry Armory purchased four stock-turning lathes, 12 milling machines, and various other production equipment.[16]

Continues on page 75

Second generation Blanchard lathe (above) and lock-bedding machine (right). May 20, 1859 drawings reproduced in Carolyn C. Cooper, "A Whole Battalion of Stockers: Thomas Blanchard's Production Line and Hand Labor at Springfield Armory." IA, The Journal of the Society for Industrial Archeology (Volume 14, Number 1, 1988).

All the remaining machines for the Harpers Ferry Armory were purchased from private firms located in such widely dispersed locations as Boston, Massachusetts; Keene, New Hampshire; Windsor, Vermont; West Troy, New York; Philadelphia, Pennsylvania; Baltimore, Maryland; and Alexandria, Virginia. But two firms in the Springfield, Massachusetts area—the Ames Manufacturing Company and the American Machine Works—furnished the bulk of the new armory machinery.

In 1853, the Ames Co. began manufacturing Cyrus

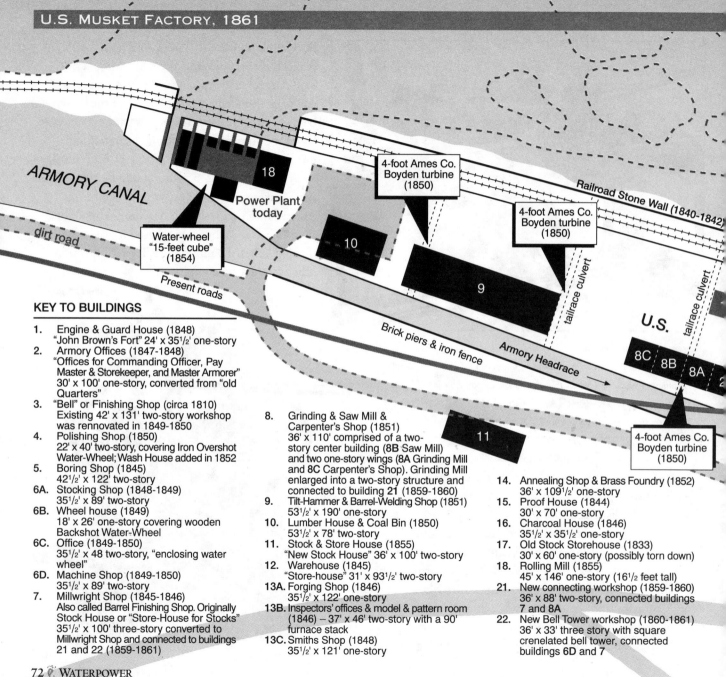

ARMORY CANAL

dirt road

Present roads

Power Plant today

Water-wheel "15-feet cube" (1854)

4-foot Ames Co. Boyden turbine (1850)

Railroad Stone Wall (1840-1842)

4-foot Ames Co. Boyden turbine (1850)

tailrace culvert

tailrace culvert

U.S.

18

10

9

Brick piers & iron fence

Armory Headrace

8C 8B 8A

11

4-foot Ames Co. Boyden turbine (1850)

KEY TO BUILDINGS

1. Engine & Guard House (1848)
   "John Brown's Fort" 24' x 35$\frac{1}{2}$' one-story
2. Armory Offices (1847-1848)
   "Offices for Commanding Officer, Pay Master & Storekeeper, and Master Armorer" 30' x 100' one-story, converted from "old Quarters"
3. "Bell" or Finishing Shop (circa 1810)
   Existing 42' x 131' two-story workshop was rennovated in 1849-1850
4. Polishing Shop (1850)
   22' x 40' two-story, covering Iron Overshot Water-Wheel; Wash House added in 1852
5. Boring Shop (1845)
   42$\frac{1}{2}$' x 122' two-story
6A. Stocking Shop (1848-1849)
   35$\frac{1}{2}$' x 89' two-story
6B. Wheel house (1849)
   18' x 26' one-story covering wooden Backshot Water-Wheel
6C. Office (1849-1850)
   35$\frac{1}{2}$' x 48 two-story, "enclosing water wheel"
6D. Machine Shop (1849-1850)
   35$\frac{1}{2}$' x 89' two-story
7. Millwright Shop (1845-1846)
   Also called Barrel Finishing Shop. Originally Stock House or "Store-House for Stocks" 35$\frac{1}{2}$' x 100' three-story converted to Millwright Shop and connected to buildings 21 and 22 (1859-1861)

8. Grinding & Saw Mill & Carpenter's Shop (1851)
   36' x 110' comprised of a two-story center building (8B Saw Mill) and two one-story wings (8A Grinding Mill and 8C Carpenter's Shop). Grinding Mill enlarged into a two-story structure and connected to building 21 (1859-1860)
9. Tilt-Hammer & Barrel-Welding Shop (1851)
   53$\frac{1}{2}$' x 190' one-story
10. Lumber House & Coal Bin (1850)
    53$\frac{1}{2}$' x 78' two-story
11. Stock & Store House (1855)
    "New Stock House" 36' x 100' two-story
12. Warehouse (1845)
    "Store-house" 31' x 93$\frac{1}{2}$' two-story
13A. Forging Shop (1846)
    35$\frac{1}{2}$' x 122' one-story
13B. Inspectors' offices & model & pattern room (1846) – 37' x 46' two-story with a 90' furnace stack
13C. Smiths Shop (1848)
    35$\frac{1}{2}$' x 121' one-story

14. Annealing Shop & Brass Foundry (1852)
    36' x 109$\frac{1}{2}$' one-story
15. Proof House (1844)
    30' x 70' one-story
16. Charcoal House (1846)
    35$\frac{1}{2}$' x 35$\frac{1}{2}$' one-story
17. Old Stock Storehouse (1833)
    30' x 60' one-story (possibly torn down)
18. Rolling Mill (1855)
    45' x 146' one-story (16$\frac{1}{2}$ feet tall)
21. New connecting workshop (1859-1860)
    36' x 88' two-story, connected buildings 7 and 8A
22. New Bell Tower workshop (1860-1861)
    36' x 33' three story with square crenelated bell tower, connected buildings 6D and 7

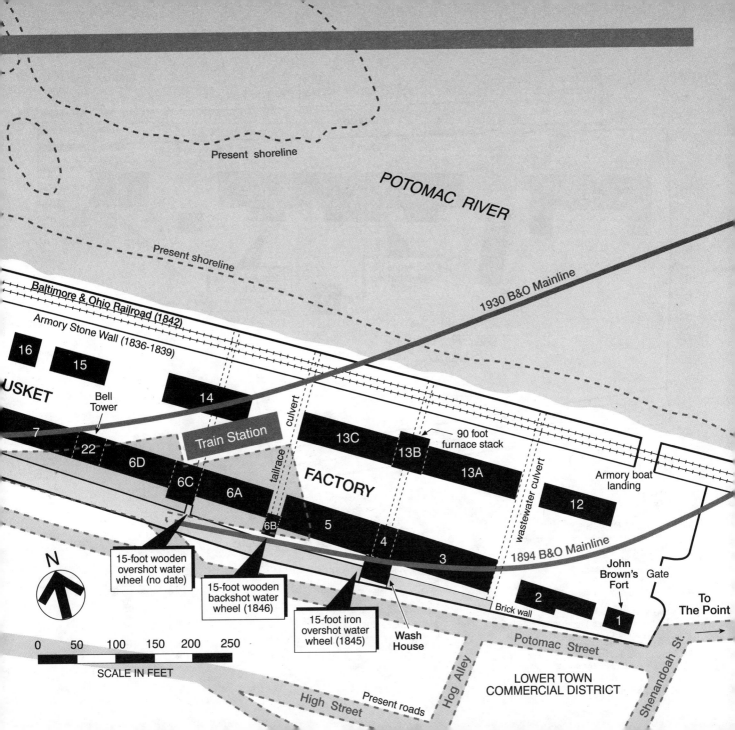

POTOMAC RIVER

Present shoreline

Present shoreline

Baltimore & Ohio Railroad (1842)

1930 B&O Mainline

Armory Stone Wall (1836-1839)

16

15

USKET

Bell
Tower

7

22

6D

6C

6A

6B

Train Station

14

Culvert

tailrace

FACTORY

13C

13B

13A

90 foot
furnace stack

wastewater culvert

12

Armory boat
landing

5

4

3

1894 B&O Mainline

John
Brown's
Fort

Gate

To
The Point

N

15-foot wooden
overshot water
wheel (no date)

15-foot wooden
backshot water
wheel (1846)

15-foot iron
overshot water
wheel (1845)

Wash
House

Brick wall

2

1

Potomac Street

0   50   100 150 200 250

SCALE IN FEET

Hog Alley

Shenandoah St.

LOWER TOWN
COMMERCIAL DISTRICT

Present roads

High Street

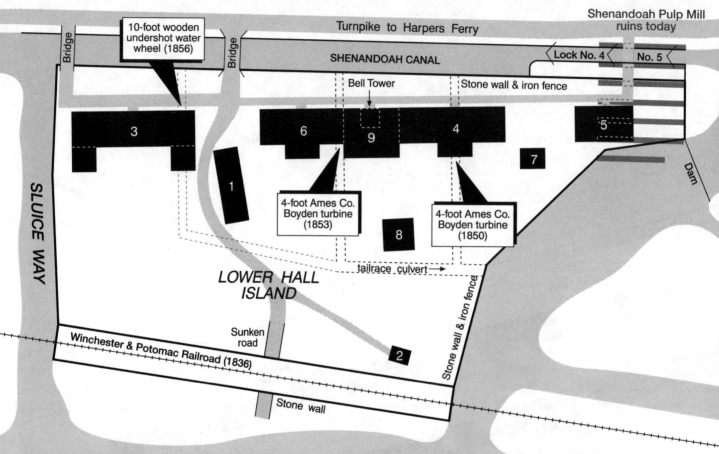

10-foot wooden undershot water wheel (1856)

Bridge

Bridge

Turnpike to Harpers Ferry

SHENANDOAH CANAL

Shenandoah Pulp Mill ruins today

Lock No. 4

No. 5

Bell Tower

Stone wall & iron fence

Dam

3

6

9

4

5

1

7

4-foot Ames Co. Boyden turbine (1853)

4-foot Ames Co. Boyden turbine (1850)

8

LOWER HALL ISLAND

tailrace culvert

SLICE WAY

Sunken road

Winchester & Potomac Railroad (1836)

Stone wall & iron fence

2

Stone wall

SHENANDOAH RIVER

KEY TO BUILDINGS

1. Filing Shop (1843-1844)
   74' x 25' two-story
2. Proof House (1845)
   19 1/2' x 15' one-story
3. Finishing & Machine Shop (1847-1848)
   128' x 35 1/2' two-story with two 24' x 24' one-story wings
4. Tilt-hammer & Forging Shop (1849-1851)
   110' x 35 1/2' one-story with 14 1/2' x 35 1/2' rear center projection
5. Annealing Furnace & Proof House (1851-1852) – 60' x 36' one-story

6. Machine Shop (1852-1853)
   87 1/2' x 35' one-story with 14' x 36' rear center projection
7. Coal house (1853-1854)
   25' x 21' one-story
8. Stock House (1853-1854)
   Originally the old Forging Shop at Hall's Rifle Works (1819); 30' x 30' two-story
9. Barrel Drilling & Finishing Shop (1859-1860)
   57 1/2' x 49 1/2' two-story

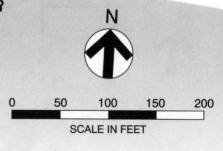

N

| 0 | 50 | 100 | 150 | 200 |

SCALE IN FEET

By 1854, mechanized production of interchangeable firearms was well underway throughout the Harpers Ferry Armory. Attesting to the significantly improved state of both national armories following the government's nine-year renewal program, Colonel H.K. Craig, the Chief of Ordnance and former superintendent at Harpers Ferry, wrote that "the buildings are now of a decidedly superior character to what they formerly were, and the machines, which have been almost entirely renewed, are of the best kind and most improved patterns." [17]

∞

The geographical diversity of the government's machinery suppliers reflects the broad national context in which industrial technology was now being shared. The enormous technical challenges imposed by interchangeable manufacture on a factory-wide basis had been largely overcome by the planning, expertise, and ingenuity of John H. Hall, John Symington, Benjamin Moor, and James Burton. Equally important was their access to the ideas and improvements of others, and their willingness to adopt them at Harpers Ferry.

Successfully applying waterpower to this expanded and highly mechanized production process called for a similarly Herculean effort. As early as 1830, Hall had understood the shortcomings of traditional waterpower systems in supporting mechanized production on a reliable basis. Between 1845 and 1854, Symington, Moor, Burton, and others were forced to draw upon their extensive mechanical expertise and their willingness to adopt new waterpower devices to meet the increased power demands of the armory's new machinery.

One particularly innovative hydraulic device was the reaction wheel. Like the tub wheel, reaction wheels were affixed to a vertical shaft, were relatively cheap, required little space, and ran at greater velocities than conventional water wheels. But reaction wheels operated according to significantly different hydraulic principles from tub wheels. Whereas a tub wheel was set in motion by the impact or impulse of water striking and splashing off horizontal blades, a reaction wheel was "one propelled by the pressure of the water in the direction of the circular motion of the wheel developed by the discharge of the water in a contrary direction." Water actually moved *through* a reaction wheel, exerting force upon wheel passages through reactive pressure. [18]

Tub wheels typically possessed an estimated efficiency of only about 10 percent; a reaction wheel's efficiency was closer to 40 percent. Reaction wheels were also able to run submerged, a significant advantage in sites prone to backwater; tub wheels could only operate above the level of the tailwater. Still, a good reaction wheel did not match the horsepower output or efficiency of a well-built conventional water wheel, which often could convert from 60-75 percent of the energy available in falling water to power.

One of the first reaction wheels in America was patented by James Rumsey of Shepherdstown, Va., in 1791. Rumsey had served as the first superintendent of the Patowmack Company and had toured the Potomac River with George Washington in August 1785 (*see page 23*). "Rumsey's improved principle of reaction" featured an enclosed rotor which was acted upon both by pressure and reaction of water exiting from the casing. Rumsey also introduced a wooden flume that directed the flow

Sketch of "a new and most efficacious Hydraulical Machine" by Joseph Barnes, September 21, 1792. Barnes, an associate of James Rumsey, based his water wheel design upon "Rumsey's improved principle of reaction." Water was admitted to the hollow wheel from below through a wooden trunk or penstock (A, right), then expelled from the periphery of the wheel through six apertures (numbered 1-6, bottom left). The reaction of water exiting the wheel in tangents gave "the rotatorey [sic] motion and force to the Machine." (Joseph Barnes to John Vaughan, Sept. 21, 1792. American Philosophical Society, courtesy Nick Blanton, The Rumseian Society, Shepherdstown, W.Va.).

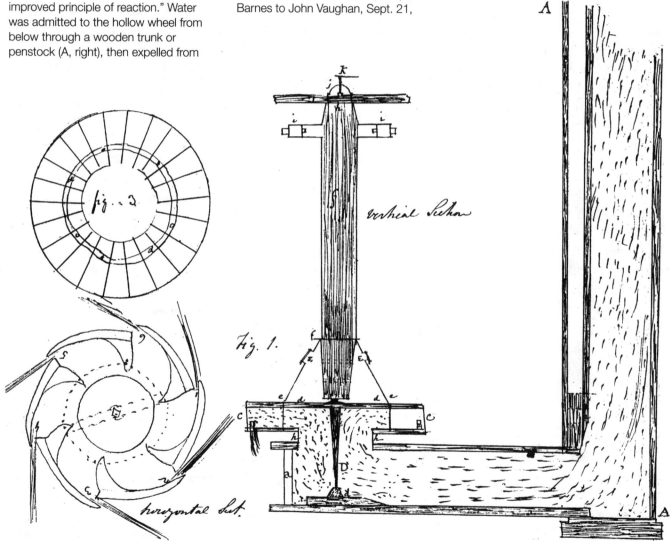

of water up, rather than down, into the rotor; this removed the weight of the headwater from the wheel and consequently reduced wear and strain on the device's wooden components. Rumsey's reaction wheel was further developed by his associate Joseph Barnes, who drew up detailed sketches of "a new and most efficacious Hydraulical Machine" in 1792 (*see illustration on facing page*). Barnes added multiple curved exits or apertures to the wheel casing, directing the water exiting through these apertures in a tangential direction, further increasing the force of reaction upon the rotor.[19]

During the early decades of the 19th century, millwrights expended "a vast amount of ingenuity" on the fabrication of improved reaction wheels. The introduction of iron gave these devices greater strength and durability, provided greater precision in design and construction, and made possible smoother and more efficient operation. On the subject of reaction wheels, James B. Francis, chief engineer and superintendent of the Locks and Canals at Lowell, Mass., wrote:

not less than three hundred patents relating to them, had been granted by the United States Government. They continue, perhaps as much as ever, to be the subject of almost innumerable modifications. Within a few years, there has been a manifest improvement in them, and there are now several varieties in use, in which the wheels themselves are of simple forms, and of single pieces of cast-iron, giving a useful effect

approaching sixty per cent of the power expended.[20]

On November 30, 1844, Major John Symington requested $550 "For the purchase and fitting up of a turbine wheel and bevel gearing" at the Harpers Ferry Armory. The new wheel was not reported in place, however, until June 30, 1846:

Machinery constructed and put in Operation during the year At the Musket Factory— 1 Turbine reaction Water Wheel, with Penstock and Cast iron gates, Shafting and bevel gearing, for driving the Fan-Blast for Smith's forges and grindstones.[21]

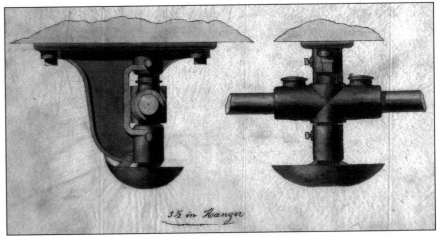

3½-inch ceiling hangers for overhead line shafting. Cups or catch basins were affixed beneath the hangers to catch lubricant dispensed from small reservoirs. At the time these drawings were made in the early 1850s, tallow or animal fat would have been used to lubricate the line shafts. Burton Drawings, Harpers Ferry NHP (Cat. No. 13668).

Although the terms "reaction wheel" and "turbine" were often used interchangeably, there were important differences between the two devices. An early reaction wheel, like the one Symington described above for the Harpers Ferry Armory, was typically assembled in a local machine shop from stock patterns using crude, un-machined castings. Turbines, on the other hand, "were built in some of the most advanced machine shops of the country." As a consequence, reaction wheels "usually gave a very small effect in proportion to the quantity of water expended" whereas the first turbines exhibited "a useful effect of seventy-five per cent. of the power expended."[22]

No mention is made in surviving Armory records on the operation or performance of this particular "Turbine reaction Water Wheel," but Symington's interest in the new technology was apparently piqued. On January 7, 1847, he submitted the following request to the Ordnance Department:

> From the various reports touching the merits of different water wheels improved from the French Turbines, and put in operation throughout this country. I am at a loss to determine which to select for the Armory. Two wheels of this description, highly spoken of especially as to cheapness, and known as Dripps Wheel, and Parkers Wheel, are in operation at various factories & mills at and near Coatesville and Manyunk near Phila.
>
> I propose therefore, provided you think proper to give me an order to that effect, to proceed to those places, will access to judge by a personal examination, and inquiries, as to the relative

advantages of these wheels. and how they compare with the Turbine Wheel now in operation at the Armory . . .[23]

The "Parker Patent Percussion and Reaction Water Wheel" was based upon James Rumsey's original wheel. Water entered the cast-iron Parker wheel from below through a central opening and was discharged horizontally through channels formed by iron plates. Austin and Zebulon Parker made several important improvements of their own, including the addition of a "helical sluice"— a spiral guide which channeled incoming water in the same direction as the motion of the wheel. This modification dramatically increased the speed of their own reaction wheel—from 80 to 280 rpms—and required a smaller volume of water. They also added a draft box or tube, comprised of an airtight casing which extended from the wheel outlet into the tailrace. This permitted the wheel to operate above the level of the tailrace with no adverse effect on efficiency, and furnished millwrights with easy access to the wheel for examination, maintenance, and repair. Patents for the Parker wheel were taken out in 1829 and again in 1840, and the wheels were built under licensing arrangements by small machine shops all across the country.[24]

In 1845, William Dripps of Coatesville, Pa., received a patent for his own "Improvement in Water Wheels." The Dripps wheel differed from the Parker wheel in that water entered the wheel casing through narrow slots arranged in a circular pattern around the casing's top, made a 90 degree inward turn through straight guide vanes surrounding the wheel, then passed downward, pressing against curved wheel buckets, and giving the wheel motion. In 1847, Joseph R. Anderson installed two Dripps wheels at the Tredegar Iron Works in Richmond, Virginia. The performance of these wheels, however, proved very unsatisfactory, requiring "4 times as much water as an overshot wheel" to do the same amount of work. Within a year, both Dripps wheels were scrapped.[25]

There is no record that Symington acquired either a Parker Wheel or a Dripps Wheel for the Harpers Ferry Armory. Nonetheless, he was certainly becoming familiar with the operating characteristics of these new types of wheels, and learning about the differences between simple reaction wheels and true turbines. After 1847, Symington turned his attention almost exclusively to the more highly developed "water wheels improved from the French Turbines."

~

In 1827, Benoit Fourneyron, a French engineer, introduced a hydraulic turbine—a device that channeled water through an enclosed chamber fitted with an inner ring of fixed guide blades. These guide blades deflected the water outward against the moving vanes of a "runner." The vanes of this outer runner were curved in the opposite direction from the fixed inner guide blades, reversing the direction of water flow within the device and creating a reactive force. Fourneyron's patent, obtained in 1832, described his invention as "a wheel of universal and continuous pressure or hydraulic turbine." Unlike conventional water wheels, where water operated only upon a portion of the buckets or floats at a given time, all the working surfaces of the turbine were simultaneously subject to the pressure and reaction of

the water passing through the wheel. Careful experiments showed that the Fourneyron wheel operated with an efficiency ranging from 70 to 75 percent.

Fourneyron's design, commonly known as an "outward flow" turbine, was adopted by several American engineers, including Ellwood Morris of Philadelphia; Uriah A. Boyden of Lowell, Mass.; and George Kilburn of Fall River, Mass. Kilburn, master mechanic of the print-works of Andrew Robeson & Sons, built a copy of the Fourneyron turbine based upon a description provided by his employer, who had seen the wheel in operation in France. Kilburn's wheel, fabricated in 1844, was a complete success. In 1846, E.C. Kilburn and Company was formed, and the firm began building George Kilburn's turbine-wheel for the market (*see illustrations on following page*). Within a very short time, the company's "Fourneyron or Outward Discharge Turbine Water-wheel," more commonly known as "The Fall River Turbine," was being used by textile mills throughout New England and in such far-flung places as Alabama, Georgia, and Tennessee. As we will shall soon see, this new turbine was also used on Virginius Island at Harpers Ferry.[26]

While George Kilburn was fabricating his new turbine in 1844, Uriah A. Boyden visited Andrew Robeson & Sons, and "received from Mr. Kilburn every facility for examining both the construction and operation of the wheel."[27] The following year, Boyden patented an improved version of the "outward flow" turbine to meet the exacting requirements of the great Lowell textile mills (*see illustrations on following page*). Boyden's design featured a conical approach passage, giving the incoming water a gradually increasing velocity and a spiral motion that corresponded to the direction of the motion of the wheel; an improved gate mechanism for regulating the flow of water to the wheel; improved guide vanes which directed the flow of water through the wheel passages more efficiently; and a "diffuser" similar in principle to the Parker Wheel's draft box, helping control the passage of water leaving the wheel and contributing an additional three to five percent to the wheel's efficiency. In tests conducted by James B. Francis in 1845 and documented in the *Lowell Hydraulic Experiments*, the Boyden turbine was found to convert 88 percent of the energy available in the falling water into power. This compared extremely favorably with the 60-75 percent efficiency rating of a conventional water wheel, and the 40-60 percent efficiency of a typical reaction wheel.

Hydraulic turbines shared all the advantages of reaction wheels: they required relatively little space, not needing large and expensive masonry wheelpits typically required for conventional water wheels; they operated at a greater velocity than conventional water wheels, resulting in more perfect regularity of machine speeds; they ran submerged, reducing the adverse effects of backwater and ice; and, being fabricated from iron, they required very little maintenance. Unlike reaction wheels, hydraulic turbines were engineered to very high standards in some of the nation's most advanced machine shops, resulting in greater horsepower output and much more efficient operation.

∿

On June 30, 1848, Symington reported that a "6 feet diameter Turbine wheel with main driving gear and drums" was constructed in the new Finishing Shop at the Rifle Factory. A second six-foot turbine was subsequently installed in that shop, and both wheels were

Disk (left) and turbine wheel or runner (right) from the Fall River Turbine. The turbine wheel engaged into the fixed disk from below and received the outward discharge of water from the disk's spiral guide vanes. Unlike a conventional water wheel, where water operated only upon a portion of the buckets at a given time, all the working surfaces of the turbine were simultaneously subject to the pressure and reactive force of water passing through the wheel. Courtesy The American Textile History Museum.

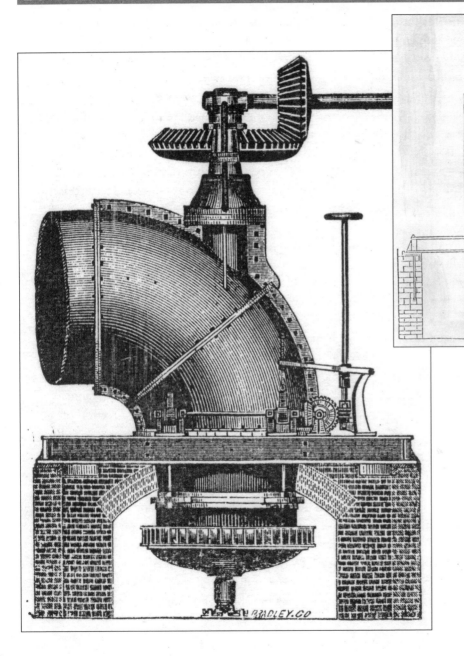

Boyden turbine illustration and section, from a Bradley Company catalog. "In this cut **A** is the quarter turn through which the water is admitted to the turbine; **D** is the wheel; **E** is the plate for securing the wheel to the shaft; **F** is one of the girders for supporting the turbine, &c, of which there are two extending entirely across the pit; **H** is a pipe which encloses the shaft **S** from contact with the water; and **R** is one of the toothed racks attached to the gate rods, of which there are four for operating the gate by means of pinions whose shafts are connected and moved by a worm and gear." Courtesy Smithsonian Institution.

operating by June 30, 1849. The total cost for these two wheels was $4,200, a price consistent with large Fourneyron-type outward flow turbines. Unfortunately, Symington gave no further details, nor did he name the manufacturer, so the origin of these wheels is not known.[28]

Within just a few years, however, these two turbines proved unsatisfactory. On October 31, 1855, Armory superintendent Henry Clowe complained about the defective condition of these wheels to Colonel Henry Craig at the Ordnance Department:

> Permit me to call your attention, to the great necessity, which I also explained verbally to you, at your last visit to the Armory, of substituting for the two Turbine water wheels at the Rifle Factory, a new Undershot Wheel.
>
> I am at no time certain of the availability of those wheels for efficient service, and a full description of the trouble they give us for repairs, is recited in my Estimates for the ensuing fiscal year.[29]

As promised, Clowe's full description of the problems with these turbines was furnished in his Estimates for Fiscal Year 1856-1857:

> The two turbine water-wheels now in use in this shop are placed so low in the pit, that it is difficult to make the necessary repairs when required; at some seasons of the year they cannot be made at all. Should any accident happen during the winter, or in the sickly season during the summer, the exposure of the health of the workmen incident to the repairs would be such as to preclude to a great extent, and perhaps entirely, its accomplishment with reasonable cost.
>
> All this being occasioned by back-water arising from the dam across the Shenandoah river, erected by the Harper's Ferry and Shenandoah Manufacturing Company, in connexion [sic] with the deep position of the turbine wheels, which back-water is liable to stop the works for necessary repairs for two or three weeks at a time.
>
> It is proposed to substitute for these a new undershot wheel with cut-stone head-blocks, cut-iron frame, fitted, framed, and erected upon the most approved plan.[30]

Colonel Craig subsequently authorized the replacement of the two turbines with a single conventional undershot wheel. The new wheel, "designed to perform the service lately performed by the two old ones," was put into operation in the Finishing Shop by June 30, 1856. In details of construction and direction of rotation, an undershot wheel resembled a typical breast wheel. It lacked, however, the tight-fitting apron that served to keep the falling water in the wheel buckets during rotation, and averaged an efficiency of no more than 40 percent. The new undershot wheel measured 10 feet in diameter by 12 feet wide, was made of wood with a cast-iron shaft, and was supplied with water by a cast-iron penstock 21 feet long, three feet wide, and three feet high. The main driving drums, shafts, and other millwork in the Finishing Shop were also renovated and improved.[31]

This episode demonstrated the imperfect results sometimes obtained from the adoption of new reaction devices. Just as Joseph R. Anderson had learned at the Tredegar Iron Works, Henry Clowe, too, realized that the introduction of new but untested water wheels provided no guarantees for success. Throughout the 1840s and 1850s, millwrights and engineers everywhere struggled to understand the operating principles of these unfamiliar new devices. The fact that reaction wheels and turbines were so often described interchangeably demonstrates the confusion that existed about the precise merits of these different hydraulic devices. Even a single wheel configuration might exhibit widely different operating characteristics from one millseat to another depending upon streamflow, headwater, and machinery load. Wrote one 19th century mechanical engineer:

> As is the case of vertical water wheels, in the economical use of turbines much depends on their exact adaptation to the stream and site where they are employed, and in every case these points should be carefully studied and the turbine constructed accordingly . . . . The introduction into general use of the turbine has been considerably retarded by these points not being borne in mind, and by the construction of a number of wheels of exactly the same pattern, whether they met the requirements of the case or not, when a few simple modifications might have secured a far higher practical result.[32]

The efficiency ratings claimed by different wheel manufacturers added to the confusion. Since wheel efficiency claims were not confirmed by independent testing during the early days of turbine manufacture,

Conventional water wheels at the U.S. Musket Factory: the remains of a 15-foot diameter wooden overshot water wheel are visible near the ruins of the Smith & Forging Shop, circa 1869. This wheel was located between the Stocking Shop and Machine Shop. Harpers Ferry NHP (HF-685).

Conventional water wheels at the U.S. Musket Factory: remains of a wooden "Backshot Water Wheel, 15 feet diameter, 10 feet wide." The water wheel and large masonry wheel pit were completed in 1846. A wheel house originally covered the water-wheel and main driving gear. The wheel was located between the Boring Shop and Stocking Shop. Harpers Ferry NHP (HF-1727).

millwrights had no accurate way to measure the claims of one manufacturer against another, or to even ensure that manufacturers were being honest.

Confusion, lack of familiarity, and the expensive mistakes that sometimes resulted served to retard the adoption of these important new hydraulic devices. Just as Henry Clowe at Harpers Ferry showed no hesitation in replacing his two new turbines with a tried and true

conventional water wheel, so too other millwrights found comfort and security in the traditional and thoroughly familiar old water wheels. This helps explain why the Harpers Ferry Armory, while experimenting with and adopting new reaction wheels and turbines, continued to construct, repair, and rely upon conventional water wheels right up until the Civil War. In addition to the new undershot wheel placed in the Rifle Factory Finishing Shop in 1856, four conventional water wheels continued to operate at the Musket Factory during the 1850s: **1**) a 15-foot wooden overshot water wheel was located underneath the two-story brick office connecting the Stocking Shop and Machine Shop; **2**) a wooden "Backshot Water Wheel" 15 feet in diameter by 10 feet wide was constructed in 1846 and enclosed by a brick wheelhouse connected to the Stocking Shop; **3**) a 15-foot cast-iron overshot wheel was located beneath the two-story brick Polishing Shop connected with the Boring Shop and "Bell" or Finishing Shop; and **4**) a "water-wheel, 15 feet cube, master wheel and gearing" was installed in the new Rolling Mill in 1854.[33]

❧

In 1849, the Ames Manufacturing Company—one of the government's principle suppliers of arms-making machinery—began manufacturing Boyden turbines under a licensing arrangement at their machine shop in Chicopee, Mass. A year later, in May 1850, the Harpers Ferry Armory purchased their first Boyden turbine from Ames for the new Tilt Hammer Shop at the Rifle Factory. Described as a "4 feet cast iron Turbine wheel & Flume," the water-wheel, fixtures, cast-iron forebay and penstock cost $1,157, including freight from Boston.[34]

In September 1850, three more Boyden turbines were purchased from the Ames Manufacturing Company and installed at the Musket Factory—one in the new Grinding & Saw Mill, and two in the new Tilt-Hammer Shop. These turbine wheels measured 42 inches in diameter by 4½ inches deep. The cost, including "cast-iron flumes, wrought-iron forebays and fixtures complete," totaled $6,137—$2,000 for each turbine and $137 for freight from Boston. These turbines also included water-wheel regulators or governors—an important component of these new waterpower systems.[35]

Remains of a turbine pit on the site of the U.S. Rifle Factory's Machine Shop. An Ames Company Boyden turbine was installed here in 1853. February 1987 photo by the author.

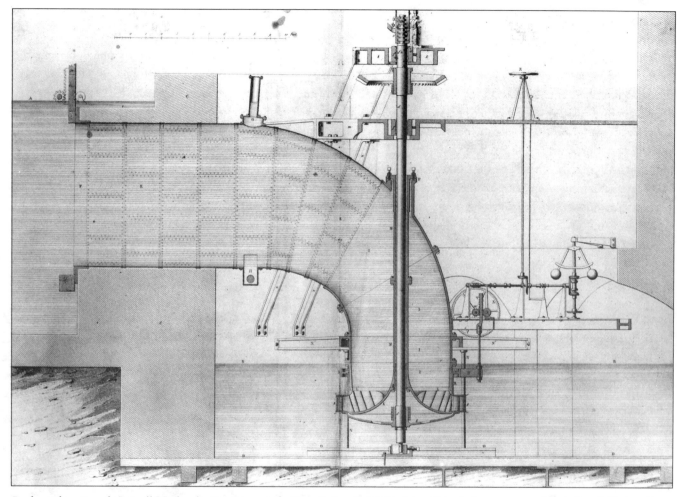

Boyden turbine, from the Lowell Hydraulic Experiments *by James B. Francis, 1868 edition. This wheel was constructed by the Lowell Machine Shop in 1851. The wheel's gate mechanism included a water wheel governor (right). Hagley Museum and Library (#75.461.1).*

One of the earliest and most accurate descriptions of water-wheel governors appeared in an 1825 government report:

These machines are calculated to raise the gate, and give additional power by increasing the column of water on the wheel when the motion is too slow, and depress the gate and diminish the column when the motion of the wheel is too rapid. By this means a regular and nearly uniform motion is preserved in the operation of all the wheels and machinery.[36]

Water-wheel governors became a common and increasingly sophisticated appendage to waterpower installations during the age of the hydraulic turbine.

The Harpers Ferry Armory purchased its fifth Boyden turbine from Ames in early 1853. It was placed in a wheel-pit of cut stone beneath the new Machine Shop at the Rifle Factory. The installation included a new stone and cast-iron forebay, a new culvert that drained the tailwater from the wheel pit, and a "large force pump, for throwing water in case of fire," that was attached directly to the turbine casing.[37]

The sixth and last Ames Company Boyden turbine ordered by the Harpers Ferry Armory was never delivered to the Virginia manufactory. During Fiscal Year 1858-1859, the government placed a $10,000 order with James T. Ames for a barrel-rolling machine and a Boyden turbine measuring 36 inches in diameter by 3 inches deep to drive the new machine. When armory managers subsequently decided to place the barrel-rolling machine in the Tilt-Hammer Shop and use the building's existing turbines to power the device, they found they had no need for the new turbine. Ames

Detail of a Boyden turbine runner. Boyden fitted a Diffuser, comprised of two stationary discs (shaded in drawing), around the outside circumference of the runner. This device served to slow the velocity of water leaving the wheel and thereby retained a portion of the water's energy otherwise lost. Hagley Museum & Library (#75.461.4).

offered to omit the new turbine from the order and reduce the barrel-rolling machine contract by $500. Such a small reduction, however, suited neither Armory Superintendent Alfred M. Barbour nor Master Machinist Armistead Ball, who estimated the actual cost of the turbine and cast-iron flume to be closer to $2,500. Unable to reach an acceptable compromise, and having no need for the new turbine at Harpers Ferry, the Ordnance Department had Ames deliver the turbine to the Springfield Armory in September 1859. The barrel-rolling machine was delivered to the Harpers Ferry Armory at about the same time.[38]

During the two decades prior to the Civil War, the government waterworks at Harpers Ferry received constant attention from Armory managers determined to capture the maximum streamflow available from the Potomac and Shenandoah rivers. The Armory's annual Reports of Operations submitted to the Ordnance Department reveal that funds were expended for repairs or improvements to the government's dams and canals in all but four years between 1842-1861.[39]

An example of the type of work performed appears in the Armory's Report of Operations for June 30, 1843:

> During the past Season, the canal which supplies the power from the Dam on the Potomac, has received extensive and thorough repairs, in new Head Gates, a Pier head and Ice breakers, and new Gates to the Lock which admits boats with Coal and other supplies for the Armory; indeed, the whole mass of masonry at the head of the Canal, and lock, have been renewed and the Canal cleared out—whereby the power will be much increased in periods of low water, and a more uniform supply of water be obtained . . .[40]

Undated drawing of a Boyden turbine with cast-iron flume and shafting at the Springfield Armory. A notation on the drawing instructs the millwright to "place the top of the wheel 1½ ft below top of water line in race." Springfield Armory NHS (NHSD #400).

The most common annual expenses included repairs to damaged stone masonry caused by ice and high water; replacement of stone facing, timber cribbing, and rock fill on the Potomac and Shenandoah dams; renewal of wooden headgates feeding the canals; and removal of sand, silt, and other debris from the canals and raceways. The most significant cause of damage during this period was the flood of April 18, 1852, an account of which appeared in the *Virginia Free Press*:

GREAT FRESHET AT HARPERS-FERRY.

Our county has been visited by an awful calamity.—The oldest inhabitants never before witnesses [*sic*] such a rise in the waters of the Potomac and Shenandoah river.—The inundation came upon us like an avalanche—sudden, unexpected and overwhelming . . .

By Tuesday morning the streets of Harpers Ferry, had become channels for mighty rivers, and the second and third stories and house-tops, resting places for its distressed inhabitants . . .

The destruction of property is beyond all description. Every house on Shenandoah and Potomac streets was almost entirely submerged—the water being six feet higher than at any other period within the recollection of man . . .

The loss of property belonging to the U.S. Armory, as well as to private citizens, cannot at present be estimated, but is very great . . .[41]

The flood left behind considerable "sandbars and obstructions" in the Armory Canal, caused extensive

Boyden turbine, from a Bradley Company catalog. Smithsonian Institution (No. 43-10).

damage to the "walls and embankments" of the Shenandoah Canal, and necessitated the replacement of 1083 perches of stone and 916 cubic yards of filling on the "Dam over the Potomac, which was much injured by the flood of 1852."[42] (*See **Floods at Harpers Ferry**, pages 164-165*).

Continues on page 94

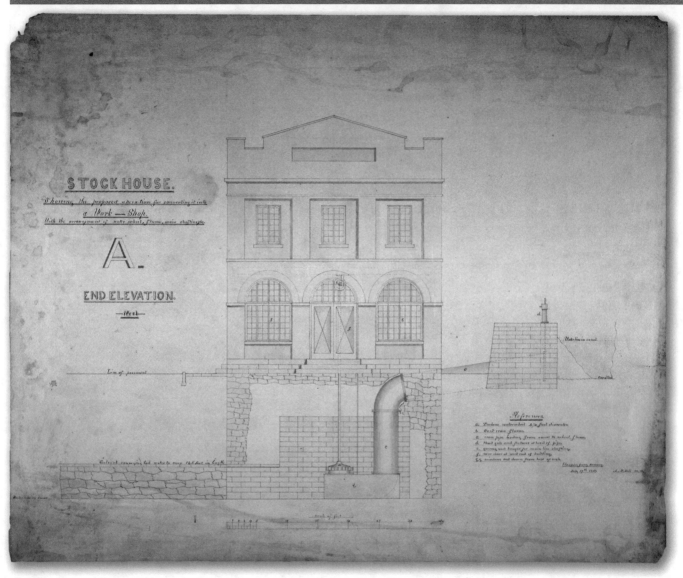

"End Elevation" of the Stock House, showing the proposed alteration for converting it into a workshop with the arrangement of water wheel, flume, main shafting, etc., drawn by Master Machinist Armistead M. Ball, July 17, 1858. Burton Drawings, Harpers Ferry NHP (Cat. No. 13694).

In November 1855, the Ordnance Department asked superintendent Henry W. Clowe to commence the fabrication of "Dragoon Swords and Artillery Sabres" at the Harpers Ferry Armory. Clowe responded to this request on November 23:

There is a Building, located immediately on the line of our Canal at the Musket Factory, the old Stock House, about 45 feet West of the Machine Shop, which is suitable in location, and with some alterations would be convenient as a Shop, where most of this Sword work might be done. There is likewise ample water power, that can readily be applied to driving the necessary machinery in the Building, either by putting in proper position a small Turbine, now on hand with all the fixtures, which was purchased for a Fan Blast in the Rolling Mill and not used, or by gearing to the power afforded in the Water Wheel of the Machine Shop, by underground shafting. [1]

The turbine Clowe described was probably the "Turbine reaction Water Wheel" acquired by the Armory in 1846, which included "Penstock and

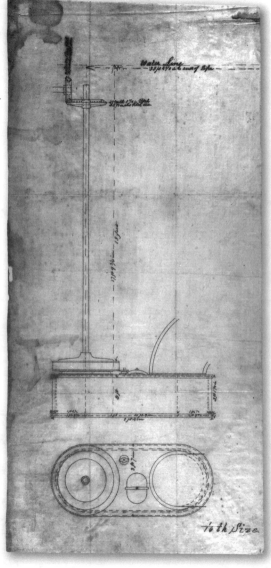

Detail of a 4½ foot diameter turbine water wheel with vertical shaft and cast-iron penstock, for the proposed improvement of the Stock House. Burton Drawings, Harpers Ferry NHP (Cat. No. 13703).

Cast iron gates, Shafting and bevel gearing, for driving the Fan-Blast." [2]

Four drawings, completed in 1858 by Armistead M. Ball, the Armory's Master Machinist, show the proposed conversion of the Musket Factory Stock House into a workshop for the manufacture of Dragoon Swords and Artillery Sabres. The drawings illustrate the proposed installation of a "Turbine waterwheel 4½ feet dimension" in the basement of this shop. [3]

In Ball's *End Elevation* drawing, the Penstock is situated *underneath* the 4½-foot turbine wheel. This arrangement differed significantly from the prescribed installation of a Boyden turbine, but was typical of early reaction wheel installations—including those of the well-known Parker Wheel (*see also Rumsey's Improved Principle of Reaction on page 76*).

---

1. H.W. Clowe to H.K. Craig, Nov. 23, 1855.
2. Report of operations for the year ending June 30, 1846.
3. Armistead Ball's Stock House drawings are part of the James H. Burton collection, which includes over 100 hand-tinted drawings, pencil sketches, and hand-written notes from the Harpers Ferry Armory. The drawings, many of them signed by Acting Master Armorer James. H. Burton, date from the 1850s. The drawings were found during a home restoration project in Winchester, Va., in 1984, and were subsequently acquired by the Harpers Ferry Historical Assn. and donated to Harpers Ferry NHP.

STOCK HOUSE.

Exhibiting the alteration for converting it into a workshop &c. &c.

H.K.Armory

FRONT ELEVATION

B.

Above: "Front Elevation" of the Stock House. Burton Drawings (Cat. No. 13695); Opposite page: "Plan" of the Stock House (Cat. No. 13696).

Millwrights who adopted these early reaction wheels had learned the importance of "bringing the head water to bear underneath the wheel, so as to cause the upward pressure of the head water to exactly balance the downward pressure and weight of the wheel with its upright shaft."[4] By this arrangement, the friction and wear on the bearings was considerably reduced, and the life of the cast-iron wheel prolonged.

In October 1858, just a few months after Armistead Ball had completed his Stock House drawings, Chief of Ordnance H.K. Craig authorized superintendent Clowe to proceed with the conversion of the workshop. Apparently not satisfied with the water wheel proposed by Ball, and no doubt mindful of the recent failure of the two turbines at the Rifle Factory (*see page 82*), Craig then added:

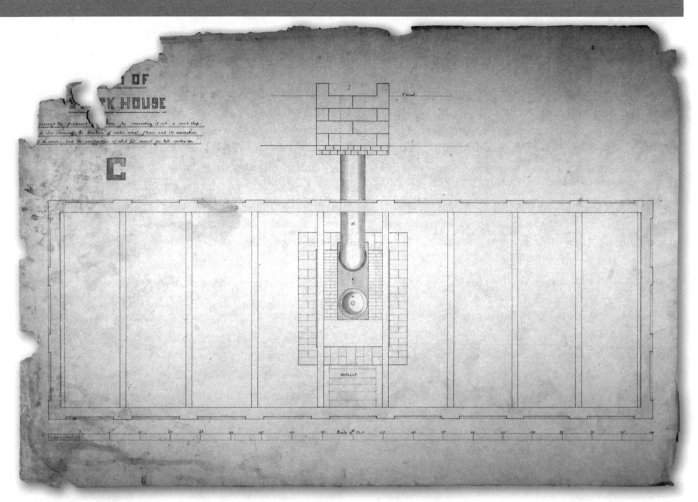

I have however to remark that it will be adviseable [sic] to have recourse to some experienced manufacturer to procure the Turbine Wheel you propose to introduce. Mr. J.T. Ames of Chicopee has deserved reputation in such work; and I understand there is another manufacturer of these Wheels, in, or near Worcester Massachusetts.[5]

The conversion of the Stock House into a Millwright Shop, which commenced in 1859, was not completed until 1861. No new turbine was ever installed in this shop; instead, power was delivered by underground shafting from the adjacent Machine Shop.

4. M. Powis Bale, *Saw-Mills* (London: Crosby Lockwood and Co., 1883), 54.
5. H.K. Craig to Henry W. Clowe, October 9, 1858. The firm in Worcester manufactured Monroe's wheel, a "center-vent" turbine of 60 horsepower. (*Springfield Daily Republican*, October 30, 1858).

During the next few years, the dirt banks along the canals adjacent to both the Musket Factory and Rifle Factory were replaced with cut stone walls. These improvements helped prevent the accumulation of silt and debris washed into the canals from adjacent roads and hillsides, and promoted the more efficient flow of water into the various water wheel flumes. In 1853, the entire canal basin at the Rifle Factory was walled in with "409 feet of dry wall nearly 6 feet high by 3 wide" along the road to Harpers Ferry, and "a dry wall, 224 feet long, 6½ feet high, and 3 feet thick" alongside the workshops. At the Musket Factory, the headrace was also walled in: a cut stone wall was built along the south bank of the canal adjacent to Potomac Street in 1855, and "a substantial wall of cut stone the whole way up to the rolling mill" alongside the workshops was completed in 1860 (*see **Ruins of the Armory Headrace**, page 174*).[43]

Despite these improvements to the Musket Factory raceways, the supply of water from the Potomac River was apparently still not adequate. By all accounts, the original Armory Dam, which had been completed in 1800, rebuilt in 1809, 1820, and 1828, and repaired or renewed countless more times, remained deficient. On February 18, 1859, the government contracted with the firm Snovell & Company for the erection of a new armory dam across the Potomac River. On about March 3, 1859, under the supervision of government engineer Thomas Patterson, the contractor began laying masonry for the new dam on the Maryland side of the river. A dry season proved most favorable to the contractor and his workmen, and construction of the dam was "rapidly

"Plans For A Dam For The Use Of The U.S. Armory At Harper's Ferry, Va." The drawing, which dates from about 1858, describes the proposed dam as a "dressed stone structure" and illustrates both the stone coping (left) and timber protection (right). Hagley Museum and Library (Accession 1534, Oversize Material).

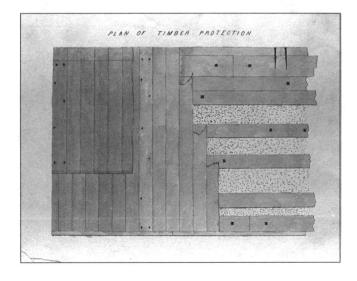

progressing" throughout the summer. In October 1859, however, John A. Snovell disappeared with $1,500 of the firm's funds, and the United States canceled its contract with Snovell & Company.[44]

A new contract was awarded to Hugh L. Gallaher in March 1860, and work on the dam resumed shortly thereafter. But in September 1860, engineer Patterson reported that work had been much delayed by frequent high water during the year. Of a proposed total length of 1,470 feet, only 420 feet of masonry was complete, and just 300 feet of the dam was timbered and sheeted. Of approximately $60,100 appropriated for dam construction, about $40,000 had been spent, and the dam was only one-third complete. In January 1861, Patterson was dismissed, and construction was put under the direct supervision of Armory superintendent Alfred M. Barbour. The contractor awaited the arrival of spring to resume construction, but the Civil War erupted in April 1861, and the new dam was never completed.

COMMERCIAL MANUFACTURING ON VIRGINIUS ISLAND

The period 1844-1861 witnessed some startling changes on Virginius Island. A robust national economy, growing popular support for Southern manufacturing, new mechanical innovations, and the recent arrival of both railroad and canal stimulated the introduction of corporate enterprise and the expansion of commercial manufacturing on the island. At the same time, many of the relatively small establishments here continued to operate much as they had in the past, serving primarily the modest needs of the local community.

Entrepreneurs who ignored the expansion of commercial manufacturing did so at their own peril, as goods arriving by rail and canal from such far-away places as Alexandria, Baltimore, Philadelphia, and other east coast locations could now compete with locally-made products. Businesses that chose to compete aggressively with distant manufactories faced risks too: large commercial establishments required ample waterpower and considerable capital for factory buildings and machinery. Business enterprise on Virginius Island after 1844 experienced some notable successes and failures in the new commercial marketplace.

Two events had a particularly important impact on the development of commercial manufacturing at Virginius Island. On August 12, 1843, Lewis Wernwag, one of the founders and original trustees of Virginius Island, died. The renowned bridge builder and accomplished millwright was 74 years old. In 1844, Wernwag's Tract 4 property, which included the saw mill and machine shop, was put up for sale by his son, John Wernwag, and son-in-law Jesse Schofield. These two men, operating under the name Wernwag & Schofield, appointed James Giddings of Frederick County, Maryland, to act as their agent to sell the property.

The bankruptcy and resulting sale of the Island Mill—the largest establishment on Virginius Island—precipitated another significant change. In March 1844, Abraham H. Herr and John Herr, Pennsylvania natives, acquired Tract 2 and the Island Mill from the court at a public auction. The firm Herr & Brother operated the Island Mill until 1848, when Abraham Herr acquired his brother's interest in the property; the establishment soon was known as Herr's Mill.

James Giddings and Abraham Herr became the two most prominent entrepreneurs on Virginius Island, and their business activities shaped the development of commercial manufacturing at the place for the next several years.

❧

Wernwag and Schofield had set the asking price for their Tract 4 property at $30,000, and Giddings produced a circular to attract new buyers. This detailed flyer included a plat of Virginius Island (*see page 99*), and promoted the:

> splendid and well known property, being and laying at Harper's Ferry, in the State of Virginia, called and known as the Island of Virginious [*sic*], and possessing improved water power unequalled at this time in the Basin of the Potomac, having a natural dam distributing nearly all the water contained in the Shenandoah River, over a fall of 12 feet. The undersigned deems it superfluous to say any thing as to the superior advantage of this property for the purposes of manufacturing, as every person of Science and Geographical knowledge of the United States, will see that this situation is not surpassed by any in the United States.[45]

No buyers stepped forward, however, and business at the saw mill and machine shop continued as usual for the next two years. In 1845, Wernwag & Schofield advertised their availability to saw wood for the following rates: "40 cents per 100 ft. board measure; 20 cents per 100 feet running, for shingling, lathing and paling; or we will saw for the third log."[46] New machinery installed around this time included a "double Saw Mill, of Crosbey's Patent, together with two carriages, Straps, and all the Irons belonging to said Mills, and two Circular Saws, of about 24 inches in diameter."[47]

Pearson Crosby's patent *Sawmill for Resawing Boards and Other Timber* was an interesting device particularly well suited to the requirements of the sawmill on Virginius Island (*see illustrations on page 98*). Ever since the Shenandoah Canal had opened in 1807, gundalows that discharged their cargoes at Harpers Ferry had been broken up and sold for lumber. For instance, in 1840, George Mauzy of Virginius Island advertised:

> I have a considerable quantity of GONDALO PLANK, SCANTLING, &c. on hand, which I will sell low for *Cash,* or to *punctual men.* The price for the plank is $1 per hundred feet, and the scantling at a *fp a piece.*[48]

According to Crosby's 1841 patent application, the principal object of his water-powered sawmill was to "re-saw boards and plank so as to divide them into parts much smaller than has been done by any mill heretofore constructed . . . ." This machine was well-suited to re-sawing gundalow planking, and for converting the boards into shingling, lathing, and paling. Today, hull planking, ribs, and side boards from these old boats can still be found in the rafters and framing members of 19th century buildings throughout Harpers Ferry.[49]

In the years following Lewis Wernwag's death, the sawmill continued to operate on a limited commercial

"View of the Island Virginius, in the Shenandoah, at Harpers Ferry. Taken near Jefferson's Rock," from an 1857 lithograph. Also visible, on the far right, is the U.S. Rifle Factory and Shenandoah Canal. Harpers Ferry NHP (HF-490).

basis, with a succession of operators serving the modest needs of the local community. The fact that the saw mill operators continued to advertise sawing logs on a toll-exchange basis suggest the establishment was a relatively small commercial operation. As late as April 1850, saw mill operator A.S. Ruddock advertised: "Farmers wishing sawing done for their own use, will be accom-

modated as soon as they will bring their logs to the mill . . . ." [50]

In 1844, operation of the machine shop was managed by John Wernwag, and although ownership of the establishment changed hands in May 1846 and again in July 1854, Wernwag apparently continued to operate it throughout the period. Wernwag principally produced

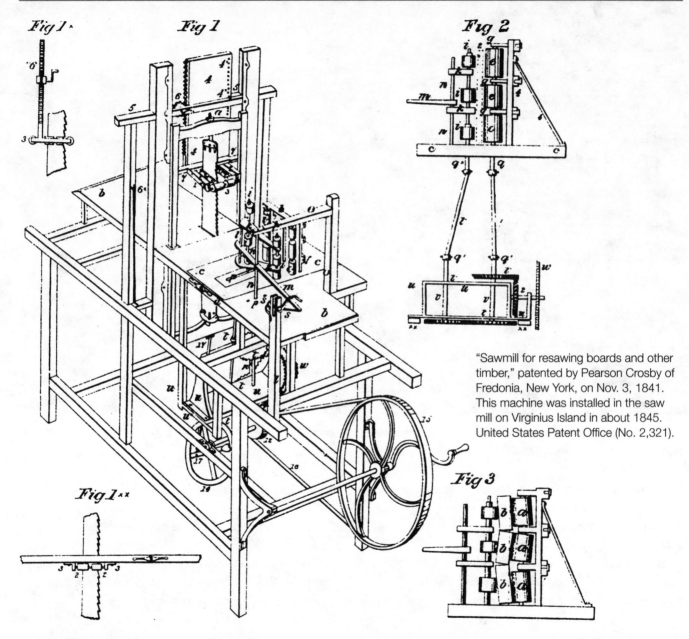

"Sawmill for resawing boards and other timber," patented by Pearson Crosby of Fredonia, New York, on Nov. 3, 1841. This machine was installed in the saw mill on Virginius Island in about 1845. United States Patent Office (No. 2,321).

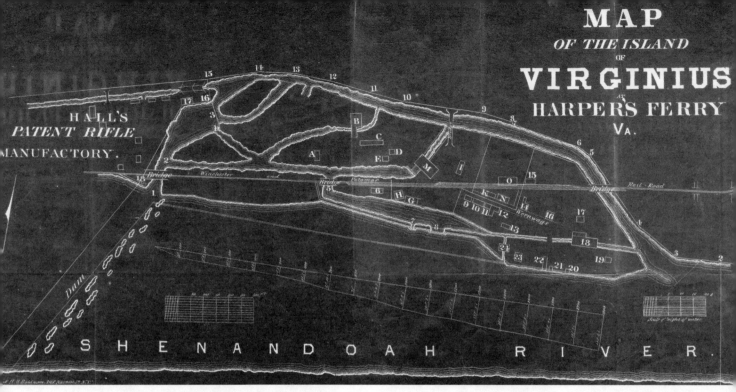

*"Map of the Island of Virginius at Harpers Ferry, Va.," prepared in May 1844. The map accompanied a circular produced by James Giddings which identified the principal waterpower features and industrial structures on Virginius Island: (**1**) "the entrance of the water from the Shenandoah under the rail-road bridge;" (**2**) "Entrance of race running parallel with the railroad;" (**3**) "A dam across the channel, with a sluice to supply boats with water passing the canal;" (**18**) "Large double Saw Mill;" (**21** & **22**) "2 Large Smith shops;" and (**24**) "machine shops occupied by John Warnwag [sic], and now in full operation." Also shown are the (**B**) Iron Foundry and (**M**) Island Mill. Harpers Ferry NHP (Map 40, Drawer 3, Item 29).*

machine parts and castings for the Harpers Ferry Armory, and probably filled machinery and millwork orders for various private manufactories in the area.

Another relatively small business establishment on Virginius Island was Hugh Gilleece's iron foundry. Throughout the 1840s, in addition to the contract work he did for the Harpers Ferry Armory, Gilleece continued to produce farm implements, wagon parts, and residential hardware. Gilleece gradually expanded the size and capacity of his establishment, adding the *Great Western Cook Stove* to his product line in 1843. By 1850, the iron foundry employed eight male workers, consumed 150 tons of pig iron annually, and produced $12,000 worth of castings. The business was valued at $7,000.[51]

This manufactory, however, apparently grew no further. On August 31, 1855, Abraham Herr acquired the property. By 1860, the establishment, operating under the name Herr and Snapp Foundry, was valued at only $2,000, employed just three men, consumed 100 tons of pig iron, and produced just $7,000 worth of castings.[52]

Abraham Herr's principal business interest, the Island Mill, proved much more profitable. The 3½-story, 96 feet by 48 feet stone flour mill was the largest building on Virginius Island. In 1850—two years after Herr had acquired sole possession of this establishment—the mill employed five men, ground 90,000 bushels of wheat annually, and produced over 20,000 barrels of flour and 300 tons of plaster with a total value of $100,000. Ten years later, Herr's Mill employed ten men, ground 145,000 bushels of wheat annually, and produced 32,000 barrels of flour worth $233,400. An adjacent cooperage employed another 14 men and manufactured 30,000 flour barrels annually valued at $11,250.[53]

The scale of production and its associated value clearly show that Herr's Mill was a prosperous commercial manufactory serving a market much larger than the local community. In fact, as late as 1850, Virginia was the nation's fourth largest wheat producer, and Jefferson County, Virginia, ranked third in state wheat production. The location of Herr's Mill served as an ideal collection point for the wheat harvests of the remote and still relatively undeveloped Shenandoah and Potomac valleys. Rail cars, canal boats, or gundalows delivered grain right to the mill's doorstep. Flour packed in barrels was then shipped by canal or railroad at very reasonable rates to either Georgetown or Baltimore—two of the east coast's larger commercial marketplaces. In 1850, Herr's Mill ground 15,000 more bushels of wheat than the largest mill in nearby Washington County, Maryland. Ten years

later, the value of flour produced at Herr's Mill was nearly 18 times the average annual value of flour produced by other mills in Jefferson County, and about 13 times the national average.[54]

An astute and enterprising businessman, Herr was also involved in transportation projects designed to tap the lucrative grain markets in neighboring Loudoun County, Virginia, which ranked second in state wheat production. He served as chairman of the stockholders of the Hillsborough & Harpers Ferry Turnpike, served as president of the stockholders of the Shenandoah Bridge Company, and helped raise capital for the Alexandria & Harper's Ferry Railroad Company. The proposed rail line never reached Harpers Ferry, but the toll road and toll bridge facilitated grain shipments by wagon from western Loudoun County to Herr's Mill. Herr soon became the most prominent and prosperous businessman on Virginius Island, and began acquiring the holdings of other island entrepreneurs. By August 1855, Herr became the sole owner of Virginius Island.

Between 1844-1846, despite his best efforts, James Giddings was unable to find buyers for Wernwag and Schofield's Tract 4 property on Virginius Island. Seeing an opportunity in this circumstance, Giddings apparently persuaded his associates to answer the growing call for southern manufacturing and to embark on one of the region's most ambitious commercial enterprises.

In January 1846, James Giddings, John Wernwag, Jesse Schofield, Gerard B. Wager, and Calvin Page formed the Harpers Ferry & Shenandoah Manufacturing Co. The act of incorporation permitted the new company to manufacture any item it wanted, and also to sell water privileges, waterpower, and land. From the outset, the company decided to erect at least two cotton factories on the Tract 4 property along the Shenandoah River. Giddings, the principal promoter of the new enterprise, served as agent for the company, solicited stock subscriptions and construction bids, and became company president in July 1846.

In May 1846, the Harpers Ferry & Shenandoah Manufacturing Company purchased Tract 4, including the saw mill and machine shop, from John Wernwag and Jesse Schofield—concluding the property sale for which Giddings had originally been hired. No doubt Giddings had suggested this arrangement in order to persuade Wernwag and Schofield to join the new enterprise.

The corporation generated considerable enthusiasm and excitement throughout the Harpers Ferry area, fueled by the popular support for southern manufacturing in general—and a southern textile industry in particular—then sweeping across the South. William Gregg, the South Carolina businessman and mechanic who started much of this interest in 1845 with his articles in the *Charleston Courier,* put words into action when he established his own textile mill in Graniteville, South Carolina, in 1846.

Coincidentally, passage of a new tariff bill on July 30, 1846, removed excessive duties which southern states had long opposed on manufactured cotton fabrics, and served to further stimulate domestic textile manufacturing. According to the *Spirit of Jefferson,* the new tariff had a significant impact on the Harpers Ferry & Shenandoah Manufacturing Company: "The stock was subscribed, the buildings erected and the immense and costly machinery purchased under and in view of the new Tariff." [55]

The promoters of the Harpers Ferry & Shenandoah Manufacturing Company enjoyed widespread support in the local press, and many members of the community subscribed enthusiastically to the company's stock. On May 22, 1846, the *Spirit of Jefferson* wrote:

> We are gratified to learn that the Harpers-Ferry and Shenandoah Manufacturing Company are progressing rapidly in obtaining the Stock, (sixty thousand dollars,) of said Company, a large portion of which has been subscribed in Jefferson county. The Agent, Mr. Giddings, informs us that he hopes to be able to lay the foundation stone of the first factory in about two months.—The great amount of water power on the Potomac and Shenandoah, bounding and running through Jefferson county, points out this location as equal, if not superior to, any in the U. States for Manufacturing purposes. We should be glad to see our friends of the county take hold of the Stock, as it promises to be a profitable investment. [56]

The following year, as the company's new cotton factory neared completion, the *Spirit of Jefferson* exalted in the excitement, enthusiasm, and optimism that characterized the entire enterprise:

> 'What new building is that?' is daily asked, and the stranger is surprised to hear for answer, that in the

Valley of Old Virginia, a large Cotton Factory has sprung into existence and the busy Spindle and Loom are about to send forth as fine shirtings and sheetings as any other establishment of the kind in the country. The Harpers-Ferry Manufacturing Company, with a capital of $60,000, and the experienced and indefatigable Giddings at their head, will now in a few weeks commence operations, and surely we should hail the day when the first yarn is twisted as a bright and glorious epoch in the history of the Valley of Virginia. Harpers-Ferry has every requisite for becoming a distinguished Manufacturing town, and we doubt not, now the first step has been taken, that such, before many years, will be the case. With an enterprising population, a sufficiency of labor, cheap and abundant food, a fine water power to almost any desired amount, and above all, surrounded by, and connected, by means of the best communications, with one of the finest and most productive Valleys in the world, furnishing a home market, and having at the same time an equal chance in other markets, we cannot see how it can possibly be otherwise.[57]

Giddings began soliciting proposals for construction of the company's first cotton factory building in July 1846. The specifications called for a four-story structure 100 feet by 45 feet. The foundation was to be four feet thick at the base, 16 feet high, and three feet thick at the top. Bids were also solicited for 320,000 bricks and for carpenter's work.[58]

In August 1846, Giddings obtained permission from the government to quarry stone for building foundations from the steep cliffs along "the road leading to the Rifle Factory." Construction of the cotton factory foundation commenced a short time later, and was "completed up to brick wall" by October 22, 1846. On May 4, 1847, work began on the four-story factory building, and the establishment was put into partial operation by February 1848.[59]

One month later, the company placed the following advertisement in newspapers up and down the Shenandoah Valley:

To Dry Goods Merchants.
The undersigned would respectfully call the attention of Merchants to the article of yard wide **Sheetings** and **Shirtings**, now manufactured by the Harpers-Ferry and Shenandoah Manufacturing Company at Harpers-Ferry.

He believes the goods of their Mill to be fully equal to any manufactured in the country, and therefore solicits the attention of purchasers.

The contiguity of the Mill to the Baltimore & Ohio Railroad, the Winchester & Potomac Railroad and the Chesapeake & Ohio Canal, will enable the undersigned to fill orders for any portion of Western Virginia with promptness, and at less than Baltimore prices. He would ask Merchants to give these goods a trial before purchasing elsewhere.

W. Giddings, *Agent,*
for Harpers-Ferry & Shen. Man'g Co.[60]

Virginius Island in 1865. The principal buildings, from left to right, are the four-story cotton factory, saw mill, former residence of Lewis Wernwag, three-story machine shop, and another dwelling house. The tracks of the Winchester & Potomac R.R. are visible in the foreground. Harpers Ferry NHP (HF-70).

By all accounts, the new building was a marvel of 19th century architecture and industrial technology. The four-story brick structure featured a bell tower and a polished tin roof. The building was fitted with gas lights and heated by steam. The production machinery was particularly noteworthy:

The Machinery and shafting, built by Chas. Danforth, Esq., of Patterson, N.J., is, we are told, of the latest improvement, and highest possible finish; admitted, on all hands, to be superior to any thing of the kind, ever brought into this region of country. He has supplied every thing from the first shaft to the shuttle bobbin; and his work, in this mill, goes to prove that he deservedly ranks with the best machinists of the age.[61]

Charles Danforth had begun working in a Massachusetts cotton mill when he was just 14 years old. On September 2, 1828, at the age of 31, he designed and patented a significant improvement in the standard spinning frame known as the cap spinner. This new device, which featured an inverted cup suspended from a fixed spindle, enabled yarn to be spun much faster and more uniformly than was previously possible. Danforth took his new invention to Patterson, New Jersey, which was second only to Lowell, Massachusetts, in the number of its textile manufactories. Here he obtained a job as machinist, and perfected and patented at least five improvements to the original cap spinner. In 1840, Danforth purchased his own machine shop, and embarked on a highly successful and profitable career in the textile machinery business.[62]

At the new cotton factory on Virginius Island, Danforth's machinery was organized into four departments. Typical of textile mills of the period, flow production was probably organized from the first floor upward.

May 4, 1841 patent drawings of an improved version of the original Danforth Cap Frame or Cap Spinner. United States Patent Office (No. 2,077).

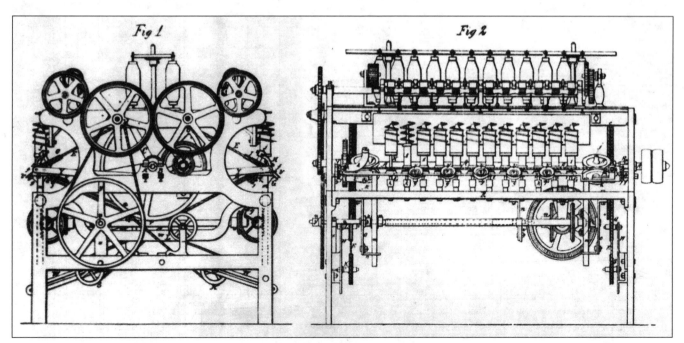

The Carding Department, located on the first floor, contained one cotton opener and cleaner, two pickers, eighteen 36-inch carding engines, three drawing frames, and six double roller beam speeders. Here the cotton bales were opened, cleaned, and passed through the cylinders of the carding engines. Wire teeth fitted on these cylinders combed out the cotton fibers, rolled the cotton into several layers called the *lap*, and then combed this *lap* into a thick rope or *sliver*. The loose, irregular *sliver* was fed into the drawing frames, which made it more uniform. The *sliver* then passed through the double roller beam speeders, which produced a course, slightly twisted continuous strand of fibers called a *roving*.[63]

Cotton factory building, circa 1900. Erected in 1848, the building served as a Cotton Factory (1848-1852), a Union hospital (1863-1865), and the Child & McCreight flour mill (1867-1889). Harpers Ferry NHP (HF-62).

The *roving* went on to the Spinning Department on the factory's second floor. Here were 18 spinning frames—called the *Danforth Cap Frame* or *Cap Spinner*—each one possessing 132 spindles (*see illustrations on facing page*). On these machines, spools of *roving* passed to an equal number of wooden bobbins mounted on fixed spindles. Each bobbin was circumscribed by a smooth stationary polished ring which was suspended from the top of the spindle. This stationary ring was a cap similar in shape to an inverted tumbler, from which the *Cap Spinner* derived its name. The *roving*, which passed through the lower edge of the stationary ring, was drawn and

simultaneously twisted under tension as lifters rose and fell on either side of the machine. The resulting yarn was wound onto the bobbins, which were set in motion by an endless driving band. The reciprocating motion of the lifters, and uniform tension on the thread passing through the stationary ring onto the bobbins, resulted in yarn that was both uniform and elastic.

Yarn that was used for the *warp*—the strands of thread that ran the length of the cotton cloth—went

Power loom weaving in a 19th century textile mill. Courtesy The American Textile History Museum.

to the Dressing Department. This room was equipped with four dressing frames and six cradle warpers. On the dressing frames, yarn gathered from several bobbins was wound together onto a reel or spool and a starch paste was applied to strengthen the thread. The material was then transferred to the cradle warpers, which collected the *warp* thread onto a warp beam.

Weaving was the final stage in the production of cotton cloth. The Weaving Department, located on the factory's third floor, was equipped with 97 water-powered looms. Here the warp beams were mounted on the looms. Each piece of *warp* yarn was drawn through a loom harness onto a front roller. A bobbin of filling yarn or *weft* yarn was mounted on a flying shuttle. The loom was then engaged: the warp beam rotated to unwind the *warp* threads, a cloth beam rotated to wind up the cloth, and the flying shuttle was propelled back and forth by a treadle mechanism attached to shuttle cords, carrying the *weft* across the *warp* as the odd and even threads were alternately lifted.

The finished cloth was then pressed, brushed, and banded for shipment to market. The finishing room or a small machine shop may have been located on the factory's fourth floor. Finishing equipment included "one cloth press, I scraper and brush machine, banding machines, lathe and tools for roller covering."[64]

The managers of the new cotton factory estimated that the power looms would turn out from 40,000 to 45,000 yards of sheetings, and consume from 12,000 to 15,000 pounds of cotton per day. They planned to employ from 85-100 operatives. According to the 1850 Census, the factory actually employed 70 workers—35 men and 35 women. In an average month men earned $16, while women earned just $4.57. The mill manufactured $32,000 worth of sheetings annually.[65]

❧

Two E.C. Kilburn & Company iron turbine water wheels, each 70 inches in diameter, powered the production machinery in the new cotton factory. These wheels were the first hydraulic turbines used on Virginius Island. E.C. Kilburn & Company of Fall River, Mass., was a prominent manufacturer of textile machinery; the firm had

clients throughout New England and across the deep south.

In 1846, E.C Kilburn & Company began the commercial production of standard "Fourneyron" turbines in various stock sizes (*see illustrations on page 80*).

767 Shenandoah River.

Herr's Dam, circa 1882. The dam and stone headgates were originally built by the Harpers Ferry & Shenandoah Manufacturing Company in about 1848. The ruins of Herr's Mill are visible on the right. The row houses on the left were erected during the 1850s, when Virginius Island reached its peak population of about 200. Harpers Ferry NHP (HF-29).

Many of these water wheels, commonly known as "The Fall River Turbine," became the workhorse of the cotton milling industry. The two 70-inch turbines purchased by the Harpers Ferry & Shenandoah Manufacturing Company operated under a 14 foot head of water, and probably developed about 60-70 horsepower.[66]

The company also erected new water-works, including a new dam across the Shenandoah River, new headgates at the upstream end of Virginius Island, and a centralized water distribution system for holding and delivering waterpower to all the manufactories situated on Tract 4.[67] Under a provision in the firm's charter—modeled after the Locks and Canals, a highly success-ful company devoted to the development, disposal, and management of waterpower in Lowell, Massachusetts—the Harpers Ferry & Shenandoah Manufacturing Company was prepared to sell this waterpower to tenants who leased any of the firm's properties. These included the saw mill, machine shop, and a small water-powered smith's shop located on Tract 4 just upstream from the new cotton factory.

The new water distribution system included a small millpond or inner basin, designed to store water until it was needed to develop power. In connecting this inner basin to their new cotton factory, the company appar-ently spared no expense:

> To supply this mill with water, the company have constructed arched raceways of stone, under

Water tunnel ruins on Virginius Island. These stone arched culverts, erected in 1848, conveyed water from the inner basin to the cotton factory on Virginius Island. April 1979 photo by the author.

ground, of sufficient capacity to pass the entire water of the river; thus avoiding the unsightly open canals, (which we understand, disfigure many of our manufacturing towns,) and at the same time affording additional space for buildings.[68]

The Harpers Ferry & Shenandoah Manufacturing Company soon began construction of a second cotton mill just a few yards upstream from their first factory. Completed in July 1849, the new four-story brick mill was smaller than its sister mill, measuring just 57 feet by 48 feet. Although the new factory was powered by water, there is no record of the type of water wheel used.

On August 2, 1849, the *Virginia Free Press* reported that the new establishment:

> has just commenced operations under the charge of Messrs. STANBROUGH & JOHNSON. This factory is capable of manufacturing 400 lbs. of Cotton yarn, 100 lbs. of Batting, and 50 lbs. of Candle wick per day . . . . The Machinery consists of seven Carders, four Spinning frames (called the Danforth Cap Frame), two Reels, and Warning Mill, &c. This establishment employs some of the best and most experienced hands now in this country—some of them from establishments in Manchester, England.[69]

The firm of Stanbrough & Johnson apparently leased the new building from the Harpers Ferry & Shenandoah Manufacturing Company, and operated the establishment under the name Valley Mills. They specialized in the manufacture of cotton yarn, warp, batting, and candle wicking, and invited "the citizens of the Valley and surrounding country [to] give us their patronage to promote the spirit of enterprise begun in this part of Virginia."[70]

In 1850, Ira Stanbrough formed a new partnership with John R. Holliday, and the firm Stanbrough & Holliday operated the cotton mill. This firm employed six male and eight female workers, and produced $22,000 worth of yarn, warp, and batting. The men earned an average monthly wage of $14.50, while the women earned $10.87—significantly more than the $4.57 monthly salary earned by women in the adjacent cotton factory.[71]

On January 15, 1852, Stanbrough and Holliday went into partnership with Mark A. Duke of Baltimore, agreeing to continue the manufacture of cotton yarns, warps, batting, and candlewick for a period of one year. This new partnership was short-lived however: on or about Nov. 19, 1852, fire destroyed the Valley Mills (*see* **Waterpower Ruins on Virginius Island**, *pages 172-173*).

By early 1852, the Harpers Ferry & Shenandoah Manufacturing Co. had fallen into considerable debt. Riding a wave of national economic prosperity and great enthusiasm for southern manufacturing, the company had been formed with very high hopes, but insufficient capital.

During the period 1840-1860, the number of cotton spindles across the country more than doubled, rising to over 5,200,000 by 1860. Spindles in the textile manufacturing center of Lowell, Massachusetts, alone rose from 300,000 in 1850 to 400,000 in 1860. By comparison, the cotton factory on Virginius Island possessed just 2,376 spindles.[72]

The astonishing growth of the cotton industry—which expanded nearly twice as fast as the nation's population—was accompanied by swings of prosperity and depression. The industry experienced a particularly difficult period shortly before 1850, when the construction of new textile factories outpaced both crops and markets. As a result, cotton prices soared while the price of yarn and cloth remained stationary or declined. The

Continues on page 112

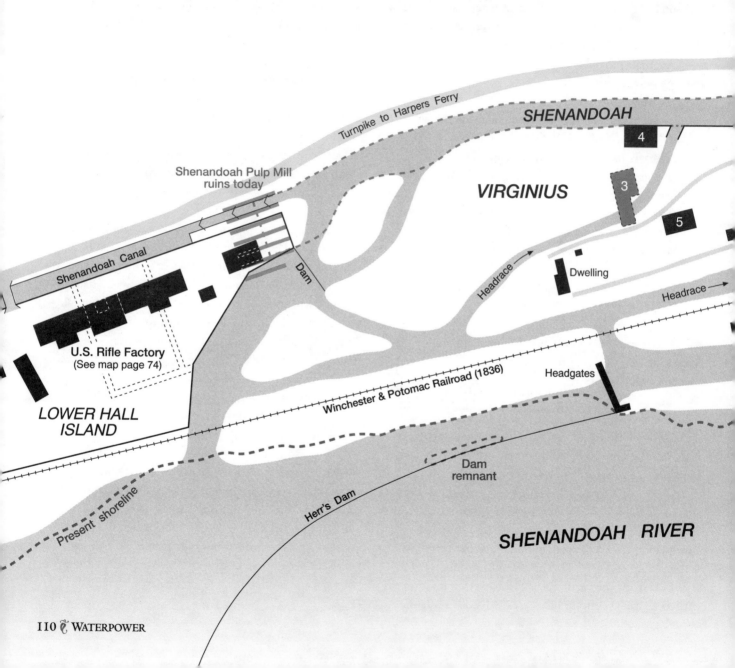

Turnpike to Harpers Ferry

SHENANDOAH

Shenandoah Pulp Mill
ruins today

VIRGINIUS

4

3

5

Shenandoah Canal

Dam

Headrace

Dwelling

Headrace

U.S. Rifle Factory
(See map page 74)

LOWER HALL
ISLAND

Winchester & Potomac Railroad (1836)

Headgates

Present shoreline

Herr's Dam

Dam
remnant

SHENANDOAH RIVER

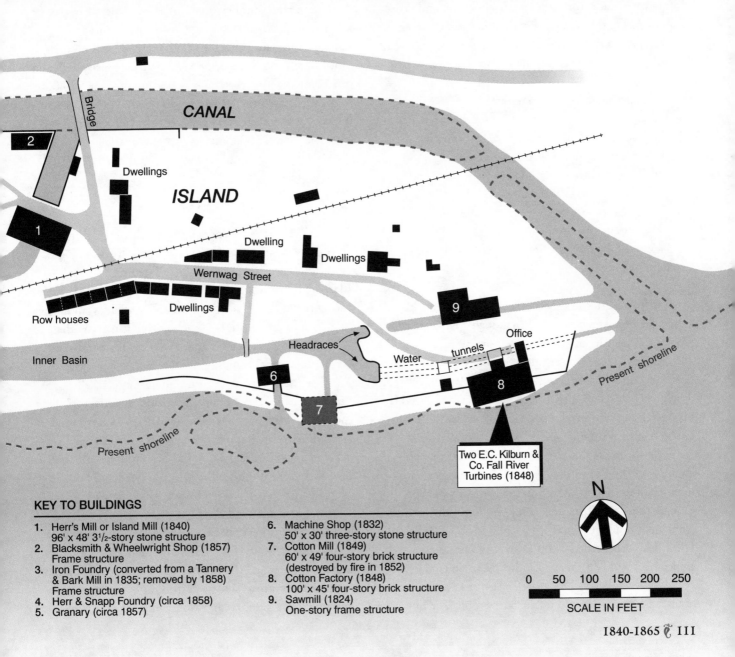

CANAL

Bridge

ISLAND

Dwellings

Wernwag Street

Dwelling

Dwellings

Row houses

Dwellings

Inner Basin

Headraces

Water   tunnels   Office

Present shoreline

Present shoreline

Two E.C. Kilburn &
Co. Fall River
Turbines (1848)

N

KEY TO BUILDINGS

1. Herr's Mill or Island Mill (1840)
   96' x 48' 3½-story stone structure
2. Blacksmith & Wheelwright Shop (1857)
   Frame structure
3. Iron Foundry (converted from a Tannery
   & Bark Mill in 1835; removed by 1858)
   Frame structure
4. Herr & Snapp Foundry (circa 1858)
5. Granary (circa 1857)

6. Machine Shop (1832)
   50' x 30' three-story stone structure
7. Cotton Mill (1849)
   60' x 49' four-story brick structure
   (destroyed by fire in 1852)
8. Cotton Factory (1848)
   100' x 45' four-story brick structure
9. Sawmill (1824)
   One-story frame structure

0   50   100 150 200 250

SCALE IN FEET

margin of manufacturing profit disappeared, and those establishments that lacked the necessary capital to endure the slump were driven out of business. Frances Robb, in her study of industry along the Potomac River, writes:

Entrepreneurs in the Potomac River Valley failed to note that local conditions did not parallel those so favorable to the successful ventures in New England. Most notably missing were the well-financed investors willing to risk capital and able to make substantial reinvestments in a project. This inability to sustain an enterprise without immediate return on the investment severely hampered the industrial growth of the Potomac River Valley.[73]

With liabilities in excess of $50,000, the stockholders of the Harpers Ferry & Shenandoah Manufacturing Company, meeting in March 1852, ordered the sale of all company assets. As early as April 8, 1852, the sale of both the cotton factory and cotton mill was announced. The great flood of April 18, 1852, however, delayed the proposed sale, and no doubt caused considerable damage to the company's dam, headgates, and raceways.

The company was also named in at least three lawsuits filed by creditors, and the court subsequently intervened to direct the sale of the company's property. One of these creditors was James Giddings, the former company president, who filed a claim for $4,110.28 in 1852. The court ruled in his favor, and Giddings' association with Virginius Island came to an end.

On December 9, 1852, the *Virginia Free Press* announced a court-ordered public auction of "All The Property, Real and Personal," of the Harpers Ferry & Shenandoah Manufacturing Company. Additional notices were published during the next several months, until finally, on July 25, 1854, Abraham Herr purchased the company's property at a public auction for $25,000.

Herr leased the cotton factory to the firm Cramer & Hawks, who advertised brown cottons for sale in 1856 and 1857. By 1860, however, the establishment was no longer operating, and Herr was using the building to store grain.[74]

❧

The failure of the Harpers Ferry & Shenandoah Manufacturing Company marked the end of the island's most ambitious commercial enterprise. The promise that Harpers Ferry would become "a distinguished Manufacturing town," and that the loom and spindle would usher in a "bright and glorious epoch in the history of the Valley of Virginia" faded amid a flurry of lawsuits and bankruptcy proceedings.

The entrepreneurs on Virginius Island lacked sufficient capital to sustain the cotton manufactory, but there is no evidence they lacked sufficient waterpower. According to one report: "The water, in this river, *measured during the dryest season*, has been found sufficient to propel 50,000 spindles; the effective head and fall being 15½ feet."[75]

The new dam and distribution system completed by the Harpers Ferry & Shenandoah Manufacturing Company in about 1848 apparently delivered enough water to operate all the island's water-powered manufactories—the cotton factory, cotton mill, machine shop, saw mill, iron foundry, and flour mill. Of all these establishments, only the two cotton manufactories required dependable, daily waterpower on a year-round basis to operate profitably. The cotton factory's two Fall River Turbines probably proved adequate to the operational needs of this establishment. Herr's Mill required sufficient waterpower only during the fall harvest season, and the profitability of this enterprise throughout the 1850s suggests that sufficient power was usually available. The other island manufactories, which were much smaller in scale, most likely used waterpower only sporadically during a typical work day. Taken collectively, the manufacturing establishments on Virginius Island probably required only about half the waterpower of the nearby Rifle Factory for their routine operations.

WEVERTON MANUFACTURING COMPANY

Two and a half miles downstream from Harpers Ferry, the Potomac River breaks out of the Blue Ridge Mountains over a final flurry of steep rock ledges. George Washington called these rapids "Pains falls." Today they are known as Knoxville Falls.

On August 7, 1785, Washington and the directors of the Patowmack Company—having carefully inspected the course of the Potomac River at Harpers Ferry by canoe—held a meeting at the foot of these falls. Washington wrote:

> These are best passed on the Maryland side. They are pretty Swift—shallow—and foul at bottom but the difficulties may be removed. From the bottom of these Falls, leaving an Island on the right, & the Maryland Shore on the left the easy & good Navigation below is entered.[76]

The site where Washington and his comrades met—commanding a head and fall of 15 feet and receiving the combined flow of the Potomac and Shenandoah rivers—offered a prime location for the development of waterpower. The place also shared important ties to Harpers Ferry, including geography, transportation, and the development of commercial enterprise.

In August 1821, Caspar Wever, a construction superintendent on the National Road, purchased just

Ruins of "A large stone Flour Mill" at the foot of Short Hill Mountain in Loudoun County, Virginia, just across the Potomac River from Weverton. The mill was erected by John Peacher in about 1824, and was subsequently acquired by Caspar Wever. April 1979 photo by the author.

over 16 acres along the Potomac River at the falls. Wever extended his holdings in 1823 and again in 1825, acquiring 274 additional acres. In 1824, Wever bought a large stone flour mill which stood alongside Israel Creek near its junction with the Potomac River. The mill, which had been established in 1774, contained two pair of burrstones and one corn stone. Subsequently, the entire property became known as "Wever's Mills."

Just across the river, at the foot of Short Hill Mountain in Loudoun County, Virginia, John Peacher purchased "ten acres and seven perches of land" on March 20, 1824. Peacher, who had erected the first gristmill on Virginius Island between 1822-1823, also erected "a large stone Flour Mill" on this site.[77]

The development of transportation along the Potomac River in the early 1830s opened new commercial opportunities for Caspar Wever and other entrepreneurs in Maryland and Virginia. The Chesapeake & Ohio Canal, Baltimore & Ohio Railroad, and Frederick & Harpers Ferry Turnpike passed directly through Wever's property.

In November 1834, Wever consolidated his property holdings into a single tract comprising 556 acres. The following April, Wever and several associates formed the Weverton Manufacturing Company. Among the first stockholders was Gerard Bond Wager of Harpers Ferry, who later served as one of the original partners in the Harpers Ferry & Shenandoah Manufacturing Company.[78]

The promoters of the new enterprise saw great promise in the development of the site. Raw material, for instance, might be "as readily and cheaply procured at Weverton as it can any where else, whilst the great improved high-ways which pass it, furnish a cheap carriage for the manufactured articles, to markets in every direction."[79] They clearly appreciated the importance of abundant waterpower, raw materials, and transportation in facilitating the large scale manufacture of commercial goods. In this respect, they were more farsighted and more ambitious than were the entrepreneurs on nearby Virginius Island in 1835.

The Weverton Manufacturing Company, however, was not formed to engage directly in manufacturing operations. Instead, it was modeled on the very successful Locks and Canals company of Lowell, Massachusetts, which was devoted exclusively to the development, disposal, and management of waterpower, and to the sale or lease of adjacent real estate.

Wever, who had accepted an appointment as Superintendent of Construction of the B&O Railroad in 1828, played a direct role in the development of the region's transportation system. In the fall of 1835, he supervised construction of the masonry bridge piers of the Potomac Viaduct at Harpers Ferry. Lewis Wernwag, who was awarded the contract for the bridge's seven timber spans, began work a short time later. On May 27, 1836, Benjamin H. Latrobe, Jr.—chief engineer of the B&O Railroad—wrote that "Wernwag is preparing for the superstructure, which he will frame at Wever's Mill, 3 miles below the scite [sic]."[80]

The development of Weverton was stalled by the Panic of 1837, and by the subsequent depression which lasted from 1839-1843. As economic conditions improved, activity at the site revived. In 1844, Wever requested permission from the directors of the C&O Canal Company to erect a dam across the Potomac

River. The right to draw water from the river had been granted to the C&O Canal—and to its predecessor, the Patowmack Company—by the Maryland state legislature. This privilege was jealously guarded by the canal company.

Notwithstanding Wever's assertion that "the interests of your company will be considerably advanced by the contemplated improvements at this place," his request apparently languished before the C&O Canal's board of directors. On February 8, 1847, Wever again wrote canal company president J.M. Coale, and permission for the new dam was finally granted in April 1847.[81]

The dam was soon put under contract, and the structure was completed by 1849. Joseph P. Shannon, an associate of Lewis Wernwag and former partner in the firm Wernwag & Sons on Virginius Island, erected the dam at a cost of $25,000. The structure was comprised of large iron pins drilled and driven into the rock riverbed, with wood beams and facing attached. Wrought iron bars served to hold the timbers in place. Three large masonry intake sluices or headgates were erected along the Maryland shoreline. These diverted water into the company's large millrace, which ran parallel to the C&O Canal.

In 1847, the Weverton Manufacturing Company offered its first lots for sale to the public. Sales proved disappointing, however, and the stockholders soon became disillusioned. Following completion of the dam in 1849, the company, at Wever's suggestion, hired New Jersey civil engineer Edward N. Dickinson to thoroughly

These stone headgates were erected in about 1849 by the Weverton Manufacturing Company along the Maryland shore of the Potomac River. April 1979 photo by the author.

evaluate the waterpower potential of the site. Dickerson's report heartened many of the firm's subscribers:

The power at Weverton developed by the construction of a dam in 1849, extends the whole breadth of the Potomac and furnishes sites for factories on both shores; the water power above, between this and the mouth of the Shanandoah [*sic*] at Harper's Ferry in addition are more than double that at Lowell, Massachusetts, and both combined, when fully developed to their utmost

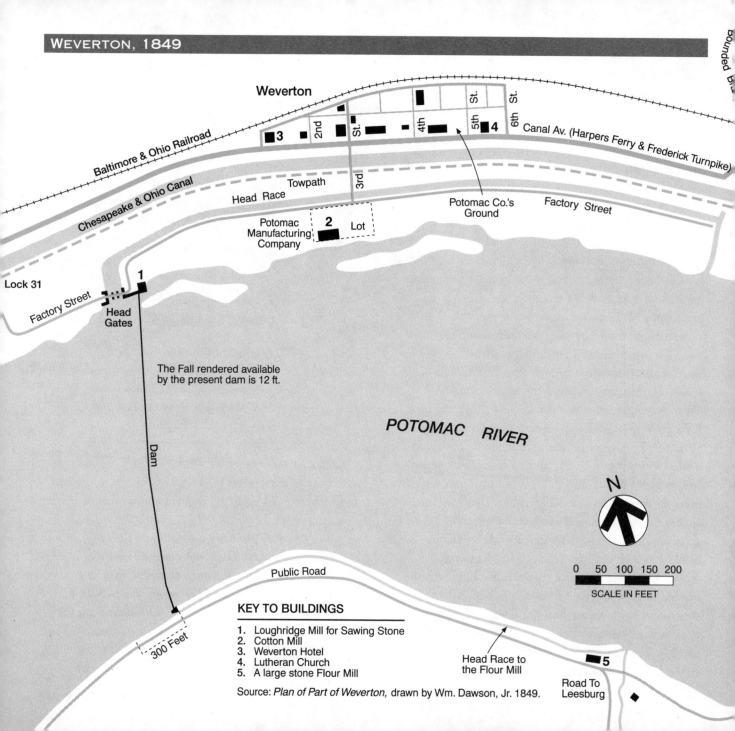

Weverton

Baltimore & Ohio Railroad

Chesapeake & Ohio Canal

Canal Av. (Harpers Ferry & Frederick Turnpike)

2nd St.

3rd St.

4th St.

5th St.

6th St.

3

4

Towpath

Head Race

Factory Street

Potomac Co.'s Ground

Potomac Manufacturing Company

2 Lot

Lock 31

Factory Street

1

Head Gates

The Fall rendered available by the present dam is 12 ft.

Dam

POTOMAC RIVER

N

0 50 100 150 200

SCALE IN FEET

Public Road

Head Race to the Flour Mill

5

Road To Leesburg

300 Feet

KEY TO BUILDINGS
----
1. Loughridge Mill for Sawing Stone
2. Cotton Mill
3. Weverton Hotel
4. Lutheran Church
5. A large stone Flour Mill

Source: *Plan of Part of Weverton,* drawn by Wm. Dawson, Jr. 1849.

capacity will be sufficient to propel 600,000 spindles. I am not aware of the relative difference in price, between the right of the water power at Weverton and Lowell, but understand it is greatly in favor of the former. Those engaged in manufactures are most competent to form a correct opinion as to their true interests, and will act accordingly.[82]

Despite lackluster property sales, several small manufacturing firms were established at Weverton. On July 7, 1849, the Weverton Steel & File Company—subsequently known as the Henderson File Company—was established. In 1850, the firm employed 20 men and produced steel and cast iron files, saws, and other cutting tools valued at $30,000. William Loughridge, the inventor of locomotive air brakes, also established a small marble works of 20 horsepower.[83]

One of the larger new establishments was a cotton factory, erected by the Potomac Manufacturing Company between 1849-1850. On January 10, 1850, the company acquired a waterpower privilege from the Weverton Manufacturing Company "to the extent of two hundred horse power."[84] Wever was apparently involved in this enterprise, and so too was James Giddings, the principal promoter of the Harpers Ferry & Shenandoah Manufacturing Company on Virginius Island. On February 6, 1849, the *Spirit of Jefferson* reported:

> For the term of a moderate lifetime, Casper [*sic*] W. Wever has been laboring to apply the immense water-power of the Potomac near Harpers-Ferry to manufacturing purposes. At last his persevering efforts are about to be crowned with triumphant success, and Weverton is destined to carry down his name in the annals of industry by the side of Lowell and Lawrence. The machinery of a large Cotton Factory will be in operation next summer. Several other Factories are under way. A church and a Hotel have been erected, and every thing about Weverton bespeaks a large manufacturing town, promising eventual employment to thousands of industrious people, and a certain market for the produce of the surrounding country.[85]

The *Frederick Examiner* also reported enthusiastically on the progress of the Weverton enterprise:

> Weverton possesses from its natural and artificial advantages all the elements that constitute a solid and permanent prosperity, and its future rapid progress is now beyond a doubt – it is a positive certainty. – There is scarcely an hour of the day or night that the cars from east or west do not pass directly through the property; the boats also; thus affording double facilities for transportation.[86]

The company's debts, however, continued to mount. In 1849, a portion of the firm's property was advertised at a public sale to satisfy the claims of creditors. The following year, the enterprise received a fatal blow: the machinery for the new cotton factory was found to be unsuitable for the new manufactory, and the establishment never operated. James Taylor, a Civil War sketch artist who traveled through Weverton in 1864, related the story:

> In our brief stop at Weverton, I was afforded an opportunity to view and glean from a fellow passenger, once a residenter of the vicinity, the history of a row of two story low pebble dash buildings betwixt us and the river, he stating that they were built at the suggestion of a well-meaning enthusiastic business man of the town, a Mr. Giddings, the structures being intended for cotton mills to be run by water power, but when the machinery was made and brought to the place, it was found the ceilings were too low to admit its entrance into the rooms, which calamitous fact so disheartened the projectors of the enterprise, that they dropped the whole thing then and there, leaving "Giddings' folly" as it has since been termed, to moulder and decay.[87]

The assets of the Potomac Manufacturing Company, which included "the Mill or factory and the lands thereto attached, the water right of said Company purchased of the Weaverton [sic] Manufacturing Company," and various other lots, were sold at a public auction in October 1869. For all intents and purposes, the Weverton Manufacturing Company also ceased to operate, although it continued to exist on paper until 1882.[88]

On January 15, 1857, Caspar Wever sold "Wever's Mill"—the flour mill he had acquired back in 1824—to Howard Paceley for $4,500. Wever subsequently became a farmer, and continued to live in a small farmhouse near Lock 31. He died on February 7, 1861. An auction of Wever's remaining farm equipment and personal effects brought just $501.88.[89]

At both Harpers Ferry and Weverton, entrepreneurs learned a hard lesson: access to both waterpower and transportation were not enough to ensure the success of large scale commercial manufacturing. Substantial capital investments were also necessary to sustain an enterprise through short-term setbacks and unforeseen circumstances. The promoters of the highly successful Boston Manufacturing Company, for instance, were all wealthy Massachusetts merchants. Their first textile mill in Waltham, Mass., was capitalized at $400,000. By comparison, the Harpers Ferry & Shenandoah Manufacturing Company was capitalized at just $60,000. In 1850, when the cotton factories on Virginius Island and at Weverton were just getting underway, the "Boston Associates" already controlled a fifth of America's cotton production at Lowell and other New England manufacturing centers. The merchants, farmers, and small scale mill operators who characterized the population of the Potomac River Valley simply could not furnish the substantial capital necessary to sustain these ambitious corporate enterprises at Harpers Ferry and Weverton.[90]

After the Flood of 1877, the C&O Canal Company purchased the dam and the abandoned cotton factory at Weverton. The dam was promptly demolished and, in 1879, the cotton mill was torn down. The Henderson

The caption on this illustration, which appeared in Harper's Weekly *in November 1859, reads: "The Harper's Ferry Insurrection.—The U.S. Marines storming the Engine-House.—Insurgents firing through holes in the wall." Harpers Ferry NHP (HF-115).*

File factory, which also suffered extensive damage from this flood, was torn down about the same time. Wever's old flour mill was still operating in 1877 under the name Weverton Milling Company. The establishment finally closed down in 1895.

JOHN BROWN'S RAID AND THE OUTBREAK OF CIVIL WAR

John Brown's raid on the "United States Armory and Arsenal at Harpers Ferry" sent a shockwave across the South and dramatically exacerbated already strained sectional tensions.[91] For the residents of Harpers Ferry, there was a mixture of shock, disbelief, and profound anger at this armed attack upon their community. On October 17, 1859, during the second day of the raid, Mary E. Mauzy wrote her daughter, Eugenia Burton (wife of James H. Burton, the former Acting Master Armorer at Harpers Ferry and now Chief Engineer of the Royal Small Arms Manufactory in Enfield, England):

> Oh my dear friend such a day as this. Heaven forbid that I should ever witness such another.
>
> Last night a band of ruffians took possession of the town, took the keys of the armory and made Captive a great many of our Citizens. I cannot write the particulars for I am too Nervous. For such a sight as I have just beheld. Our men chased them in the river just below here and I saw them shot down like dogs. I saw one poor wrech rise above the water and some one strike him with a club he sank again and in a moment they dragged him out a Corpse. I do not know yet how many are shot but I shall never forget the sight. They just marched two wreches their Arms bound fast up to the jail. My dear husband shouldered his rifle and went to join our men May god protect him. Even while I write I hear the guns in the distance I heard they were fighting down the street.
>
> I cannot write any more I must wait and see what the end will be.[92]

The raid deeply shook the armory workforce, and anxieties remained high for several weeks. Rumors that armed bands of abolitionists and fugitive slaves were roaming across the Blue Ridge Mountains added to the turmoil. Mary Mauzy's husband, armorer George Mauzy, wrote the Burtons again on December 3, 1859:

> Well the great agony is over. "Old Osawatomie Brown" was executed yesterday at noon . . . .
>
> There is an immense concourse of military at Charlestown, not less than 2000 men are quartered there, the Courthouse, all the churches & all the Lawyers offices are occupied. We have upwards of 300 regulars & 75 or 80 Montgomery Guards. These men were all sent here by the Sec. of War & Gov. Wise to prevent a rescue of Brown & his party by northern infidels and fanatics: of which they boasted loudly, but their courage must have oozed out of their finger ends, as none made their appearance. We are keeping nightly watch, all are vigilant, partys of 10 men out every night, quite a number of incendiary fires have taken place in this vicinity & County, such as grain stacks, barns & other out-buildings.[93]

As sectional fervor increasingly divided the nation, Harpers Ferry remained in a perpetual state of alarm. A company of U.S. Army regulars sent to guard the Armory was billeted in the Large Arsenal, which had fallen into such disrepair that only miscellaneous supplies were now stored there. By January 1860, nearly every able-bodied man at Harpers Ferry was a member of the local guard. Armory workmen found it almost impossible to settle back into their daily routines.[94]

Musket Factory ruins, July 1865. By the end of the Civil War, most of the Harpers Ferry Armory was destroyed. Harpers Ferry NHP (HF-38).

This same sectional turmoil also affected the life of James H. Burton. On January 21, 1860, the Virginia Assembly passed a bill "For the better defence [*sic*] of the State." The old Virginia Manufactory of Arms—renamed the Richmond Armory in 1861—was reactivated after being shut down for 38 years. J.R. Anderson & Company was awarded a large contract to supply machinery for the reactivated manufactory, and the firm engaged Burton in November 1860 to engineer the Richmond Armory contract. Burton, who had recently returned to the United States from England, accepted the new position, and on December 4, traveled to Harpers Ferry where he was allowed "free access to the drawings patterns &c. in the Armory."[95]

As the nation moved closer to armed conflict, the situation in Harpers Ferry continued to deteriorate. In January 1861, Armory superintendent Alfred M. Barbour, alarmed by anti-Union sentiment in the Shenandoah Valley, advised the War Department that he had "reason to apprehend that some assault will be made upon the United States Armory at Harper's Ferry."[96] With the bombardment of Fort Sumter on April 12-13, 1861, Virginia inched closer to secession. On April 17, a Virginia convention, which had been indecisive during the preceding months, finally passed an ordinance of secession, and the Harpers Ferry Armory became an immediate military target.

Lt. Roger Jones, a United States Army regular, defended the Armory on the evening of April 18, 1861, with 50 soldiers and 15 volunteers. In nearby Charles Town, several companies of Virginia militia totaling 360 men assembled and advanced toward Harpers Ferry. Jones, outnumbered and unable to obtain reinforcements, set fire to the Arsenal and several Musket Factory buildings. At about 10 p.m., an explosion ripped through the Small Arsenal. Townspeople acted quickly to extinguish fires in most of the workshops, but by the time the first Virginia militiamen entered town the Large and Small Arsenals were consumed by flames.

The capture of the Harpers Ferry Armory "placed at the disposal of the State of Va. two nearly complete and ample sets of machinery & other facilities for the manufacture of Rifles & Rifle Muskets." During the next several weeks, Virginia militiamen disassembled and packed over 300 machines, thousands of feet of leather belting and shafting, and 57,000 assorted tools from the Musket Factory. In addition, enough component parts for between 7,000 and 10,000 Rifle Muskets and Percussion Muskets were also seized. All this ordnance stock, machinery, and tools were loaded on railroad cars and shipped to Winchester, Virginia, for transfer to Richmond.[97]

Ruins of the Rolling Mill at the west end of the U.S. Musket Factory, photographed by Silas A. Holmes in October 1862. The brick and wrought-iron fence on the right, erected in 1856-1857, extended 1,365 feet along the Armory headrace. Library of Congress (LC-B8171-0655 DLC).

Ruins of the U.S. Rifle Factory, burned by Confederate raiders in June 1861. Standing in line, from front to back, are remains of the Tilt-hammer & Forging Shop, Barrel Drilling & Finishing Shop (with the bell tower), Machine Shop, and Finishing Shop. Locks 4 and 5 of the Shenandoah Canal—a double lift lock—are visible in the foreground. Harpers Ferry NHP (HF-37).

Removal and packing of all the equipment in the Musket Factory was not completed until the first week of June 1861. Fearing an imminent Union assault on Harpers Ferry, the governor of Virginia ordered James H. Burton, who had just been appointed superintendent of the Richmond Armory, to personally supervise the

Ruins of the Smith & Forging Shop, photographed on May 29, 1886. The workshop was torn down a short time later. The furnace stack, erected in 1846, was 90 feet tall, 10 feet square at its base, and situated on top of a "massive stone arch thrown across a tail race leading from one of the water wheels." Harpers Ferry NHP (HF-785).

task of stripping the Rifle Factory. Burton, the former Acting Master Armorer at Harpers Ferry, arrived at the Shenandoah manufactory at midnight, June 8, and "at once set about making arrangements for the removal of the remaining machinery, materials &c." When the last packed railroad cars left Harpers Ferry five days later,

another 132 machines and thousands of tools and firearm components had been confiscated.[98]

Burton's complete familiarity with the machinery for manufacturing United States firearms proved indispensable to the Confederacy. By October 1, 1861, the Richmond Armory—using the tools and machinery confiscated from the Musket Factory—"was in complete working order" and producing arms "of the U.S. pattern Rifle Musket in process of manufacture at the H. Ferry Armory." The machinery from the Rifle Factory was also serving the South at the former U.S. Arsenal in Fayetteville, North Carolina.[99]

On June 14, 1861, Confederate troops under the command of General Joseph E. Johnston blew up the B&O Railroad Viaduct, burned the Musket Factory workshops, and retreated towards Winchester. Two weeks later, on June 28, Confederate raiders burned the Rifle Factory workshops and destroyed the wagon bridge across the Shenandoah River. After just two months of civil war, the Harpers Ferry Armory had been reduced to ruins. It never recovered.

With the outbreak of the Civil War, industrial activity on Virginius Island also came to a halt. In June 1861, while Confederate forces were busy stripping the U.S. Rifle Factory of its machinery and ordnance stock, Abraham Herr sold James H. Burton "41 pieces gas pipe, 13 Hangers, oil can & grease" from the cotton factory. Burton, by this time a Lt. Col. in the Ordnance Department of the Virginia State Militia, authorized the payment of $15.50 to Isaac Strider "for services rendered in taking down shafting and gas pipes at Herr's mill."[100]

Burton was also anxious to purchase two machines from John Wernwag, who had continued to operate the machine shop on Virginius Island through the 1840s and 1850s, and to install them in the new Spiller & Burr small arms manufactory in Richmond, Virginia:

I have been corresponding with Mr. John Wernwag at H. Ferry, on behalf of Messrs Spiller and Burr on the subject of purchasing his cutting engine and cutters, and an unfinished slide lathe he has on hand. I enclose his last letter to me on this

Musket Factory buildings rehabilitated for use as a Union quartermaster depot during Major General Philip Sheridan's 1864 Shenandoah Valley campaign. The headgate for a 15-foot "Backshot Water Wheel" is visible along the Armory headrace just to the left of the two-story Boring Shop. Harpers Ferry NHP (HF-619).

subject, by which you will see that he names prices for both these tools, although he does not say he will sell them. Now, it is important that we should get them if possible, as we need them much, and I therefore enclose herewith certificate of deposit in the Exchange bank of this city for the sum of $650.00 payable to the order of Mr. John Wernwag upon which that amount in money can be drawn in Winchester.[101]

In October 1861, Abraham Herr, who supported the Union when the Civil War erupted, invited federal troops stationed across the Potomac River in Maryland to remove a large quantity of grain from his flour mill. The 13th Massachusetts and 3rd Wisconsin regiments accepted the offer, and the grain was removed in a few days. In retaliation, a Confederate raiding party, disguised in civilian clothing, entered Harpers Ferry a few days later and burned Herr's Mill. This establishment, the most profitable enterprise on Virginius Island, was never rebuilt. Herr subsequently moved to Georgetown in the District of Columbia, where he operated a flour mill after the war.

By August 1862, the cotton factory had been converted into a Union hospital. Two dwellings were also used for hospital purposes. Various other island

Circa 1865 view of Virginius Island from Jefferson Rock. A Union troop train is passing across the island on the Winchester & Potomac Railroad. The ruins of Herr's Mill, burned by Confederate raiders in October 1861, are visible in the upper right. Harpers Ferry NHP (HF-119).

buildings were occupied as offices, barracks, and stables. By the end of the war, homes and industry on Virginius Island were either in ruins or considerable disrepair, and most island residents had moved away. With the federal armory also destroyed, the prospects for recovery at Harpers Ferry were decidedly uncertain. ❧

CHAPTER 4
NEW TECHNOLOGIES & NEW ENTREPRENEURS
1865-1924

We hope its valuable water power, (said to be scarcely second to Lowell,) may be developed in its utmost degree, and that soon again the busy hum of industry will assume the place of its now riddled and gloomy aspect.

—*Spirit of Jefferson*, July 30, 1867

HARPERS FERRY EMERGED FROM THE CIVIL WAR badly scarred and largely in ruin. Both the Musket Factory and Rifle Factory were destroyed, and the industrial establishments on Virginius Island were damaged from military occupation and neglect. A series of six floods had also swept through town between 1861 and 1865, destroying milldams and leaving behind large deposits of silt and mud in the millraces and power canals (*see* **Floods at Harpers Ferry**, *pages 164-165*).

Even more troubling was the departure of the town's workforce. The armorers who produced firearms for the government had long since deserted the place, relocating to Springfield, Massachusetts; Richmond, Virginia; Fayetteville, North Carolina; or various other arms-making centers in both North and South. Abraham Herr, owner of Virginius Island and the once-prosperous merchant flour mill that now lay in ruins, moved to Georgetown 60 miles down the Potomac River.

The only armory building to escape destruction at Harpers Ferry was "John Brown's Fort"—the old fire engine and guard house. While this structure drew curious visitors to town, and in time became a popular tourist attraction, it provided no significant source of employment for the war-weary residents.

Journalist John T. Trowbridge, who visited Harpers Ferry shortly after the end of the war, described the depressing scene:

But while the region presents such features of beauty and grandeur, the town is the reverse of agreeable. It is said to have been a pleasant and picturesque place formerly. The streets were well graded and the hill-sides above were graced with terraces and trees. But war has changed all. Freshets tear down the centre of the streets, and the dreary hill-sides present only ragged growths of weeds. The town itself lies half in ruins. The government works were duly destroyed by the Rebels; of the extensive buildings which comprised the armory, rolling-mills, foundry, and machine-shops, you see but little more than the burnt-out, empty shells.[1]

Footnotes for Chapter 4 begin on Page 185.

Ruins of the Harpers Ferry Armory in 1890, showing the Armory gates, John Brown's Fort, and the chimney stack of the former Smith and Forging Shop (right). The new Harpers Ferry Paper Company, erected in 1888-1889, is visible at the far end of the Armory yard. Harpers Ferry NHP (HF-1237).

Amid this despair, however, Trowbridge saw hope for the place, writing that "the tremendous water-power afforded by its two rushing rivers, and the natural advantage it enjoys as the key to the fertile Shenandoah Valley" should allow Harpers Ferry to again ". . . become a beautiful and busy town."[2] Steadfast town residents and a handful of new entrepreneurs agreed.

CHILD & MCCREIGHT

On July 24, 1867, Abraham Herr sold his holdings on Virginius Island to Jonathan C. Child and John A. McCreight of Springfield, Ohio, for $75,000. The sale embraced "the whole Island properties, with all its valuable water rights and privileges." Of particular interest to these new entrepreneurs was the four-story cotton factory. Although the original machinery, turbines, and shafting had been removed, the building was still structurally sound. The firm Child & McCreight engaged the services of William F. Cochran—a skilled engineer, mechanic, and inventor—to superintend the rehabilitation of the old cotton factory into a merchant flour mill.[3]

During the next 15 months, Cochran employed a large force of men to fit up the new mill with water-powered flour-milling machinery. The reconfigured establishment contained ten run of burr-stones set in motion by four turbine water wheels, each rated at about 75 horsepower. Conveyor buckets fastened to leather belts moved flour through the mill, and a cooperage was situated on the building's top floor. The mill had a production capacity of five hundred barrels of flour daily, and the machinery was "said by adepts in that business, to be a marvel of ingenuity, which greatly added to the previous and well-established fame of Mr. Cochran."[4]

Child & McCreight also rehabilitated Herr's Dam, cleared out the millraces and water tunnels built two decades earlier, and erected new headgates operated by a cogwheel and ratchet system.

The mill's four new iron turbines were manufactured by James Leffel & Co. of Springfield, Ohio. Leffel, a millwright and foundry operator, received a patent for a completely new type of reaction wheel in 1862. Called the "Double Turbine Water Wheel," this device departed significantly from previous designs by combining two wheels in a single case (*see illustration on page 131*).

This improved Leffel wheel was a double bucket design, namely, with a ring of upper buckets and a ring of lower buckets immediately below them and arranged so that the water would pass through both of these sets of buckets and on out into the draft tube in the most efficient manner, thereby creating the highest results in power and speed for the amount of water and the fall of water that were being utilized.[5]

Cotton factory building, circa 1890-1913. The railroad spur track was built for the Child & McCreight flour mill in 1869. Harpers Ferry NHP (HF-897).

The upper wheel was comprised of inward-flow buckets, while the lower wheel had axial-flow buckets that curved inward and downward, This "mixed flow" design resulted in a longer, narrower, and faster turbine which, according to Leffel's patent application, was capable "of yielding from ninety-two to ninety-five per cent. of the power of the water and a greater per cent. than any other wheel heretofore constructed." Leffel's invention—elaborated by other inventors in subsequent years—became the model for the modern "American mixed-flow turbine."[6]

In addition to their demonstrated efficiency, Leffel turbines were compact and inexpensive, commonly ranging in price from $350-$500 for runner sizes of 30-40 inches in diameter. In 1862, during the first year of production, Leffel sold 47 Double Turbines. Sales in 1863 grew to 62, and increased to 153 the following year. By 1870, sales totaled as many as 400-500 turbines annually.

Three of the four Leffel turbines installed in the Child & McCreight mill measured 5 feet-10 inches in diameter (each with a runner size of about 48 inches); the fourth wheel measured 4 feet-10 inches (with a runner size of about 40 inches). Together, these four wheels developed 300 horsepower.

The turbines sat on a raised wooden floor in an enclosed penstock beneath the flour mill. Wicket (or "swing") gates around the circumference of each turbine

Above: Four Leffel turbines and drive shafts, installed by William F. Cochran in the Child & McCreight flour mill in 1867, still survive on Virginius Island. February 1987 photo by the author. ***Left:*** *Leffel turbine model on display at the Smithsonian Institution.* ***Facing page:*** *Leffel Double Turbine Water Wheel, from an 1870 catalog. Ohio Historical Society (#83-3).*

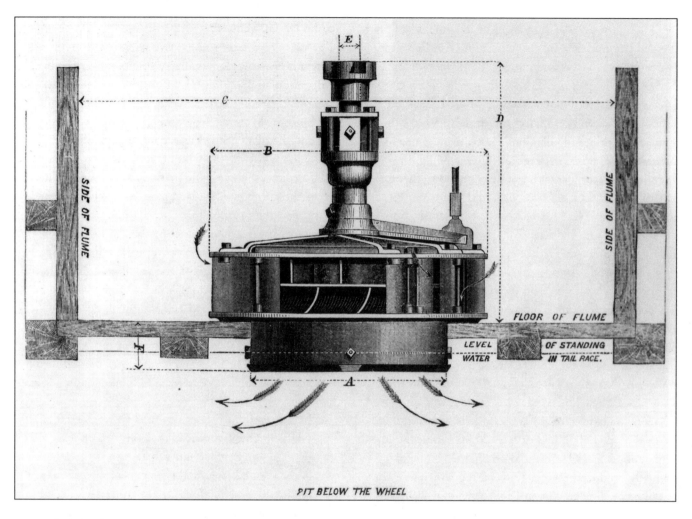

PIT BELOW THE WHEEL

controlled the flow of water onto the double runners. The wicket gates were attached by radial arms to a quadrant mechanism, which was turned by a small gate control gear connected to a hand wheel. Once the wicket gates were opened, water admitted into the penstock passed inward and downward through the turbine's double runner, engaged the runners, and powered the mill's ten burr-stones and various other mechanical contrivances. Spent water exiting the turbines was discharged from short iron skirts or draft tubes beneath the wooden floor before passing through stone arches back into the Shenandoah River.

In August 1868, Child and McCreight sold an un-divided third interest in their Virginius Island property to Solomon V. Yantis and Horatio R. Riddle for $15,000. The firm now became known as Child, McCreight & Co. The company rehabilitated several other factories and residences on Virginius Island—some 28 buildings in all—and leased them out to interested parties. The Excelsior Planing Mills and Lumber Yard, for instance, briefly operated in the old sawmill and machine shop. The Child family moved into Abraham Herr's former residence adjacent to the burned-out ruins of Herr's Mill, while the McCreight family probably occupied Lewis Wernwag's former house near the sawmill. Among the island's other residents during this period was John Wernwag, son of the famous bridgebuilder and an accomplished machinist in his own right. Wernwag lived on the second floor of the machine shop, and may have still operated the old establishment.

According to the 1870 Census, merchant flour milling on Virginius Island continued to be a prosperous enterprise. The Child & McCreight flour mill employed 20 men and converted 400,000 bushels of wheat into 80,000 barrels of flour worth $700,000 annually. The mill's cooperage, which employed another 16 men, annually produced 40,000 flour barrels worth $20,000. A railroad siding erected in 1869 permitted the trans-port of 18 carloads of wheat and flour to and from the mill daily.[7] (*See Flour Milling in the 19th Century on pages 136-137*).

Water-powered industry was alive and well on Virginius Island, and prosperity was slowly returning to the place.

SALE OF GOVERNMENT PROPERTY

The War Department never gave serious consideration to rebuilding the Harpers Ferry Armory. During the Potomac manufactory's 62-year history, unit costs for firearms it produced had exceeded those manufactured at the Springfield Armory by nine to twenty-two percent.[8] Among the many factors that contributed to the cost inefficiencies at the Harpers Ferry Armory were, as we have already seen, wide fluctuations in the streamflow of the Potomac and Shenandoah rivers. Periodic work stoppages that resulted from either too much or too little water were no longer acceptable for the highly mechanized firearms production process. Recurring annual costs associated with the repair and rehabilitation of the manufactory's waterworks had also strained the War Department's limited budget.

An Act of Congress passed on December 15, 1868, provided for the sale of all government property at Harpers Ferry. The armory property was platted into lots, and a public notice advertised the impending sale:

In pursuance of the act approved December 15, 1868, and by direction of the Secretary of War, the property of the United States at Harper's Ferry, West Virginia, and vicinity, will be sold by Public Auction, on **Tuesday, the 30th day of November, 1869,** Commencing at 10 o'clock, A.M., and continuing from day to day until all is sold.

The value of this property for manufacturing purposes is too well known to render it necessary to describe it herein; but a description of the same is being prepared, and will be sent to persons who

Ruins of the Armory Smith and Forging Shop in 1870. The new B&O Railroad bridge has been completed. Harpers Ferry NHP (HF-45).

may wish it, as soon as printed, upon their applying by letter to this office.

The property will be sold in Lots. The first will include the Musket Factory, embracing a strip of land running to the western boundary on the Potomac, the Armory Canal, and Water Power of the River. The walls of two large buildings are standing on this ground, and the foundations of several others; and the water-wheels with gearing,

and the flumes, are almost in perfect order. Three of them are Turbines of the most approved kind, and the others are mostly cast iron with Wooden Buckets.

The second will be the site of the Rifle Factory and Water-Power on the Shenandoah; the buildings upon which have been destroyed, but the Canal is in good order.[9]

Captain Francis C. Adams of Washington, D.C., purchased the two principal lots—the Musket Factory site and Rifle Factory site—for $206,000. Adams subsequently joined with several partners to form The Harper's Ferry Manufacturing and Water Power Company, and "great hopes were entertained for the revival of manufactures at the place and the renewal of the old-time prosperity." The great flood of September 30 and October 1, 1870, however, dashed these hopes with unexpected fury.[10]

The Flood of 1870 was like no flood before it. The raging waters, largely confined to the Shenandoah River, rose so rapidly that many residents living along the banks of the river were trapped in their homes and drowned. Virginius Island was particularly hard hit, and several first-hand accounts of the disaster survive. Emily Child, wife of Jonathan C. Child and mother of three, described the flood in a letter to her sister:

> I snatch a few minutes to give you a few particulars of the disaster that has happened to us here. The valuable property belonging to the firm of which John is a member is a mass of ruins and we have barely escaped with our lives. We had no idea of the danger until it was too late to escape from the Island. Last Friday towards evening the

Illustration of the devastating Flood of 1870, from Harper's Weekly. *Harpers Ferry NHP (HF-347).*

water commenced rising rapidly. Before two hours every way of escape and all hope of rescue was cut off from us. So we were compelled to stay within the crumbling walls which sheltered us from the terrible water which seethed and dashed around us . . . .

Twelve buildings on the Island (some of them heavy stone and brick walls) are leveled to the ground. Our house is considered the strongest residence on the Island and yet everyone thinks if it had not been for the walls of the old mill [Herr's Mill] which stands west of us, it would have been swept away . . . .

The one bright spot in the picture, next to the saving of our lives, is the Mill which is comparatively uninjured. They lost several hundred barrels, some feed and one of their scales but if it were not for the destruction of the race, could go to grinding in a few days, but the race is the greatest calamity of all. The head gates are gone, walls are torn down and the race filled with sand.[11]

Another remarkable account of the flood is furnished by Joseph Barry, long-time resident of Harpers Ferry and well-known chronicler of its tumultuous history. Barry writes:

About 10 o'clock, a.m., on Saturday, the crowd of spectators that covered the hill near Jefferson's Rock, heard a crash on Virginius Island and soon it was known that the noise was caused by the falling in of a portion of the building occupied by Mr. John Wernwag as a dwelling and a machine shop . . . . In a few minutes the sound was repeated, when the remainder of the building crumbled and fell into the tide. The roof floated down the stream, but at first nothing was seen of Mr. Wernwag himself . . . . Two large trees grew on the river bank about a hundred yards below the island, and, as the roof floated down the stream, it fortunately dashed against one of them and was broken in two. Through the space made between the portions of the roof Wernwag's head was seen to emerge from the water and soon the brave old man had succeeded in climbing nimbly to one of the pieces . . . .[12]

Remarkably, Wernwag survived the ordeal, floating downstream to Brunswick, Maryland, where he was rescued and put aboard an evening train back to Harpers Ferry. Wernwag later wrote, however, that all his father's papers, drawings, and intricate bridge models were lost when the machine shop was swept away.

Although no official flood records were kept prior to 1877, the estimated crest of the 1870 Flood was 29.7 feet, surpassing the previous high water marks set during the Civil War freshets of 1862 and 1865 by three feet (*see Floods at Harpers Ferry, pages 164-165*). All told, 42 lives were lost in the Harpers Ferry area. On Virginius Island, floodwaters swept away the machine shop, iron foundry, sawmill, carriage shop, schoolhouse, and several dwelling houses.

The Child & McCreight flour mill never fully recovered from the disaster, and output dropped considerably. According to the 1880 Census, the mill ground

Continued on page 138

*Above: Stone crane, bed stone, and runner stone which has been set on its side for dressing at Peirce Mill in Rock Creek Park. **Right:** Stone vat and feed hopper. May 1979 photos by the author.*

Operation of a typical mid-19th century flour mill combined mechanical ingenuity with a miller's keen sense for producing a fine, hearty flour. *Burr-stones* were the heart of the gristmill and the machinery the miller attended to with the most care. An upper runner stone and a lower, fixed bed stone were housed in a round wooden stone vat (*see illustration on opposite page*). A millstone spindle, which was powered by a train of gears connected to either a turbine or water wheel, extended up through a neck bearing in the middle of the bed stone.

The runner stone was fitted with a bow rhynd—a curved iron crossbar attached to driving irons which engaged into recesses on either side of the eye (center hole) of the stone. The cockhead, which was located at the top of the millstone spindle, engaged into a bearing socket on the bow rhynd and supported the full weight of the runner stone. A cast iron driver, which was affixed to the millstone spindle just above the neck bearing, turned the runner stone by engaging into the driving irons. The base of the millstone spindle rested on a toe bearing located on top of the bridgetree. Using a screw mechanism, a miller could raise or lower the bridgetree, thus adjusting the distance between the bed stone and runner stone.

Grain—corn, rye or whole wheat— was fed into a wooden feed hopper mounted on top of the stone vat. The burr-stones, dressed with a radial pattern of flat lands and grooved furrows, sheared the bran shell from the grain like scissors as the grain moved from center to circumference. The flour then fell through small trunnion holes around the circumference of the bed stone and down a discharge spout to the meal floor for sifting and bagging.

The most popular millstones in the 19th century were French *burr-stones*, comprised of "burrs," or small pieces of quartz from the Marne Valley of northern France. These small burrs were pieced together, joined with cement, and then tightly bound with a round iron hoop.

*Left: Runner stone at the Burwell Morgan Gristmill in Millwood, Va. September 1981 photo by the author. **Right**: Illustration of typical mid-19th century flour milling machinery, from* The Roller Mill and Silo Manual *(Northern Publishing Co. Ltd., 1921).*

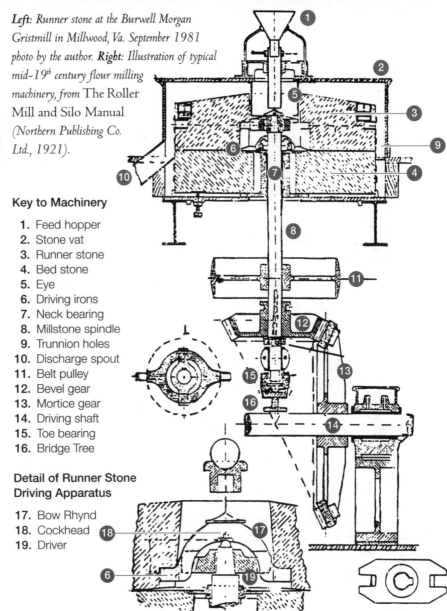

Key to Machinery

1. Feed hopper
2. Stone vat
3. Runner stone
4. Bed stone
5. Eye
6. Driving irons
7. Neck bearing
8. Millstone spindle
9. Trunnion holes
10. Discharge spout
11. Belt pulley
12. Bevel gear
13. Mortice gear
14. Driving shaft
15. Toe bearing
16. Bridge Tree

Detail of Runner Stone Driving Apparatus

17. Bow Rhynd
18. Cockhead
19. Driver

A good pair of burr-stones could grind an average of about 50 tons of grain before redressing was required.

Because too much speed, pressure or heat could destroy the texture of the flour, a miller kept his ear tuned to the noise of his machinery and periodically checked the flour for coarseness or fineness. According to Oliver Evans, author of *The Young Mill-wright and Miller's Guide*, proper grinding did not result from any specific rule but from "a knowledge depending upon that skill which is only to be obtained by practice."[1] The sharpness of the burr-stones, how close together they were set, the speed of the stones, and the rate at which grain was fed to the stones all affected the quality of the flour.

1. Oliver Evans, *The Young Mill-wright & Miller's Guide* (Philadelphia: Lea & Blanchard, 1850), 266.

just 131,000 bushels of wheat annually, producing flour and feed worth $214,324—roughly one-third the output of just a decade earlier. One cause of the firm's problems was a lack of reliable streamflow, which interrupted milling operations during much of the 1870s and 1880s. George W. Smith, an employee at the flour mill for many years, testified in 1887 that between the first of August and the last of October during a typical season, it was often "necessary to suspend operations during the day for want of the necessary supply of water the river being too low to furnish the requisite power." Smith added that prolonged periods of low water would "suspend entirely the work of the said mill."[13]

The firm Child, McCreight & Co. was dissolved in 1880 when Jonathan Child sold his interest in the business and retired. John McCreight and Solomon Yantis, however, continued to operate the flour mill under the name McCreight & Yantis. In 1884, McCreight and Yantis sold their interest in the business to the Harpers Ferry Mill Company, but McCreight remained connected with the business and was still serving as general manager of the flour mill in April 1885.

The new owners, who resided in Philadelphia, introduced several improvements to the flour mill requiring a "large outlay of money." The original burr-stones were replaced with a new roller system comprised of 24 Stevens' improved rollers, six Smith's No. 1 purifiers, three Smith centrifugal reels, a double scalping chest, an aspirator, six Princess dust collectors, two bran separators, three bolting chests with six reels each, and various packers, cleaners, separators, and smutters. The

Harpers Ferry Mill Company, however, became entangled in a series of lawsuits, and the establishment apparently operated only intermittently during the 1880s. The mill was damaged by the record Flood of 1889, and it never operated again.[14]

The great flood of 1870 caused Captain F.C. Adams to delay payment for the armory property at Harpers Ferry, and Congress agreed to extend the terms of payment to five years. It soon became clear, however, that Adams had no real interest in developing the waterpower of the Potomac and Shenandoah rivers. Rather, he believed that the Baltimore & Ohio Railroad's right-of-way through the old armory grounds had been granted on certain conditions, and that there was considerable profit to be made by instituting a suit of ejectment. The attempt failed, however, and Adams defaulted on his purchase.

Congress authorized a second public sale of the Armory Grounds and Rifle Factory site to take place on Tuesday, May 25, 1880. The public notice for this sale described what still remained of the Musket Factory lot:

United States Sale of Valuable Waterpower and Machinery:
LOT ONE, embracing the Water Power entire of the Potomac River, the Canal and Locks, and a strip of land and bluff bordering on that river, lying between the same and the streets and lots as laid down on the map aforesaid, beginning at Shenandoah street and extending to the Western line of the United States property. The wall of two large buildings, the John Brown Engine House

and the foundations of several other buildings are standing, and large quantities of dressed building, flagging and other stone are upon the ground. The Machinery consists of three Turbine Wheels and four Cast Iron Wheels of large dimension, with Gearing, Flumes, &c . . . .[15]

No new buyers stepped forward, however, and a visitor later wrote ". . . it seems a pity that so beautiful a spot with so fine a water power should remain in the dilapidated condition in which I saw it in 1880."[16]

Anxious to sell the property, Congress authorized a third public sale. On October 22, 1884, Thomas Savery of Wilmington, Delaware, purchased the Musket Factory lot for $25,100, outbidding the Baltimore & Ohio Railroad by $100. There was no competition for the old Rifle Factory site alongside the Shenandoah River, and Savery secured this tract for just $810. On March 2, 1885, both the Musket Factory lot and the "old rifle factory on the Shenandoah River . . . together with the water power of the Shenandoah River and the rights conveyed to the United States by John Strider," were formally conveyed to Thomas Savery.[17]

Thomas H. Savery. Hagley Museum and Library (#76.299.2).

The timing of Savery's Harpers Ferry property acquisitions coincided with the Tenth Census *Reports of Water Power of the United States,* conducted in 1880 and published in 1885. The government report was particularly favorable toward the development of waterpower along the Potomac River at Harpers Ferry, remarking:

> The facilities for transportation are excellent, building materials are abundant, and there seems to be no reason why a large and fine power could not be utilized here. The site is probably the most favorable one on the river.[18]

Regarding the development of waterpower along the Shenandoah River on Virginius Island, the *Water Power* report recommended improvements that Savery and his engineers ultimately adopted:

> By building a dam at the head of the island and turning the water into the old [Shenandoah] canal, this fall could be used without difficulty, and with considerable building-room on the island; and a much greater fall than 14 feet could be used, if necessary, depending on the height of the dam.[19]

Savery planned to erect "ground wood pulp" mills, and he possessed a complete familiarity with this emerging new industry.

During most of the 19th century, the basic raw material for paper was cotton and linen rags. Rag paper was durable and attractive, but as early as the 1850s the supply of rags could not keep pace with the demand for paper. The idea of using wood as a raw material for paper had been considered back in the early 1700s. But it wasn't until about 1858, when German inventor Henry Voelter obtained a U.S. patent for a new wood pulp grinder, that a "mechanical process" for reducing wood to fiber was widely adopted in this country.

Savery, himself an inventor, had obtained 32 U.S. patents for improvements to machinery for manufacturing paper. He also served as a foreman, operations manager, vice-president, and ultimately as president of the Pusey & Jones Company in Wilmington, Del., a recognized leader in the manufacture of pulp and paper machinery during the late 19th century.

At Harpers Ferry, Savery had access to several key ingredients for the successful manufacture of mechanical wood pulp: abundant raw materials in the forests of the Potomac and Shenandoah valleys; connections by railroad and canal to the expanding paper mills of the East coast; and an abundance of water. Large amounts of water, in fact, were used throughout the mechanical pulp-making process. Logs were commonly suspended in water to await grinding; logs were mixed with water in the mechanical pulp grinders; pulp-slurry from the grinders was conveyed by pipes to the shaking screens; and waste material from the grinders was discharged from water pipes back into the river.

Between 1887 and 1889, Savery erected two pulp mills at Harpers Ferry. The combined waterpower developed and utilized by these two mills totaled 4,944 horsepower, dwarfing all previous attempts to tap the power of the Potomac and Shenandoah rivers.

SHENANDOAH PULP COMPANY

The Shenandoah Pulp Company was incorporated in the State of West Virginia on November 10, 1886. Formed for the purpose of manufacturing "ground wood pulp," the company's original shareholders included Thomas Savery (President), William Luke (Secretary-Treasurer), and John F. Quigley (General Manager).[20] A few months later, on April 20, 1887, construction of the new pulp mill commenced on the site of the former locks of the Shenandoah Canal adjacent to the old rifle factory.

John F. Quigley, who superintended construction of the mill, also erected new stone headgates at Shenandoah City (Strider's Mill) and completed a new Shenandoah dam sometime during the late summer of 1887. The dam—1,300 feet long, 13 feet wide, and 5-6 feet high—consisted of timber cribbing bolted by iron spikes to the river bottom and filled with stone rip-rap. The structure extended diagonally across the entire width of the river. Just as John H. Hall's dam on this site in 1832 had caused a riparian dispute between the government and John Strider (*see page 47*), so too Quigley's new dam prompted a lawsuit against the Shenandoah Pulp Company.

Thomas H. Savery encountered many difficulties at Harpers Ferry arising from the imprecise and indefinite wording of old government deeds. There were several conflicting claims made by property holders at the place. Many of these landowners, it turned out, were not aware

This circa 1888 view of Virginius Island shows the new Shenandoah Pulp Company mill (upper right) and the ruins of Herr's Mill (center). The covered railroad bridge about one mile upstream (upper left) is adjacent to Shenandoah City and the new Shenandoah dam. Harpers Ferry NHP (HF-1240).

of just what riparian privileges they actually possessed.

In 1851, John Strider's property at the upstream end of the old Shenandoah Canal had been purchased by the Shenandoah City Company for $51,700. The purchase included Strider's Mill—commonly called "Gulf Mills" in the county deed books—and 127 acres of land on both sides of the Shenandoah River. The place subsequently became known as Shenandoah City.[21]

The Shenandoah City Co., by virtue of its holdings on both sides of the river, assumed it possessed all the necessary riparian privileges to fully develop the waterpower at the site. Although the company failed, all the assets of the firm were sold by court decree to E.W. Miller in 1868. Miller, too, apparently believed he possessed an exclusive right to the waterpower at Shenandoah City. On January 19, 1885, however, attorney James D. Butt advised Thomas H. Savery that "all parties who have held under Strider since 1833 have lost sight of the fact that he had conveyed his water privileges to the U.S. and that said privileges pass by sale to the Vendees of the U.S." According to Butt, "The Strider Deed to the U.S. of 1833 conveys the right to diminish the flow of the water to the U.S. Factory," and he assured Savery that the Shenandoah Pulp Company "will have the same right."[22]

Nonetheless, when construction of the new Shenandoah dam threatened to subject the Shenandoah City property to backwater, Miller filed suit against Savery. As Butt had correctly predicted, the merits of *Miller v. Shenandoah Pulp Company* did not stand up in court, and Savery prevailed in the dispute.

At the same time that Butt was defending the Shenandoah Pulp Company against E.W. Miller, the owners of the merchant flour mill on Virginius Island also filed suit against Savery. In *Harpers Ferry Mill Company v. Thos. H. Savery and others*, the plaintiffs argued that the new dam would prevent the operation of their flour mill by severely diminishing the flow of the Shenandoah River. At the center of the dispute was Quigley's plan to divert virtually the entire flow of the river into the old Shenandoah Canal—now a 1½-mile-long millrace—bypassing Virginius Island and returning the flow to the main river channel below the flour mill. The state courts issued an injunction, and pulp mill construction was halted.

Waterpower historian Louis Hunter documents the growing trend of disputes like this during the late 19th century. He describes them as an inevitable outcome of the rapid expansion of manufacturing:

It became increasingly difficult to meet expanding power requirements without interfering to some extent with the needs and operations of other mills on the same stream. Questions of the apportionment of water and priority of its use among several claimants at the same privilege had to be resolved. With a succession of privileges on the same stream, the lower mills were dependent upon the upper ones for the release and regular supply of water, especially during the low-water seasons.[23]

Attorney James Butt had the case removed to federal court. Several local residents called to testify were divided over the key issue of whether waste water from the old rifle factory had passed back into the Shenandoah River *above* or *below* Virginius Island. John H. King, who worked at Hall's Rifle Works from 1824-1847, testified that the "Shenandoah Street channel was the tail-race from the rifle factory" and that any attempt to discharge waste water directly back into the Shenandoah River above Virginius Island "would have involved flowing the water up hill."[24] King's testimony was persuasive: water from the Shenandoah River that passed through the rifle factory property had never been available to the mills and factories of Virginius Island. On July 19, 1887, the United States Circuit Court in Parkersburg, West Virginia, dissolved the injunction and ruled in favor of the pulp mill company, reaffirming the waterpower rights previously enjoyed by the government and acquired by Savery.

After a delay of two months, pulp mill construction resumed. During August 1887, 197 men and 28 carts were employed on construction of the new pulp mill. Six months later, on February 1, 1888, the Shenandoah Pulp Company manufactured its first pulp.[25]

The new manufactory was a large and impressive structure:

> Its front and sides are of brick and the back of wood. It stands on foundation walls of stone four foot thick, laid in Portland cement, and is composed of two buildings, designed as one, and connected. The main building is 118 feet wide and 60 feet long, and spans the old canal, which runs along the Shenandoah river. The smaller building joins the main one in the rear, extending down stream 30 feet, and is 99 feet wide. At the ridge the building is about 25 feet high. The under part of the mill is divided into six flumes, each 15 feet wide, in which the water is held back by semicircular sheet iron bulkheads 15 feet high and one-quarter inch thick.[26]

Five of the six flumes contained paired sets of horizontal shaft 36-inch "Special New American" turbine water wheels, each pair discharging into a common draft chest (*see illustrations, pages 147 and 148*). These turbines were manufactured by The Dayton Globe Iron Works Co. of Dayton, Ohio. The sixth flume was reserved for overflow from the headrace.

The paired sets of horizontal shaft runners provided power by direct drive line shafting to ten Pusey & Jones Company three-pocket wood grinders located in the Wood Grinder Room on the lower (downstream) side of the mill. The horizontal shafts passed through water-tight diaphragms in the semicircular sheet iron bulk-heads which separated each flume from the grinding room (*see **Harpers Ferry Paper Company** illustration, page 155*). This arrangement provided direct drive of the grind-stones and eliminated the need for costly and troublesome bevel gearing, which could rob from 10-20 percent of the available power through friction. Operation of the shafting proved more reliable, less noisy, and maintenance costs were substantially reduced.

Rear (upstream) view of the Shenandoah Pulp Company mill and Lake Quigley. Harpers Ferry NHP (HF-1791).

A single vertical shaft 25-inch "New American" turbine initially drove all the machinery on the mill's main (top) floor: a circular saw 40 inches in diameter, two Holyoke Machine Company disc barkers, a splitter, six Gould patent shaking screens, and six Pusey & Jones Company 62-inch one-cylinder wet press machines. This vertical shaft turbine was placed directly on top of a draft chest which housed a pair of horizontal wheels. Thomas H. Savery described the arrangement in a testimonial letter to The Dayton Globe Iron Works:

> In response to your favor of the 17th inst., would say at Shenandoah Pulp Co's mill there are five draft chests, each containing two of your 36-inch Special Wheels, running under a head of about 24 feet, and driving ten Wood Pulp Grinders. Upon the top of one of these draft chests we placed one of your 25-inch Special Wheels to drive the saws, barkers, splitter and wet machines.[27]

By 1895, the Shenandoah Pulp Company had replaced one pair of its 36-inch horizontal runners with a smaller pair of 33-inch runners. At about the same time, a second 25-inch vertical shaft "New American" wheel was added to meet the power requirements of the mill's main floor machinery.

Each pair of horizontal shaft turbines in the pulp mill was rated at 532 horsepower—266 horsepower per wheel—operating under a 24 foot head of water. Each of the two vertical shaft turbines was rated at 106 horsepower. By comparison, each of the four Leffel turbines in the old Child & McCreight flour mill had developed just 75 horsepower.[28]

During the second half of the 19th century, the Dayton Globe Iron Works Co. of Dayton, Ohio, pioneered development of the "American mixed-flow" turbine, and was a leader in the manufacture of stock wheels for sale in a range of standard sizes.

Throughout North America during this period, increasingly specialized and sophisticated turbine manufacturers began to

Winter activities on Lake Quigley behind the Shenandoah Pulp Company, circa 1893. Harpers Ferry NHP (HF-423).

Downstream view of the Shenandoah Pulp Company ruins. April 1979 photo by the author.

replace the all-purpose machine shops of the early 19th century. These new firms now used more advanced metal working equipment, had access to larger financial resources, and successfully adopted the "American system" to produce large numbers of turbines in standard dimensions at significantly reduced costs. Stiff competition between companies also led to constant product improvements. Changes in wheel shape, dimension, or proportion were regularly introduced to achieve improved performance, greater efficiency, or better methods of production.[29]

In 1859, Stout, Mills & Temple—predecessor to the Dayton Globe Iron Works Co.—had introduced the "American" turbine. This wheel was patterned on an "inward flow" turbine built by Samuel Howd in 1838 and further developed by James B. Francis in 1847. Unlike the traditional "outward flow" wheels developed by Benoit Fourneyron, Uriah A. Boyden, and George Kilburn, water entered inward flow turbines from openings around the circumference of the wheel. The water passed through an outer ring of fixed guide blades, struck the moving vanes of an inner runner, and then exited from the bottom of the wheel. Despite considerable attention to its design and construction, however, the mean efficiency of the Howd-Francis wheel was only about 69 percent. This rating fell well below the best performance of the Boyden turbine, and the inward flow wheel was not widely adopted.

James Leffel's "Double Turbine" of 1862 was one of the first wheels to demonstrate the effectiveness of axial flow runner vanes beneath inner flow vanes. In 1876, John B. McCormick, a Pennsylvania inventor, found that by adding spoon-shaped discharge sections to the bottom of a turbine's inner flow runner vanes, even more energy could be captured from water leaving the wheel.

In 1884, William M. Mills of Stout, Mills & Temple adopted McCormick's design and patented the "New American Turbine Water Wheel" (*see patent drawings on facing page*). The buckets of this turbine were lengthened and curved downward, increasing the bucket area subject to the pressure and reaction of the water. The power of this new wheel, which was nearly identical in diameter to the 1859 "American" wheel, was almost doubled. Mills wrote:

We believe we will be sustained by impartial judges when we broadly assert that the New American is the most substantially and best-built Turbine now made. There is not a single part or detail but is made in a thorough mechanical manner with a view to strength, durability, and efficiency.[30]

The "New American" turbine featured several notable design innovations. Experience with the older "American" turbine had shown that steel buckets, held to the rim of the wheel runner by bolts or screws, were deficient in strength and sooner or later became detached from the rim. Consequently, the runner of the "New American" turbine was comprised of a solid or continuous casting formed entirely in dry sand molds, without a bolt or rivet in any part of the wheel. The result, according to a company catalog, was "a perfect wheel, with even, true, and smooth surfaces, and of unquestioned strength, and which we will guarantee to stand the pressure of any head."[31]

The wheel case of the "New American" turbine was also significantly improved. Graduated chutes or gates around the circumference of the wheel were hinged and angled in such a manner to provide a gradual, even, and efficient application of water to the runner when the gates were either opened or closed. "Fenders" or "gate guards" attached to these gates also relieved them from the pressure of the headwater, further easing the process of opening and closing the gates. A ring and lever mechanism, located on the dome or crown plate of the turbine and attached directly to the gates, was operated by a segment and pinion. Using a hand wheel connected by a shaft and coupling to the pinion, mill operators

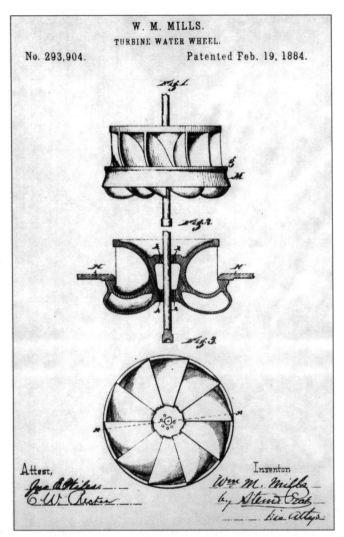

W. M. MILLS.
TURBINE WATER WHEEL.

No. 293,904.   Patented Feb. 19, 1884.

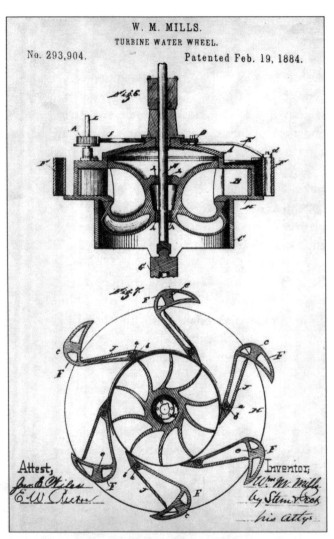

W. M. MILLS.
TURBINE WATER WHEEL.

No. 293,904.   Patented Feb. 19, 1884.

were able to engage the turbines and start up all kinds of machinery gradually, steadily, and with perfect safety.

The Dayton Globe Iron Works Co. was also a pioneer in the design and installation of paired horizontal turbines, and the "Special New American" units

Left: "New American" turbine runner. *Above*: Section and plan of the "New American" turbine runner and gate mechanism. From the patent drawings of William Mills, February 19, 1884 (United States Patent Office, No. 293,904).

installed in the Shenandoah Pulp Company were the company's earliest model. By placing the runners of these turbines on a horizontal shaft, the company departed from the long-standing tradition of building vertical shaft turbines. The new arrangement, however, permitted direct drive of horizontal shaft machinery, and did away with the need for expensive and troublesome bevel gearing. Using a single "shaft chest" (or "draft chest") and a single draft tube for a pair of turbines also reduced cost. But this innovative arrangement did not come without some penalty. Interference between the two converging streams of discharge water, and the considerable eddying that resulted, caused a loss in wheel efficiency of several percent. The company's later models featured curved partitions between the paired turbines, directing the water discharge stream downward into the common draft tube and alleviating much of the interference.[32]

Above: "Design No. 11. Represents a pair of 36-inch Special New American Turbines discharging into an iron draft-chest. This engraving was taken from an outfit we furnished the Shenandoah Pulp Co., of Harper's Ferry, West Virginia, to work under a 24-foot head." **Left:** "Design No. 12. Represents an outfit consisting of three turbines discharging into the same draft-chest, which we furnished the Shenandoah Pulp Co." *From the* Catalogue of the New American Turbine Manufactured by The Dayton Globe Iron Works Co., 1892.

Water diverted from the Shenandoah River at Strider's Mill passed down the old channel of the Shenandoah Canal to Lake Quigley, "a lovely lake, in some places over 300 feet wide, which has very little current." [33] This millpond was named for John F. Quigley, who superintended construction of the mill and served as its first General Manager. Water from Lake Quigley was then admitted into the pulp mill:

> The water of the headrace enters the mill from the upper or front side, filling each of the flumes, running thence to the water wheels, placed on a four-inch white oak floor, passing through the draught tubes, 78 inches in diameter and 17 feet deep, whence it is discharged into the tailrace. [34]

The pulp mill's twelve turbines were completely submerged by headwater in the flumes. Iron draft tubes, which extended down into the tailrace from the bottom of the turbines, made it possible to situate the wheels above the level of the tailwater. Draft tubes, in fact, had become an integral component of the "American mixed flow" turbine. According to a 19th century hydraulic engineer, they permitted "the utilization of the full head by action of the draft or suction pull exerted on the wheel by the water leaving the turbine through the tube from which all air has exhausted." [35]

A 1922 Manager's Report from the Shenandoah Pulp Company demonstrated the importance of a properly fitted draft tube. According to the report, the four-inch white oak flooring under one side of a "Wheel Case" had rotted away and the lug screws no longer held the case down tight on the floor. This permitted water and air to leak into the draft tube, "greatly reducing the power of the wheels." Bolts were substituted for lug screws and ten inches of cement was run into forms around the wheel case, apparently correcting the problem. [36]

Through experience, millwrights learned that any break in the vacuum which permitted air to leak into the draft tube caused unequal pressure across the turbine runner vanes, irregular running, and serious corrosion. This "cavitation"—characterized by constant flexing, bending, and pitting of the runner surfaces—might reduce a wheel's life span by several years. Cavitation usually resulted from failure of the turbine casing, an improperly constructed draft tube, or too much turbulence in the headrace.

In addition to permitting direct drive of the wood grinders by horizontal shafting, an important advantage of locating the turbines above the tailrace at the Shenandoah Pulp Company was ease of maintenance. Since each of the mill's flumes could be sealed off with independent headgates and the water drained, periodic inspection and repair of the turbines was reasonably simple and convenient.

❧

The manufacture of "ground wood pulp" involved several distinct steps. Spruce and poplar logs, the most common types of wood used for mechanical pulp, were delivered by rail car to Lake Quigley and floated down to the pulp mill. Spruce was generally preferred because of its "long fibers, softness, and whiteness." [37] The logs were conveyed onto the mill's main floor by either a log hoist or an endless chain belt mechanism. Inside the mill, disc barkers stripped off the tree bark, a circular saw cut the logs into 15-inch lengths, and the logs were split in half.

The pulpwood was then run down chutes into the Wood Grinder Room on the mill's lower (downstream) floor and loaded into the pockets of a three-pocket wood grinder. Each wood grinder housed a large grindstone four feet in diameter and 10 inches thick. The grinder pockets measured nine inches high, 15 inches wide, and 18 inches deep. Each pocket was fitted with a brass plunger 10 inches in diameter, actuated by hydraulic pressure, 40 pounds to the square inch. The brass plunger forced each

Above: Pusey & Jones Company wet press machine, circa 1890. Two screen cradles sit on the raised platform to the left; press rolls and drying cylinders are on the right. Hagley Museum and Library (#72.369.158).
Left: Pusey & Jones Company three-pocket wood grinder, from a circa 1901 company catalog. Courtesy Hagley Museum and Library.

log against the 18 inch face of the grindstone, which made 200 or more revolutions per minute and slowly ground the wood into pulp.[38]

A large amount of water was piped through the wood grinders, helping lubricate the grindstones but also producing "a continuous amount of steam and humidity which rises against the rafters overhead and rots them very rapidly."[39] The water was mixed with the freshly ground pulp to create a slurry, called "stuff." This "stuff" was piped from pits under the grinders by centrifugal pumps to oak "Screen Cradles" on the mill's main floor. The "stuff" was then dropped onto shaking screens comprised of finely meshed wire cloth. The vibration of the shaking screens, which were turned by rollers, removed excess water from the wood pulp.

In 1922, a system of shower pipes was installed in the Screen Cradles to help separate pulp fibers from unground wood slivers. Prior to this improvement, there was "much wastage of material because of the fact that all slivers from grinders and screens are dumped directly into the river without even washing off the good pulp which adheres to them."[40]

From the screens, a layer of pulp from 1½ to 2½ inches thick was conveyed onto a 62-inch one-cylinder wet press machine (commonly called a "Wet Machine"). Typically, two Screen Cradles were attached to each Wet Machine, allowing one cradle to supply pulp to the screens while the slivers and other waste were emptied from the second cradle. Rollers covered with endless woolen felts guided the pulp between press rolls and drying cylinders, which bonded the "stuff" into sheets. The pulp, about 40%-45% dry, was rolled into bundles of one hundred pounds each, loaded onto rail cars at a siding alongside the mill, and shipped to paper mills for final processing.

The production capacity of the Shenandoah Pulp Company was 40 tons for a 24-hour day, and the firm reportedly employed as many as 51 men who worked 10-12 hour shifts. The record flood of June 1, 1889 briefly interrupted operations, destroying the headgates at Shenandoah City, washing away the embankment of Lake Quigley in two places, and carrying off about $2,000 worth of pulp lumber.[41] The mill, however, suffered only minor damage, and was back in operation within six weeks. A second pulp mill along the banks of the nearby Potomac River also began operation in 1889.

HARPERS FERRY PAPER COMPANY

Construction of the Harpers Ferry Paper Company—Savery's second "ground wood mill" at Harpers Ferry—began in May 1888 on the former site of the Armory's Rolling Mill parallel to the Potomac River. This new manufactory was virtually identical in design and construction to the Shenandoah Pulp Company.

When mechanical operations commenced on March 23, 1889, the mill contained ten turbines which developed 2,604 gross horsepower (*see illustration, page 155*).[42] Water for power was taken from the side of the headrace—the former Armory Canal—and discharged directly into the Potomac River below the mill. The working head for the site was about 24 feet. Supplying the long headrace was the old Armory Dam, a combination masonry and crib structure which extended diagonally across the Potomac River:

> The dam is low throughout its entire length. The northerly portion which connects with the Maryland shore is laid up in stone masonry while the other portion is composed of stone filled cribs . . .[43]

Potomac (Armory) Dam undergoing repair, circa 1922. This photo is attributed to William Savery, who served as General Manager of the Harpers Ferry Paper Company. This dam provided power to the mill, and to the subsequent Power Plant, from 1889-1991. Harpers Ferry NHP (HF-814).

Just nine weeks after the Potomac dam and the new pulp mill were put into operation, however, the Flood of 1889 temporarily halted production. According to Minutes of the Harpers Ferry Paper Company, the dam "was found to be a complete wreck and it was found impossible to maintain anything like the former head of water without extensive repairs to the Dam and they were begun at once."[44] Floodwaters also swept away a small frame office adjacent to the pulp mill and a considerable portion of the canal raceway wall.

Just as litigation had interrupted construction of the nearby Shenandoah Pulp Company, a riparian dispute threatened to halt Savery's development of waterpower along the Potomac River. On October 1, 1885, L. Victor Boughman, president of the Chesapeake & Ohio Canal Company, wrote Thomas H. Savery:

I am informed by Superintendent Biser that you contemplate drawing water from <u>our</u> <u>dam</u> on the Potomac River above Harpers Ferry. Under no circumstance can we permit you to do so, as the C&O Canal Co. own the water privilege of the Potomac River or so much thereof as is necessary to keep said canal open for navigation. You will be held responsible for any infringement of these rights and liable to arrest and damage.[45]

This was the first open claim made by the Canal Company to the dam, which was erected by the Harpers Ferry Armory in 1801, and had been maintained by the government until the outbreak of the Civil War. In November 1833, the dam also began serving the C&O Canal as a feeder dam (*see pages 32-34*). The Flood of 1877, which was particularly severe along the Potomac River, apparently destroyed part of the old dam, and the damage was discussed during a Canal Company meeting. The minutes of this meeting, for the first time, referred to the structure as "Dam No. 3."[46]

The dispute prompted Thomas Savery to have his attorneys conduct a thorough search through the property records of the lands he had purchased from the government. The attorneys subsequently reported:

The canal of the Chesapeake & Ohio Canal skirts the river at this point on the Maryland side, and it is probable that the Canal Company owns the land between the Canal and the river at the abutment of the dam, but there are so many deeds to the Canal Company for its right-of-way that we cannot identify this particular location among the many descriptions. We find no record of any deed between the Canal Company and the Government, nor between the Government and the old Patowmack Company.[47]

On April 12, 1887, Savery's original deed to the Musket Factory property, recorded on March 2, 1885, was amended. The revised deed conveyed "the water power entire of the Potomac river with a strip of land and bluff bordering that river and lying between the streets and lots laid down on the plat of Harpers Ferry of 1869."[48] Plans for construction of the Harpers Ferry Paper Company proceeded, and the Canal Company apparently made no further claims to an exclusive water privilege here.

Eight of the ten turbines installed in the Harpers Ferry Paper Company were 36-inch horizontal shaft "Special New American" wheels arranged in four pairs. Each runner developed 283 horsepower—or 566 horsepower per pair. The mill's two remaining turbines were vertical shaft 27½-inch "Improved Success" water wheels, manufactured by the S. Morgan Smith Company of York, Pa. Each of these wheels developed 170 horsepower, 62% more than the two vertical shaft "New

Ruins of the Harpers Ferry Armory, circa 1870. The Harpers Ferry Paper Co. was built directly on top of the Rolling Mill ruins (left foreground). Ruins of the Lumber House & Coal Bin, Tilt-Hammer & Barrel-Welding Shop, and Smith & Forging Shop are also visible. (Stereograph by J.W. & J.S. Moulton, Salem, Mass.)

American" wheels installed at the Shenandoah Pulp Company—showing just how quickly turbine manufacturers were improving their wheels during this period.

Mechanical operations at the Harpers Ferry Paper Company were virtually identical to those at the Shenandoah Pulp Company:

> The grinder room is at low level to permit direct connection of the grinders to the horizontal shafts of water wheel units. The wet machine room floor is something like 4' above the level of the water in the head race. On the wet machine room level are the screens, cutting-off saw, barkers, etc.[49]

The horizontal shaft turbines powered eight three-pocket wood grinders in the "Wood Grinder Room," while the vertical shaft turbines operated all the equipment on the mill's main floor.

Even as the Shenandoah Pulp Company and Harpers Ferry Paper Company were being constructed, the economics of paper production began to change. Pulp mills like the two built at Harpers Ferry were springing up across the nation, expanding from eight manufactories in 1870 to 82 in 1890. In 1865, the cost of print paper averaged 24½¢ per pound. By the early 1890s, the boom in pulp and paper manufacture across the country had lowered the price of print paper to less than 3¢ per pound.[50] Operating a profitable pulp manufactory under these market conditions proved extremely difficult during the late 19th and early 20th centuries.

Another obstacle to profitable pulp mill operation at Harpers Ferry was the seasonable variability of streamflow. In 1908, a thorough inspection of the hydraulic properties of the Shenandoah Pulp Company found that the waterpower developed at this site was reduced by as much as 25% "on account of low water for three months in the year." According to

Harpers Ferry Paper Company, circa 1900. Harpers Ferry NHP (HF-1143).

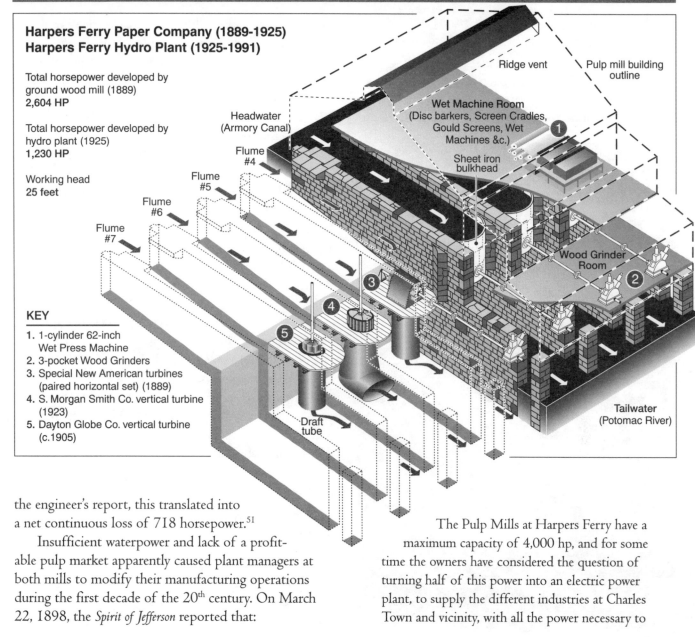

Harpers Ferry Paper Company (1889-1925)
Harpers Ferry Hydro Plant (1925-1991)

Total horsepower developed by
ground wood mill (1889)
2,604 HP

Total horsepower developed by
hydro plant (1925)
1,230 HP

Working head
25 feet

Headwater
(Armory Canal)

Flume
#4

Flume
#5

Flume
#6

Flume
#7

Ridge vent

Pulp mill building
outline

Wet Machine Room
(Disc barkers, Screen Cradles,
Gould Screens, Wet
Machines &c.)

Sheet iron
bulkhead

Wood Grinder
Room

Tailwater
(Potomac River)

Draft
tube

KEY

1. 1-cylinder 62-inch
   Wet Press Machine
2. 3-pocket Wood Grinders
3. Special New American turbines
   (paired horizontal set) (1889)
4. S. Morgan Smith Co. vertical turbine
   (1923)
5. Dayton Globe Co. vertical turbine
   (c.1905)

the engineer's report, this translated into
a net continuous loss of 718 horsepower.[51]

Insufficient waterpower and lack of a profitable pulp market apparently caused plant managers at
both mills to modify their manufacturing operations
during the first decade of the 20th century. On March
22, 1898, the *Spirit of Jefferson* reported that:

The Pulp Mills at Harpers Ferry have a
maximum capacity of 4,000 hp, and for some
time the owners have considered the question of
turning half of this power into an electric power
plant, to supply the different industries at Charles
Town and vicinity, with all the power necessary to

run their plants as well as lighting Harpers Ferry and Charles Town.[52]

In July 1899, Thomas H. Savery joined with others to form the Harpers Ferry Electric Light & Power Co. On May 25, 1905, the new firm leased Flume #6 in the

Harpers Ferry Paper mill to generate electricity from 6:00 p.m. until 6:00 a.m. at a rate of 50¢ per horsepower per month. At about this same time, the company installed a new 51-inch 330 horsepower Dayton Globe Co. vertical shaft turbine in Flume #6 to power a single "dynamo" or generator situated on the mill's main floor. By 1907, the company was generating electricity from "2 Dynamos operated by Water Power" inside the mill. During this same period, the Harpers Ferry Paper mill reduced the number of its wood grinders from eight to four. By driving just one wood grinder rather than two from each pair of horizontal turbines, more efficient and reliable operation was probably obtained.[53]

In 1904, the Shenandoah Pulp Company also leased the use of one water wheel with its shafting and connections—representing about 100 horsepower for an average of 12 hours a day—to the Harpers Ferry Electric Light & Power Company. The lease carried a rate of $600 a year for a period of five years, and provided sufficient floor space in the mill to accommodate the electrical apparatus.[54] About the same time, the Shenandoah mill also reduced the number of its wood grinders from ten to four. Manufacturing operations at the Shenandoah Pulp Company, however, did not appear to suffer. According to a 1908 report by hydraulic engineer E.A. Flanagan:

Remains of a horizontal turbine shaft protrude from a semicircular sheet iron bulkhead in Flume #4 of the former Harpers Ferry Paper Company. The large hand wheel and spur gear operated a gate control mechanism on a pair of Special New American turbines. Fall 1980 photo by the author.

This circa 1894 view shows, from right to left alongside the Potomac River, the new Baltimore & Ohio Railroad mainline tracks and passenger depot, the old B&O mainline tracks, the former Armory Yard, the Harpers Ferry Paper Company, and part of the Armory Canal. Harpers Ferry NHP (HF-92).

The physical condition of its Mill Buildings and Machinery is excellent and a uniform production of twenty-two tons of Ground Wood Pulp (dry weight) per day shows the mill to be in good running order and under able and careful management.[55]

As time went on, however, both pulp mills at Harpers Ferry began to suffer increasing losses. Limited space for growth, a limited and erratic supply of water-power, and the depletion of nearby timberlands prevented either company from expanding its scale of production to meet the challenges of widespread competition in the commercial marketplace. According to the records of the Harpers Ferry Paper Co., mechanical pulp imported from Europe during the early 1920s was often priced below their own cost of production. By the end of 1924, the Shenandoah Pulp Co. reported a loss of $20,945 for the year, while losses at the Harpers Ferry Paper Co. for the same period totaled $25,694.[56]

By contrast, the Harpers Ferry Electric Light & Power Co. was "run on a very economical basis," and the owners continued to make improvements to their power equipment and transmission lines. By 1913, the company had 305 customers, providing power for 4,869 interior lights and 92 street lamps, principally in Harpers Ferry, W.Va., and Brunswick, Md. In 1916, the company invested some $17,000 in new equipment, including a 240 kilowatt General Electric generator which was installed above Flume #6 in 1917.[57]

By 1921, the number of customers had jumped to 1,023. To handle the additional load, the company installed a new 57-inch 900 horsepower S. Morgan Smith Co. vertical shaft turbine in Flume #5 during the summer of 1923. This powerful new water wheel was designed to run a 500 kilowatt General Electric generator, and the prospects for expanding electric operations at the plant were decidedly favorable.[58]

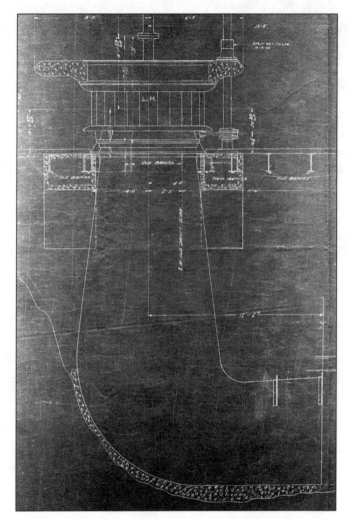

Blueprint of an S. Morgan Smith Co. vertical shaft turbine prepared for the Harpers Ferry Paper Company on Dec. 29, 1922. The drawing includes a flaring draft tube with a 90 degree elbow at the bottom. The wheel was installed during the summer of 1923. Courtesy Hagley Museum and Library.

CHAPTER 5
THE LEGACY OF WATERPOWER
1924-1991

Innovative technology could not guarantee successful operation given the irregular streamflow conditions that existed along the Potomac River.

—Patricia Chickering, unpublished report on the Potomac Power Plant

WHILE THE PROSPECTS FOR DEVELOPING HYDROELECTRIC power at Harpers Ferry were most promising, the outlook for the pulp manufacturing business was not. Hard pressed by foreign competition and by large, capital-intensive, high-volume American companies, the Shenandoah Pulp Company and Harpers Ferry Paper Company found it more and more difficult to compete in the commercial marketplace. By the 1920s, the Savery family realized that the capacity of their two mills to generate electricity was much more valuable than their capacity to manufacture ground wood pulp:

> [T]he WHEELS used by the Elect. Light Co., are income producers when water is high, low, muddy or otherwise when Pulp cannot be made and in a general way our properties have a greater value due to the present Electric development . . . .[1]

Nationally, energy produced by hydroelectric power doubled between 1912 and 1920. During the 1920s,

Footnotes for Chapter 5 begin on Page 187.

more hydroelectric plants were placed in service than during any other decade in American history. Indeed, many pulp mill owners across the nation began replacing their wood grinders with electrical generators:

> Quite a few paper companies created hydroelectric plants by simply unbolting and discarding obsolete pulp grinders, then mounting alternators in their place.[2]

In 1924, the Savery family consolidated their three Harpers Ferry companies—the Harpers Ferry Electric Light & Power Co., Shenandoah Pulp Co., and Harpers Ferry Paper Co.—when the Harpers Ferry Paper Company bought up the common stock of the other two concerns. Developments at Harpers Ferry directly reflected the nationwide momentum which was now propelling the expansion of hydroelectric power.

During the 18th, 19th, and early 20th centuries, Harpers Ferry mirrored both the ups and downs of America's

Upstream view of the Shenandoah Pulp Company and Lake Quigley, circa 1888. Herr's Dam is visible on the right. Harpers Ferry NHP (HF-613).

early dependence on waterpower. Here plant operators routinely adopted the latest water wheel designs and turbine technologies to power increasingly mechanized production systems. Virtually every significant hydraulic design known to exist was used at one time or another at Harpers Ferry: breast wheel, tub wheel, overshot wheel, undershot wheel, backshot wheel, Fourneyron turbine, and American mixed-flow turbine.

Across America, falling water remained the primary source of industrial power from Colonial times through the Civil War. Interruptions to factory operations that resulted from variations in streamflow and occasional flooding were generally accepted by plant managers and mill workers accustomed to planning their work routine around the ebb and flow of their water supply. Sustained by a long tradition of use, completely familiar to mill operators, and relatively inexpensive to harness, waterpower endured along the banks of rivers and streams all across the country. Only as the scale of manufacturing grew—and mechanization, production capacity, and cost efficiency became an integral part of the industrial landscape—did seasonal interruptions to operation become increasingly unacceptable for water-powered manufactories.

A major factor in 19th century American industrialization was the rise of steam power. Steam engines released entrepreneurs from their dependence on waterpower, and industry gradually moved away from the rivers. Much of the nation's industrial production now became increasingly concentrated in urban areas and in ever-larger manufacturing establishments. By 1870, steam horsepower actually led water horsepower in manufacturing by a ratio of about 52-48. Ten years later, in 1880, steam surpassed water as a power source both in power produced and in number of units in use.[3]

Efficient, low-cost turbines introduced by such companies as The Dayton Globe Iron Works and S. Morgan Smith Company actually encouraged many mill operators to prolong their reliance on waterpower. But the success of these new turbine technologies served only to slow the shift by many from waterpower to steam power:

> The share of direct-drive waterpower, despite a marked recovery in absolute terms in the 1890s, continued its decline from 21 percent in 1889 to 15 percent in 1899 and 11 percent in 1909. Conversely, steam power use doubled in the decade of the 1870s and again in the 1880s.[4]

Pulp manufacture, however, defied this trend. Because water played such a key role in pulp manufacture, it remained both convenient and economical to apply waterpower to the mechanical pulp production process. According to federal census records kept between 1870 and 1900, pulp manufacture was

New American Turbine (The Dayton Globe Iron Works Co., 1892 catalog).

the only major industry in America that did not participate in the nationwide move from waterpower to steam power. In 1870, water furnished 72 percent of the power used by the paper and wood pulp industry; as late as 1909, the industry still employed 60 percent waterpower. In terms of the gross horsepower used in pulp manufacture nationwide, water increased from 42,000 horsepower in 1870 to 505,000 horsepower in 1900, while steam grew from 12,000 horsepower to just 256,000 horsepower during the same period.[5]

For firms like the Shenandoah Pulp Company and Harpers Ferry Paper Company that relied on water for much of the pulp making process and had large capital investments in milldams, power canals, and turbines, there were few compelling reasons to convert their manufacturing operations from waterpower to steam power. Thomas H. Savery, for instance, wrote in a testimonial letter to The Dayton Globe Iron Works Co. that the "36-inch Special Wheels" put into operation both at the Shenandoah Pulp mill and Harpers Ferry Paper mill "have worked very well, and have given general satisfaction."[6]

Another compelling reason why Savery continued to rely on waterpower was addressed in a report submitted by hydraulic engineer E.A. Flanagan in 1908:

> The cost of one Horse Power produced by the Water Power at Harpers Ferry would not exceed $5.00 per year, which is one eighth the cost of a Horse Power produced by Coal. If, in order to be perfectly safe and conservative in our estimates, we

would consider the cost of a Horse Power produced by Water to be $10.00 per year, the difference in the cost, between Coal and Water would be $30.00 per Horse Power per Year, in favor of Water. Three Thousand Horse Power can therefore be produced by Water for $90,000.00 per Year less than by use of Coal.[7]

Such persuasive economic arguments gave Savery and other water-powered mill operators little reason to invest in expensive new steampower systems. As a result,

operations at both the Shenandoah Pulp Company and Harpers Ferry Paper Company remained bound to the streamflow of the Potomac and Shenandoah rivers long after waterpower had passed its prime elsewhere in America.

Bound to river streamflow as they were, the flood of May 13, 1924, was one more event that diminished the capacity of the two pulp mills at Harpers Ferry to compete in the commercial marketplace. Expensive (and increasingly scarce) pulpwood was swept away, and the dams, power canals, and related components of the water power system were badly damaged, crippling plant operations for several weeks (*see* **Floods at Harpers Ferry**, *pages 164-165*).

The pulp mill managers learned that interruptions like these, which had plagued operations at the Harpers Ferry Armory throughout its life, were still a chronic problem. The Flood of 1889, for example, shut down operations at both the Shenandoah Pulp Company and Harpers Ferry Paper Company for several weeks. Ice flows on the Potomac River in February 1918 caused a 400 foot breech in the Potomac dam, reducing the mill's capacity by half and "seriously" interrupting the electric power operation. Another ice flow in March 1920 again

Pulpwood from the Shenandoah Pulp Company clogs the streets in Lower Town Harpers Ferry during the flood of May 14, 1924. Harpers Ferry NHP (HF-305).

damaged the Potomac dam, and repair work on the structure continued through October of that year. To ensure a reliable supply of electricity during interruptions like these, a new 200 kilowatt belted generator was installed in the Shenandoah Pulp Company about this time.[8]

Erratic and widely fluctuating streamflow was discussed in several company General Manager's Reports, and the owners were forced "to spend considerable money over the years to repair the dam and other features of the water power system."[9] But the

Charred remains of the Harpers Ferry Paper Company after fire destroyed the building on January 15, 1925. The standing walls were incorporated into the Potomac Power Plant, erected on the site a short time later. Harpers Ferry NHP (HF-1574).

disaster that struck next was completely unexpected.

At 3:00 a.m. on January 15, 1925, a spark from a faulty electrical generator in the Harpers Ferry Paper mill ignited the roof of the main brick building. The roof collapsed and three carloads of pulpwood on the first floor burned, leaving the building and its contents a "charred mass." The *Farmers Advocate* reported that the fire loss was an estimated $300,000.[10]

The building was not a total loss, however, as portions of the mill's four brick walls apparently withstood the conflagration. With a fire insurance policy payment of $25,000, the Savery family decided to abandon pulp-making operations at the site and instead to reconstruct a smaller plant designed exclusively to generate hydroelectric power. Within six months a small power plant measuring 74 feet by 42 feet was completed

on the site. This building reused the original brick walls from the pulp mill's east (downstream) and south sides, and included new brick walls on the north and west (upstream) sides. These new walls were built with bricks salvaged from the old Child & McCreight Flour Mill on Virginius Island, which had been abandoned since 1889, and was heavily damaged by the 1924 flood.[11]

Compared to many hydroelectric plants erected during the 1920s—typically characterized by flat roofs, square steel frames, and nondescript brick exteriors—

Continued on page 166

Floods at Harpers Ferry, 1852-1996

1852 (April 18) The *Virginia Free Press* wrote: "Every house on Shenandoah and Potomac streets was almost entirely submerged—the water being six feet higher than at any other period within the recollection of man…" The Shenandoah Canal, Armory Canal, and Armory Dam were heavily damaged.

1861-1865 A series of floods during the Civil War severely hampered efforts to keep the B&O Railroad bridge open, destroying all or part of the structure on five separate occasions.

1870 (September 30-October 1) The Shenandoah River rose so rapidly that residents were trapped on Virginius Island. Floodwaters swept away much of the island's homes and industry, and claimed 42 lives at Harpers Ferry. Although the

Child & McCreight flour mill survived the flood, it never fully recovered.

1877 (November 25) High water caused considerable damage to the C&O Canal and closed the old Shenandoah Canal for good. The flood crest was 29.2 feet.

1889 (June 1) The rivers rose to a record height—34.8 feet—destroying the Shenandoah wagon bridge; damaging the dams, power canals, and waterpower works of the town's two new pulp mills; and forcing the C&O Canal Company into receivership.

Approximate flood level (Official flood levels were not recorded at Harpers Ferry until the Flood of 1877).

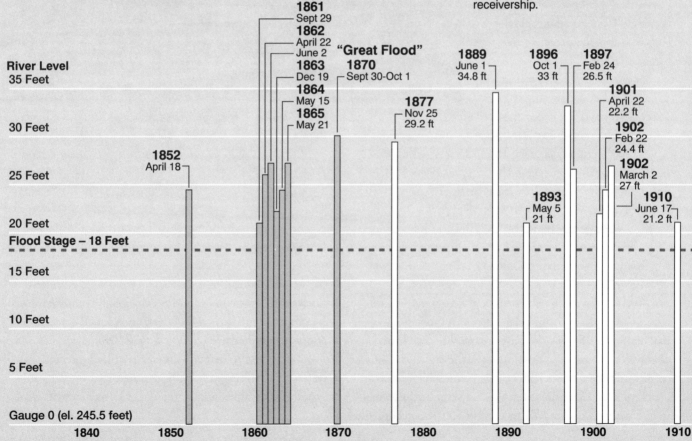

1896 (October 1) One of the town's highest floods. The rivers crested at 33.0 feet.

1924 (May 13) Floodwaters swept away three spans from the Bollman highway bridge, forced the last residents to leave Virginius Island, and permanently closed the C&O Canal.

1936 (March 18-19) 36.5 feet—the all-time record crest at Harpers Ferry. The Bollman bridge and Shenandoah bridge were swept away, while many businesses in the Lower Town were left in ruins.

1942 (October 16) All-time record crest for the Shenandoah Valley. Floodwaters reached 33.8 feet in Lower Town Harpers Ferry.

1972 (June 23) The first major flood endured by Harpers Ferry National Historical Park. Rains from Hurricane Agnes swelled the rivers to 29.7 feet in the Lower Town Historic District.

1985 (November 5-6) The Potomac and Shenandoah rivers crested at 29.8 feet, leaving behind several inches of mud in park buildings and exhibits.

1996 (January 20-21) Rain and snowmelt from the record Blizzard of Jan. 1996—which dumped more than two feet of snow in the valleys of the Potomac and Shenandoah—caused the rivers to rise to 29.4 feet in Lower Town Harpers Ferry.

1996 (September 8) Devastating rains from the remnants of Hurricane Fran fell across the Shenandoah and Potomac river basins. The rivers rose to 29.8 feet, marking the first time in the town's long history that two floods in excess of 29 feet occurred in a single year.

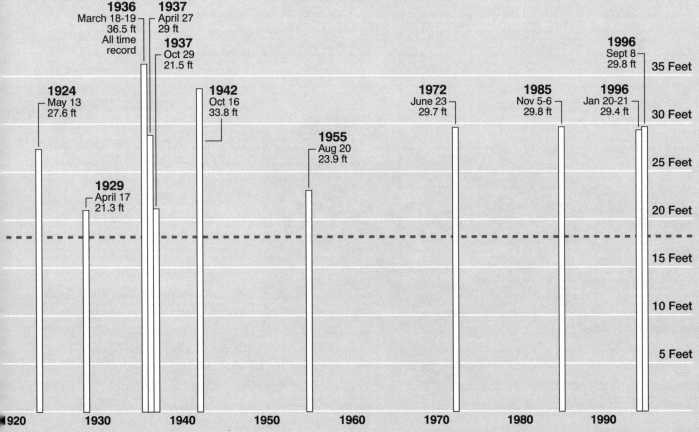

1936 March 18-19 36.5 ft All time record

1937 April 27 29 ft

1937 Oct 29 21.5 ft

1924 May 13 27.6 ft

1942 Oct 16 33.8 ft

1929 April 17 21.3 ft

1955 Aug 20 23.9 ft

1972 June 23 29.7 ft

1985 Nov 5-6 29.8 ft

1996 Jan 20-21 29.4 ft

1996 Sept 8 29.8 ft

35 Feet
30 Feet
25 Feet
20 Feet
15 Feet
10 Feet
5 Feet

1920   1930   1940   1950   1960   1970   1980   1990

the appearance of the Potomac power plant was unique. By reusing much of the brick fabric of the original pulp mill building, the power plant's external appearance reflected many of the architectural features of the 1888 structure, including a gable roof and small decorative touches in the cornice and window treatments. The addition of bricks salvaged from the Child & McCreight mill, and the likelihood that Savery had reused bricks from ruined Armory buildings in erecting the original pulp mill, all served to "connect the power house to an earlier era of Harpers Ferry's industrial past."[12]

The 240 kilowatt General Electric generator installed inside the Harpers Ferry Paper mill in 1917

Crossing guard and automobile pose at the railroad grade crossing in front of the Harpers Ferry Hydro Plant, circa 1925. A portion of the south wall of the original pulp mill extends beyond the upstream end of the new power plant. Harpers Ferry NHP (HF-808).

above Flume #6 also survived the fire. This unit was removed for repairs, rewound, and reinstalled in the plant. A new 600 kilowatt GE generator was also installed in 1925 above the S. Morgan Smith turbine in Flume #5, along with a new Woodward water wheel governor (*see page 168*). A representative from the S. Morgan Smith Company of York, Pa., was hired to inspect the two vertical shaft turbines—the 51-inch Dayton Globe wheel in Flume #6 and the 57-inch S. Morgan Smith wheel in Flume #5—and both wheels were back in service by the end of 1925 driving the plant's two electrical generators.[13]

In 1926, the company sold over 830,000 kilowatt hours of electricity—up from about 399,000 in 1920. The power plant was also now serving 1,707 customers in Harpers Ferry and Bolivar, West Virginia; Brunswick and Knoxville, Maryland; and several smaller communities nearby. Although prospects for further expanding the hydroelectric business seemed good, the power plant remained a relatively small regional operation.

There was considerable discussion between owners, plant managers, and other associates regarding their desire either to expand or sell the business. Eugene Bready, Superintendent of the Harpers Ferry Electric Light & Power Co., wrote that he was "very much interested in building something bigger here, bring factories in that would eat up all the 'juice' that we could develop."[14] Thomas

Potomac Power Plant and foundations of the former Harpers Ferry Paper Company in March 1995. Historic American Engineering Record photo by Jet Lowe (HAER WV-61-2).

Savery, Jr., on the other hand, seemed more interested in selling the business:

> We all appreciate that we must keep on developing the Power company and hope that that will be bait for some people to buy us out in near future.[15]

On August 15, 1928, a buyer finally stepped forward. The National Electric Power Company purchased the Harpers Ferry Electric Light & Power Co., Shenandoah Pulp Co., and Harpers Ferry Paper Co. for $1,100,000. About 15 years later, in 1943, the Harpers Ferry Hydro Plant was acquired by the Potomac Light &

Woodward Water Wheel Governor type HR #5649 and 500 KW General Electric generator (1), located in the Potomac Power Plant. Both the generator and governor were taken out of service in January 1991. The governor regulated the speed (and consequently the power output) of the 900 horsepower S. Morgan Smith turbine which drove this generator. The turbine (*below*) was removed from the site in April 1995.

A hydraulic pump (2) provided power to the main hydraulic power cylinder (3), which housed an 8¾-inch diameter piston. The tank (4) contained pressurized oil, monitored by a sight gauge (5). A "fly-ball" governor inside this spherical housing (6) monitored the turbine's rotational speed through a small shaft connected to the turbine wheel in the pit.

A pilot valve located on top of the hydraulic power cylinder, and controlled

Above: Woodward Governor. Historic American Engineering Record photo by Jet Lowe (*HAER WV-61-16*). *Left:* S. Morgan Smith turbine. April 1995 photo by the author.

by the rotational speed of the "fly-ball" governor through a system of levers and cams, directed hydraulic oil to either side of the piston in the main cylinder. Depending on the rotational speed of the turbine, this piston either pushed or pulled a lever arm connected by a train of gears to the turbine inlet gates in the wheel pit. To slow the wheel speed, the inlet gates were closed; to increase the wheel speed, the inlet gates were opened.

Power Co.—predecessor to the Potomac Edison Company of West Virginia.[16]

After pulp manufacturing operations at the Harpers Ferry Paper Company ceased in 1925, the Shenandoah Pulp Company remained the only water-powered manufacturing plant at Harpers Ferry. By 1927, the mill was producing just 15 tons of "ground wood pulp" daily—down from a peak production capacity of 40 tons. Losses continued to mount, and the company's liabilities soon exceeded its assets. Finally, in 1935, after forty-seven years of operation, the pulp mill shut down. The company declared its final liquidating dividend on June 23, 1936, and the corporation was dissolved by the State of West Virginia two days later.[17]

Potomac Edison Company operated the Harpers Ferry Hydro Plant as a small unmanned operation, periodically checked and serviced by a crew from another plant. On June 6, 1969, the 240 kilowatt GE generator in the power plant failed; it was not officially taken out of service, however, until 1973. Potomac Edison continued to operate the power plant until January 1991, when the 600 kilowatt GE generator was taken out of service and the hydro station was shut down.

Shenandoah Pulp Company ruins shortly before demolition in August 1938. The plant closed down in 1935 after 47 years of operation. Harpers Ferry NHP (HF-1437).

View of the Potomac Power Plant on August 13, 1931. The southwest wall of the old Harpers Ferry Paper Company is still standing in this photo. Courtesy B&O Railroad Museum, Baltimore, Md. (Compare to photograph on page 153 taken sixty-one years earlier).

Thus ended over two centuries of hydraulic operations at Harpers Ferry, W.Va. The 240 kilowatt GE generator was removed from the building sometime after 1973. In 1995, the 900 horsepower S. Morgan Smith turbine, installed in 1923, was sold to a power plant in Georgia. Today, only the circa 1905 Dayton Globe turbine, 600 kilowatt General Electric generator, Wood-

ward water wheel governor, and miscellaneous Westinghouse switchboard panels remain in the building. The National Park Service now owns the property.

Millwrights, inventors, and entrepreneurs alike learned some hard lessons about using waterpower in the 18th,

19th, and early 20th centuries. It would be wrong, however, to characterize their experience as a failure.[18] Without waterpower, the barrel lathe of Sylvester Nash, the stocking machines of Thomas Blanchard, and the special-purpose stocking, forging, and cutting machines of John H. Hall would have never been tested at Harpers Ferry; important developments and refinements in mechanized production systems at Hall's Rifle Works and the United States Armory would have likely been delayed; ambitious enterprises to manufacture cotton cloth and "ground wood pulp" would have had to wait. "Testing the limits," as many of the plant managers and entrepreneurs did at Harpers Ferry for over two hundred years, in fact characterizes the way Americans still do business. Their "success" or "failure" should be judged not by immediate economic consequences, but within the context of American technological progress, and the important contributions these people made toward it.

The Harpers Ferry Hydro Plant is inundated during the Flood of 1942. Harpers Ferry NHP (HF-1344).

It is also inaccurate to characterize Harpers Ferry's response to industrialization as "hesitant and equivocal."[19] While there are numerous documented examples of

A reminder of recent operations at the Potomac Power Plant. April 1995 photo by the author.

workers resisting change, there are also many cases where plant managers and workmen were eager to adopt new mechanized systems, only to learn that the waterpower at their disposal was simply not adequate to the task.

Because Harpers Ferry was such an important player in the nation's use of waterpower, and because the hydrological properties here have changed so little during the last two centuries, the place offers a unique setting to better understand the inseparable relationship that once connected man and river. In the many riverside ruins, there are stories of both triumph and tragedy—personal tales as well as stories that tell us much about the emergence of American industry. And judging by recent floods, the Shenandoah and Potomac rivers can *still* be as friendly or fierce as nature sees fit. ❧

Cotton mill ruins

Above: Virginius Island in 1865. The location of the cotton mill ruins are indicated on the photograph. The Valley Mills, a four-story brick establishment, was completed here in 1849. Just three years later, in November 1852, the building was destroyed by fire. Harpers Ferry NHP (HF-70).

Cotton mill ruins in February 1987 (**above**) and November 1997 (**left**). Photos by the author.

Top: Iron hub recovered from the cotton factory ruins during archeological excavations between 1966 and 1968. Photo by Eric Long.

Right: Cotton factory building, circa 1900. The location of the water tunnels (*ruins below*) and one of the mill's two remaining stone arches (*ruins on bottom right*) are indicated on the photograph. The structure was largely destroyed by the floods of 1924 and 1936. Harpers Ferry NHP (HF-62).

Lower right: remains of a leather power belt, recovered from the cotton factory building. The belt dates from the site's use by Child & McCreight as a flour mill from 1867-1889. Photo by Eric Long.

Water tunnels

Cotton factory arch

Above: Water intake tunnel ruins on Virginius Island, undergoing mechanical excavation to desilt years of flood deposits. 1998 National Park Service photo by Jeanne Lavelle.

Bottom right: Cotton factory ruins along the banks of the Shenandoah River. April 1994 photo by the author.

Above: This circa 1869 photograph shows two iron intake gates along the old Musket Factory headrace. The gate on the left admitted water to an Ames Company Boyden turbine in the Tilt-Hammer & Barrel-Welding Shop; the gate on the right supplied water to another Boyden turbine in the Grinding & Saw Mill & Carpenter's Shop. Harpers Ferry NHP (HF-646). **Right:** Remains of an iron intake gate along the old Musket Factory headrace today. April 1995 photo by the author.

FOOTNOTES

Records of the Harpers Ferry Armory cited in these footnotes, including all War Department correspondence, reports of operations, and estimates of expenses, reside at the National Archives. Duplicate photocopies of these records are available in the Harpers Ferry NHP Library.

INTRODUCTION

1. Quoted in Merritt Roe Smith, *Harpers Ferry Armory and the New Technology* (Ithaca, NY: Cornell University Press, 1977), 31.
2. Quoted in Smith, *Harpers Ferry Armory*, 32.
3. John H. Hall to Col. George Bomford, December 30, 1822.
4. *Virginia Free Press*, August 16, 1832, p.3.
5. United States Bureau of the Census, *Report of the Water Power of the United States* (Washington, DC: Government Printing Office, 1885), 46-49. See also Louis C. Hunter, *Waterpower* (Charlottesville, Va.: University of Virginia Press, 1979), 189-190.
6. *Report of Water Power*, 46-49.
7. Report of operations for the year ending June 30, 1846.
8. James Stubblefield to Col. Decius Wadsworth, February 19, 1820; James Stubblefield to Col. George Bomford, April 16, 1821.
9. Colonel Decius Wadsworth to the Secretary of War, October 14, 1817.
10. Hunter, *Waterpower*, 114-115. Riparian comes from the Latin *ripa*, "bank" or "shore."
11. John H. Hall to Col. George Bomford, September 18, 1832.
12. Hunter, *Waterpower*, 343.
13. Hunter, *Waterpower*, 202-203.
14. Hunter, *Waterpower*, 202-203, 504.
15. Kerry Hodges (editor), *Chesapeake Bay Communities, Making the Connection* (Washington, DC: EPA, 1996).
16. Joseph Barry, *The Strange Story of Harper's Ferry* (Woman's Club of Harpers Ferry District, 1903).

CHAPTER 1

1. See Smith, *Harpers Ferry Armory*, 24-26. Ironically, much of what Jefferson abhorred about the dehumanizing workshops of Old Europe came to characterize the industrial landscape at Harpers Ferry during the first half of the 19th century.
2. Corra Bacon-Foster, *Early Chapters in the Development of the Potomac Route to the West* (New York: Burt Franklin, 1912), 63. "Harper's Ferry" often appeared with an apostrophe during the 19th century. Today, the apostrophe is commonly omitted.

3. Pat Peele Darley, "Harper, Journey of Faith," 1988, 17-18 (document on file in the Harpers Ferry NHP Library).

4. Walter Dittmeyer, *Magazine of the Jefferson County Historical Society* (Charles Town, W.Va., 1935), 46-48. See also Barry, *Strange Story,* 12-14.

5. *Land Records of Virginia,* Northern Neck Book G, Page 496 and Northern Neck Book K, Page 401; Darley, "Harper," 18-19. Harper also obtained a patent to 20 acres on the Maryland shore opposite the mouth of the Shenandoah River on July 27, 1757. In March 1761, he was granted exclusive ferry rights across the Potomac River by the Virginia General Assembly. The Wager family—heirs to Robert Harper's estate—held these rights until December 1839, when they were sold to the Baltimore & Ohio Railroad. The Fairfax family held the ferry rights across the Shenandoah River until they sold them in October 1818 to the federal government.

6. Hunter, *Waterpower,* 53.

7. Thomas Jefferson, *Notes on the State of Virginia.* Edited by William Peden (Chapel Hill: University of North Carolina Press, 1982), 19.

8. Hunter, *Waterpower,* 60.

9. Hunter, *Waterpower,* 21. See also Brooke Hindle, editor, *America's Wooden Age: Aspects of its Early Technology* (Tarrytown, NY: Sleepy Hollow Restorations, 1975), 3-12.

10. The first stone building we know of at Harpers Ferry was erected as a residence for Harper and his wife Rachel. The structure was started in 1775, but scarcity of skilled masons during the American Revolution delayed completion until 1782. Harper, who died in October of that year, probably never occupied the house. The Harper House survives today as the oldest structure in Harpers Ferry.

11. War Department to Samuel Annin, May 12, 1807. See also "Explanation of the Plat," 1807, (Harpers Ferry NHP Map No. 44). "Sawmill Falls" is now called "The Staircase."

12. Will of Robert Harper, September 26, 1782 (document on file in the Harpers Ferry NHP Library).

13. Charles W. Snell, "History of the Lower Hall Island and of Captain John H. Hall's Rifle Factory, 1751 to 1841" (Harpers Ferry NHP, 1981), 6.

14. Donald Jackson and Dorothy Twohig, editors, *The Diaries of George Washington, Volume IV, 1784-June 1786* (Charlottesville, Va.: University of Virginia Press, 1978), 177. Keeptryst Furnace was situated near the mouth of Elk Run, about two miles upstream from Harpers Ferry. The "Falls" refer to "Shenandoah Falls," now commonly called "The Needles."

15. Jackson and Twohig, *Diaries of George Washington,* 178-179. Rumsey, an engineer and inventor from Shepherdstown, resigned his post in 1786 over a dispute with his assistant, Richardson Stewart. Among Rumsey's remarkable inventions were a steamboat and, in 1791, a reaction water wheel. Both designs were decades ahead of their time. See **Rumsey's Improved Principle of Reaction**, page 76.

16. "Report of President and Directors to Stockholders at meeting August 1, 1803," quoted in "Harpers Ferry Paper Company to Potomac Light and Power Company" (undated document from the archives of the Potomac Edison Company). The "Bull ring falls" were called "The Spout" by Washington, later became known as "Payne's Falls", and today are named "Whitehorse Rapids."

CHAPTER 2

1. George Washington to Secretary of War James McHenry, September 28, 1795. For a complete account of the objections raised by the War Department, see Smith, *Harpers Ferry Armory*, 28-32.

2. Secretary of War James McHenry to Joseph Perkin, August 6, 1798 (quoted in Smith, *Harpers Ferry Armory*, 38).

3. "Report of President and Directors to Stockholders at meeting August 1, 1803." *Report of Water Power*, 46-49.

4. "Mr. Brindley's Sketch of the Wheels and of all Necessary for the Potomac Works," August 4, 1801 (Harpers Ferry NHP document file, HFD-102, #17).

5. Oliver Evans, *The Young Mill-wright & Miller's Guide* (Philadelphia: Lea & Blanchard, 1850), 83.

6. Evans, *The Young Mill-wright & Miller's Guide*, 177 and 182.

7. Quoted in Hunter, *Waterpower*, 88-89.

8. James Stubblefield to Col. Decius Wadsworth, October 20, 1820. Gen John E. Wool to the War Department, May 28, 1829, quoted in Herbert H. Kissling, "United States Musket Factory, 1796-1835," (Harpers Ferry: National Park Service, 1961), 58.

9. Estimate of Expenses, Harpers Ferry Armory, 1833, quoted in Charles Snell, "A Physical History of the U.S. Musket Factory Plant, Volume I, 1794 to 1841," (Denver: National Park Service, 1981), 115.

10. James Stubblefield to Col. Decius Wadsworth, February 13, 1817; James Stubblefield to Col. George Bomford, April 16, 1821.

11. J. Newman, C.C.D.W., to Samuel Annin, August 4, 1801.

12. Samuel Annin to The Hon. William Eustis, November 14, 1809.

13. Col. Decius Wadsworth to the Secretary of War, October 14, 1817.

14. James Stubblefield to Col. Decius Wadsworth, February 19, 1820; James Stubblefield to Col. Decius Wadsworth, October 20, 1820; Kissling, "United States Musket Factory," 72.

15. James Stubblefield to Col. George Bomford, November 13, 1822; James Stubblefield to Capt. William Wade, September 19, 1825.

16. James Stubblefield to Col. George Bomford, June 14, 1826. Kissling, "United States Musket Factory," 75-76.

17. "Confidential Report," John E. Wool, U.S. Army, to Maj. Gen. Iac. Brown, November 16, 1827.

18. "Contract for Construction of Potomac Dam, 1828," quoted in Kissling, "United States Musket Factory," 107. George Rust, Jr., to Col. George Bomford, July 10, 1832, quoted in Kissling, 82-83.

19. G.C. Washington and John Abert to the Secretary of War, October 30, 1835; Kissling, "United States Musket Factory," 82.

20. George Rust to Col. George Bomford, July 18, 1832. The government dam at Harpers Ferry was variously referred to as the Armory Dam, Potomac Dam, or United States Dam, even after the structure began supplying water to the C&O Canal. In 1877, after floodwaters washed away a portion of the old government dam, Canal Company records began referring to the structure as Dam No. 3. This name is still used today.

21. Kissling, "United States Musket Factory," 83. According to research conducted by lawyers for the Harpers Ferry Paper Company in the 1880s, on January 14, 1834, Secretary of War Lewis Cass informed Speaker of the House Andrew Stephenson that "the right of the Canal Company to the use of water from the government dam was permissive only till the permanent dam below Harper's Ferry was built."

22. Kissling, "United States Musket Factory," 84; Charles W. Snell, "The Musket Factory Buildings and Grounds, Harpers Ferry Armory, 1859-1860" (Harpers Ferry National Monument, 1959), 35.

23. James Stubblefield to Col. Decius Wadsworth, May 31, 1819, quoted in Smith, *Harpers Ferry Armory*, 128.

24. W.P. Trowbridge and Charles H. Fitch, *The Manufacture of Firearms*, (Washington, DC: Department of the Interior, Census Office, 1883), 21. Smith, *Harpers Ferry Armory*, 116.

25. James Stubblefield to Col. George Bomford, February 28, 1818, quoted in Smith, *Harpers Ferry Armory*, 118.

26. Smith, *Harpers Ferry Armory*, 75, Table I.

27. James Stubblefield to Col. George Bomford, June 5, 1828; "Contract for Water Wheel," January 29, 1834, quoted in Kissling, "United States Musket Factory," 117; Estimate of expenses, Harpers Ferry Armory, 1833; Estimate of expenses for 1849-1850.

28. Evans, *The Young Mill-wright & Miller's Guide*, 167-168.

29. Hunter, *Waterpower*, 445; "Estimate for year ending June 30, 1848," Harpers Ferry Armory.

30. George Rust, Jr., to Col. George Bomford, March 3, 1832.

31. James Stubblefield to Col. George Bomford, June 10, 1816; James Stubblefield to Col. George Bomford, June 5, 1828; Gen. John E. Wool to the War Department, May 28, 1829, quoted in Kissling, "United States Musket Factory," 59.

32. Roswell Lee to Col. George Bomford, June 26, 1829.

33. John Symington to Col. George Bomford, July 12, 1829.

34. George Rust to Col. George Bomford, December 12, 1835.

35. John H. Hall to Secretary of War John C. Calhoun, March 16, 1819, quoted in Smith, *Harpers Ferry Armory*, 196.

36. John H. Hall to Col. Decius Wadsworth, May 3, 1819; James Stubblefield to Col. Decius Wadsworth, August 2, 1819; Snell, "History of Lower Hall Island," 10.

37. Bacon-Foster, *Early Chapters*, 85.

38. Snell, "History of Lower Hall Island," 3. The "Lower Falls of the Shenandoah" were commonly called "Sawmill Falls" during the 19th century, and today are known as "The Staircase."

39. "Articles of Agreement" between the United States and the Potomac Company, March 3, 1803.

40. "A Journal of Accounts, &c, Thomas Harbaugh, with, the Potomac Company, and Others. From 1803-1833" (Hagerstown, MD: Washington County Free Library), 76. Today, the Shenandoah Pulp Company ruins sit on the site of the old double locks.

41. Snell, "History of Lower Hall Island," 6; "Explanation of the Plat," 1807, (Harpers Ferry NHP Map No. 44). The Patowmack Company numbered their locks consecutively from Little's Falls downstream to Harpers Ferry: No. 1 was Little's Falls (or Lyttle's Falls or Hopewell Mills) Lock; No. 2 was Wilson's Upper Falls Lock; No. 3 was Strider's Mill (or Wilson's Lower Falls) Lock; and Nos. 4 & 5 were the double Shenandoah Canal Locks.

42. Bacon-Foster, *Early Chapters*, 120; "A Journal of Accounts," 18.

43. *Page Courier*, 24 May 1900, quoted in John W. Wayland, *A History of Rockingham County* (Dayton, VA; Ruebush-Elkins Co., 1912), 419-420.

44. Trowbridge and Fitch, *The Manufacture of Firearms*, 36.

45. Trowbridge and Fitch, *The Manufacture of Firearms*, 53.

46. Trowbridge and Fitch, *The Manufacture of Firearms*, 60.

47. Carrington Committee report, January 6, 1827, quoted in Smith, *Harpers Ferry Armory*, 237.

48. Hunter, *Waterpower*, 459; Smith, *Harpers Ferry Armory*, 244-245.

49. David A. Hounshell, *From the American System to Mass Production, 1800-1932* (Baltimore: The Johns Hopkins Press, 1984), 43.

50. John H. Hall to Col. George Bomford, July 24, 1830, quoted in R.T. Huntington, *Hall's Breechloaders* (York, Pa.: George Shumway Publisher, 1972), 95.

51. John H. Hall to Col. George Bomford, July 18, 1831.

52. John H. Hall to Gen. George Rust, August 15, 1831; John H. Hall to Col. George Bomford, September 18, 1832.

53. John Strider to the Secretary of War, November 26, 1832.

54. John H. Hall to Col. George Bomford, September 18, 1832.

55. Thomas Griggs, Jr. to Gen. George Rust, undated document.

56. Griggs to Rust. Strider's establishment was variously identified as Gulph Mills, Gulf Mills or Strider's Mill. The structure was adjacent to "Lock No. 3" of the old Patowmack Canal, and possessed a head and fall of six feet.

57. John H. Hall to Col. George Bomford, November 28, 1832.

58. George Rust to Col. George Bomford, May 21, 1833; George Rust to Col. George Bomford, June 27, 1833.

59. Snell, "History of Lower Hall Island," 50.

60. John H. Hall to Col. George Bomford, September 10, 1834.

61. John H. Hall to Col. George Bomford, October 5, 1835.

62. John H. Hall to Secretary of War John C. Calhoun, December 20, 1822.

63. Carrington Committee report, January 6, 1827, quoted in Smith, *Harpers Ferry Armory*, 240.

64. Col. George Talcott to Col. George Bomford, December 15, 1832, quoted in Smith, *Harpers Ferry Armory*, 222.

65. Jefferson County Land Grant Book I, p. 479, quoted in Mary Edith Johnson and John Barker, "Virginius Island: The Transformation of a Small Industrial Community, 1800-1936," (Harpers Ferry: National Park Service/University of Maryland Cooperative Agreement, 1992), I-2.

66. Johnson and Barker, "Virginius Island," 3.

67. Johnson and Barker, "Virginius Island," 4; Frances C. Robb, "Industry in the Potomac River Valley, 1760-1860" (dissertation submitted to the College of Arts and Sciences of West Virginia University, Morgantown, WV, 1991).

68. Petition for the Incorporation of the Town of Virginius, 11 December 1826, Jefferson County Legislative Petitions, B276, Virginia State Archives, Richmond, Virginia (quoted in Johnson and Barker, "Virginius Island," 5). Fontaine and Townsend Beckham were brothers-in-law of James Stubblefield; Edward Wager was a descendent of Robert Harper's niece, Sarah Harper Wager; and Lewis Wernwag was a renowned bridgebuilder who had recently arrived from Philadelphia. On the four tracts purchased, only Edward Wager's Tract 3 property was not developed for industrial use.

69. Johnson and Barker, "Virginius Island," 6-7; *Virginia Free Press*, March 3, 1836, p. 3, c. 5; Smith, *Harpers Ferry Armory*, 179.

70. *Virginia Free Press*, August 16, 1832, p. 3, c. 5.

71. Charles Staley to Col. George Bomford (no date), quoted in Smith, *Harpers Ferry Armory*, 163; Sawmill ledger (HAFE-283, Harpers Ferry NHP artifact collection).

72. Lee H. Nelson, *The Colossus of 1812: An American Engineering Superlative* (New York: American Society of Civil Engineers, 1990), I. See also James D. Dilts, *The Great Road, The Building of the Baltimore and Ohio, The Nation's First Railroad, 1828-1853* (Stanford, Ca.: Stanford University Press, 1993), 206-207, 218. Wager's Bridge was named for the Wager family, the descendants of John Wager. Sr. and Sarah Harper Wager, to whom Robert Harper had bequeathed the Potomac Ferry rights in 1782.

73. Snell, "History of Lower Hall Island," 27, 50-51.

74. John H. Hall to Col. George Bomford, May 28, 1834.

75. Minutes from a court of inquiry, Harpers Ferry, April 28, 1827 (records of the Harpers Ferry Armory).

76. Jack Bergstresser, HAER No. WV-35, "Virginius Island: Waterpowered Industrial Village" (Washington, DC: Historic American Engineering Record, 1987), II; Smith, *Harpers Ferry Armory*, 285.

77. *Virginia Free Press*, April 14, 1836, p. 3, c. 2, quoted in Charles W. Snell, "A Compendium of the Commercial and Industrial Advertisements of the Business and Manufacturing Establishments of Harpers Ferry and the Island of Virginius, 1824-1861" (Denver: National Park Service, 1973), 203.

78. *Virginia Free Press*, June 11, 1840, p. 3, c. 3.

79. *Virginia Free Press*, July 27, 1843, p. 3, c. 1.

80. *Virginia Free Press*, April 9, 1835, p. 3, c. 5.

81. Letter of October 13, 1837, quoted in Huntington, *Hall's Breechloaders*, 80.

82. *Land Records of Jefferson County, Virginia*, Deed Book 29, Page 37.

83. *Virginia Free Press*, October 9, 1834.

84. Thomas Cather, *Thomas Cather's Journal of a Voyage to America in 1836* (Emmaus, Pa.: The Rodale Press, 1955).

CHAPTER 3

1. *Virginia Free Press*, October 30, 1846, quoted in Robb, "Industry in the Potomac River Valley."

2. *Virginia Free Press*, October 9, 1834.

3. "Confidential Report," John E. Wool, U.S. Army, to Maj. Gen. Iac. Brown, November 16, 1827. For a complete account of the introduction of direct military control over the national armories, see Smith, *Harpers Ferry Armory*, 266-275.

4. Col. George Bomford to Secretary of War J. Spencer, November 29, 1841; Maynadier to William L. Marcy, June 18, 1846, quoted in Smith, *Harpers Ferry Armory*, 275.

5. Report of operations for the year ending June 30, 1845, quoted in Charles W. Snell, "The Musket Factory Buildings and Grounds, Harpers Ferry Armory, 1859-1860" (Harpers Ferry National Monument, 1959), 5.

6. Report of operations for the year ending June 30, 1846, quoted in Snell, "Musket Factory Buildings and Grounds," 14.

7. Report of operations for the year ending June 30, 1850, quoted in Snell, "Musket Factory Buildings and Grounds," 5.

8. Report of operations for the year ending June 30, 1851, quoted in Snell, "Musket Factory Buildings and Grounds," 10-11.

9. Report of operations for the year ending June 30, 1851, quoted in Snell, "Musket Factory Buildings and Grounds," 15.

10. "Estimate for year ending June 30, 1849," Major John Symington to the War Department.

11. Quoted in Snell, "Musket Factory Buildings and Grounds," 17.

12. Major John Symington to the Secretary of War, June 30, 1848, quoted in Snell, "Musket Factory Buildings and Grounds," 3.

13. Smith, *Harpers Ferry Armory*, 287.

14. Smith, *Harpers Ferry Armory*, 278.

15. Letter of recommendation from John Symington, April 22, 1856 (James Henry Burton Papers, Manuscripts and Archives, Yale University Library, Manuscript Group #117, Box I).

16. Trowbridge and Fitch, *The Manufacture of Firearms*, 38. Smith, *Harpers Ferry Armory*, 289-290. In 1854, James H. Burton left Harpers Ferry to take a position with the Ames Manufacturing Company.

17. Colonel H.K. Craig to Secretary of War Jefferson Davis, March 17, 1854, quoted in Huntington, *Hall's Breech-loaders*, 100.

18. Hunter, *Waterpower*, 299-300.

19. Joseph Barnes to John Vaughan, September 21, 1792 (American Philosophical Society, courtesy of Nick Blanton, Rumseian Society, Shepherdstown, West Virginia).

20. James B. Francis, *Lowell Hydraulic Experiments* (New York: D. Van Nostrand, 1868), 2.

21. Estimate of expenses for 1844-1845, November 30, 1844; Report of operations for the year ending June 30, 1846.

22. Hunter, *Waterpower*, 306; Francis, *Hydraulic Experiments*, 1-2.

23. Major John Symington to Colonel George Talcott, January 7, 1847.

24. Hunter, *Waterpower*, 309-311.

25. Michael S. Raber, Patrick Malone, and Robert B. Gordon, "Historical and Archaeological Assessment, Tredegar Iron Works Site, Richmond, Virginia" (South Glastonbury, CT: Raber Associates, 1992), 57.

26. Jonathan Thayer Lincoln, "Material for a History of American Textile Machinery," *Journal of Economic and Business History*, Volume IV, Number 2, February 1932, 268-271. *A Description of The Machinery Manufactured by Kilburn, Lincoln, & Co., Fall River, Mass., 1874* (Cambridge: Giberside Press, 1874), courtesy The American Textile History Museum, Lowell, Massachusetts. George Kilburn apparently had no financial interest in E.C. Kilburn and Company, but did provide considerable advice in constructing the turbine water-wheel.

27. William R. Bagnall, Bagnall Papers, quoted in Lincoln, "Material for a History of American Textile Machinery," 268.

28. Report of operations for the year ending June 30, 1848; Report of operations for the year ending June 30, 1849.

29. H.W. Clowe to Colonel H.K. Craig, October 31, 1855.

30. Estimate of expenses for 1856-1857.

31. Henry K. Craig to Henry W. Clowe, November 2, 1855; Report of operations for the year ending June 30, 1856.

32. M. Powis Bale, *Saw-Mills; Their Arrangement and Management; and the Economical Conversion of Timber* (London: Crosby Lockwood and Co., 1883), 50.

33. Report of operations for the year ending June 30, 1846. Report of operations for the year ending June 30, 1854. A "Backshot Water Wheel" probably denotes breast-type construction. "15 feet cube" indicates a wheel size of 15 feet diameter by 15 feet wide. Whether the wheel was overshot, undershot, breast or backshot was not indicated.

34. Report to Secretary of War Conrad, November 4, 1850. Charles W. Snell, "A Physical History of the

Plant of the United States Armory at Harper's Ferry, Virginia, 1794 to 1885, Its Evolution, Development, Destruction, and Disposal, Volume II, Reconstruction of the Armory, 1842-1851" (Harpers Ferry NHP, 1981), 210.

35. Report of operations for the year ending June 30, 1851. Snell, "A Physical History, Volume II," 136. Armistead M. Ball to Alfred M. Barbour, May 18, 1859.

36. "Report on National Armory on the Western Waters," January 18, 1825, quoted in Hunter, *Waterpower*, 87.

37. Report of operations for the year ending June 30, 1854.

38. Alfred M. Barbour to Colonel H.K. Craig, May 4, 1859; Armistead M. Ball to Alfred M. Barbour, May 18, 1859; Colonel H.K. Craig to Alfred M. Barbour, September 16, 1859. James T. Ames had been commissioned by the Ordnance Department to obtain barrel-rolling (or barrel-welding) machines from England for both U.S. Armories. This new machine was first introduced at the Springfield Armory, replacing the use of trip-hammers in barrel-welding.

39. The four years for which no expenses appear for armory waterworks were 1844, 1849, 1852, and 1858.

40. Report of operations for the year ending June 30, 1843, quoted in Snell, "Musket Factory Buildings and Grounds," 36.

41. *Virginia Free Press*, April 22, 1852, p. 2, c. 1.

42. Estimate of expenses for 1855-1856, quoted in Charles W. Snell, "Historic Structure Report for the U.S. Rifle Factory Bridges, Canal, and Dam on the Shenandoah River" (Harpers Ferry NHP, 1981), 39; Report of operations for the year ending June 30, 1853, quoted in Snell, "Musket Factory Buildings & Grounds," 37-38.

43. Report of operations for the year ending June 30, 1853, quoted in Snell, "U.S. Rifle Factory Bridges, Canal, and Dam," 20; George Mauzy to James H. Burton, July 28, 1860, quoted in Snell, "Musket Factory Buildings and Grounds," 39.

44. *Virginia Free Press*, March 3, 1859, p. 2, c. 2; *Virginia Free Press*, September 15, 1859, p. 2, c. 1; *Virginia Free Press*, October 20, 1859, p. 2, c. 3.

45. *Plan and Report with a Descriptive View of the Island of Virginius, at Harper's Ferry, Virginia*, 1844 (Harpers Ferry NHP, Map 40, Drawer 3, Item 29).

46. *Virginia Free Press*, February 20, 1845, p. 3, c. 2.

47. *Virginia Free Press*, September 3, 1846, p. 3, c. 4.

48. *The Constitutionalist*, June 18, 1840-January 28, 1841.

49. Records of the United States Patent Office, Patent No. 2,321, November 3, 1841. See also William E. Trout, *The Shenandoah River Atlas* (Richmond, Va.: Friends of the Shenandoah River, 1997), 80-81.

50. *Virginia Free Press*, April 25, 1850, p. 3, c. 1.

51. United States Census, *Products of Industry, Jefferson County, Virginia*, 1850, quoted in Bergstresser, HAER No. WV-35, 11.

52. United States Census, *Products of Industry, Jefferson County, Virginia*, 1860, quoted in Bergstresser, HAER No. WV-35, 11. In 1986, National Park Service archeologists uncovered evidence of a brick building adjacent to the iron foundry measuring 54 feet by 33 feet. This structure may have replaced Gilleece's original establishment sometime after 1855 but prior to the 1860 Census.

53. *Products of Industry*, 1850, 1860, quoted in Johnson and Barker, "Virginius Island," 37-38.

54. Bergstresser, HAER No. WV-35, 21-22.

55. *Spirit of Jefferson*, February 8, 1848, p. 1, c. 7. For a thorough discussion of the Walker tariff bill of 1846,

see Victor S. Clark, *History of Manufactures in the United States, Volume I, 1607-1860* (New York: Peter Smith, 1949), 282 and 288.

56. *Spirit of Jefferson*, May 22, 1846, p. 2, c. 6.

57. *Spirit of Jefferson*, September 3, 1847, p. 2, c. 2.

58. *Spirit of Jefferson*, July 17, 1846, p. 3, c. 4.

59. John Symington to George Talcott, August 1, 1846; *Spirit of Jefferson*, October 9, 1846, p. 3, c. 6; *Spirit of Jefferson*, February 8, 1848, p. I, c. 7. Stone quarries used by the Harpers Ferry & Shenandoah Manufacturing Company and by Lewis Wernwag were situated adjacent to Virginius Island along present-day Shenandoah Street.

60. *Spirit of Jefferson*, March 7, 1848, p. 3, c. 4. The ad also appeared in the *Winchester Republican, Staunton Democrat, Harrisonburg Register, Leesburg Washingtonian,* and *Martinsburg Gazette.*

61. *Spirit of Jefferson*, February 8, 1848, p. I, c. 7.

62. See Allen Johnson and Dumas Malone, editors, *Dictionary of American Biography* (New York: Charles Scribner's Sons, 1930), and "The Danforth, or Cap Spinner," *Journal of the American Institute, Volume I, 1836.*

63. A complete inventory of the cotton factory machinery appeared in the *Virginia Free Press*, December 2, 1852, p. 3, c. 3. Flow production in early 19th century American textile mills is described by Brooke Hindle and Steven Lubar, *Engines of Change, The American Industrial Revolution, 1790-1860* (Washington, DC: Smithsonian Institution Press, 1986), 196-198.

64. *Virginia Free Press*, December 2, 1852, p. 3, c. 3.

65. *Spirit of Jefferson*, February 8, 1848, p. I, c. 7; *Products of Industry*, 1850, quoted in Johnson and Barker, "Virginius Island," 37. The cotton factory was the first manufacturing enterprise at Harpers Ferry known to hire women. David A. Zonderman, in *Aspiration & Anxieties,* *New England Workers & the Mechanized Factory System, 1815-1850* (New York, Oxford University Press, 1992), II, points out that many young, unmarried women welcomed the opportunity to work for any wages:

For workers who were entering the wage-labor force for the first time (among them many female operatives), factory work often gave them opportunities they never had before—steady employment, cash wages, the chance to live on their own.

66. Bergstresser, HAER No. WV-35, 18.

67. Backwater from the new dam impeded operations at the Rifle Factory on Lower Hall Island, and the company was subsequently forced to modify the structure. After Abraham Herr became the sole owner of Virginius Island in 1855, this dam became known as Herr's Dam.

68. *Spirit of Jefferson*, February 8, 1848, p. I, c. 7.

69. *Virginia Free Press*, August 2, 1849, p. 2, c. 3.

70. *Virginia Free Press*, August 2, 1849, p. 3, c. 2.

71. *Products of Industry*, 1850, quoted in Johnson and Barker, "Virginius Island," 37.

72. Clark, *History of Manufactures*, 552-553.

73. Robb, "Industry in the Potomac River Valley."

74. Johnson and Barker, "Virginius Island," 44.

75. *Spirit of Jefferson*, February 8, 1848, p. I, c. 7.

76. Jackson and Twohig, *Diaries of George Washington*, 178.

77. Deed of Trust recorded July 9, 1839, in Washington County, Maryland, courtesy of David McIntosh; Deed of Trust recorded February 6, 1839, in Loudoun County, Virginia, courtesy of David McIntosh; "Plan of Part of Weverton," surveyed and drawn by Wm. Dawson, Jr., 1849.

78. An extensive account of the Weverton Manufacturing Company can be found in Peter Maynard, *Wever of the B&O Railroad and Weverton* (Brunswick, Md.: The

Brunswick Historical Press, 1996). Gerard B. Wager was a descendent of Robert Harper's niece, Sarah Harper Wager, and a prominent businessman in Harpers Ferry. He died in April 1848.

79. Weverton promotional pamphlet, 1835, quoted in Robb, "Industry in the Potomac River Valley."

80. Journals of Benjamin H. Latrobe, Jr., quoted in Dilts, *The Great Road*, 218.

81. Caspar Wever to J.M. Coale, October 7, 1844, quoted in Robb, "Industry in the Potomac River Valley."

82. Edward N. Dickerson's report is quoted in T.J.C. Williams, *History of Frederick County, Maryland, From the Earliest Settlements to the Beginning of the War Between the States* (L.R. Titsworth & Co., 1910). Dickerson was a personal friend of Caspar Wever.

83. *Products of Industry*, 1850, quoted in Robb, "Industry in the Potomac River Valley."

84. "No. 3475 Equity – In the Circuit Court for Frederick County in Equity, October 19, 1869," courtesy of David McIntosh.

85. *Spirit of Jefferson*, February 6, 1849, p. 2, c. 6, reprinted from the *Winchester Virginian*.

86. *Frederick Examiner*, September 12, 1849, quoted in Williams, *History of Frederick County*.

87. James E. Taylor, *With Sheridan Up the Shenandoah Valley in 1864: Leaves From a Special Artist's Sketchbook and Diary* (Cleveland, Ohio: The Western Reserve Historical Society, 1989), 27.

88. "No. 3475 Equity – In the Circuit Court for Frederick County in Equity, October 19, 1869," courtesy of David McIntosh.

89. Maynard, *Wever*, 114, 125.

90. Robb, "Industry in the Potomac River Valley;" *Lowell, The Story of an Industrial City* (Washington, DC: National Park Service, 1992), 34-35.

91. For a complete account of John Brown's raid, see the National Park Service publication *John Brown's Raid* (Washington, D.C.: Government Printing Office, 1974).

92. Mary E. Mauzy to Eugenia Burton, October 17, 1859.

93. George Mauzy to Mr. & Mrs. James H. Burton, December 3, 1859.

94. Smith, *Harpers Ferry Armory*, 309.

95. Smith, *Harpers Ferry Armory*, 310; Burton diary, December 5, 1860 (James Henry Burton Papers, Manuscript Group #117, Box 1).

96. Quoted in Manly Wade Wellman, *Harpers Ferry: Prize of War* (Charlotte, NC: McNally of Charlotte, 1960).

97. "Rough Draft of History of Richmond Armory," March 4, 1893 (James Henry Burton Papers); Smith, *Harpers Ferry Armory*, 319.

98. "Rough Draft of History of Richmond Armory," March 4, 1893 (James Henry Burton Papers); Smith, *Harpers Ferry Armory*, 320.

99. William B. Edwards, "One-Man Armory: Colonel J.H. Burton," *Virginia Cavalcade*, Autumn 1962, 31; "Rough Draft of History of Richmond Armory," March 4, 1893 (James Henry Burton Papers).

100. James Magalis to James H. Burton, February 5, 1862 (James Henry Burton Papers). "Herr's mill" refers to the cotton factory which Herr had acquired in July 1854, not the nearby flour mill.

101. James H. Burton to James Magalis, February 16, 1862 (James Henry Burton Papers). Whether this sale was ever concluded is not known. See also Matthew W. Norman, *Colonel Burton's Spiller & Burr Revolver* (Macon, Georgia: Mercer University Press, 1996).

CHAPTER 4

1. J.T. Trowbridge, *The South: A Tour of Its Battle-Fields and Ruined Cities* (Hartford, Conn: L. Stebbins, 1866), 66.

2. Trowbridge, *The South*, 68.

3. *Spirit of Jefferson*, July 30, 1867, p. 2, c. 3.

4. Barry, *Strange Story*, 146-147.

5. Carl M. Becker, "James Leffel: Double Turbine Water Wheel Inventor," *Ohio History* (Vol. 75, No. 4, Autumn 1966), 207.

6. Becker, "James Leffel," 204.

7. Ninth Census (1870), quoted in Johnson and Barker, "Virginius Island," 46; *Spirit of Jefferson*, December 7, 1869, p. 3, c. 2.

8. Smith, *Harpers Ferry Armory*, 323-324.

9. *Virginia Free Press*, October 14, 1869, p. 2, c. 5.

10. Barry, *Strange Story*, 146.

11. Emily E. Child to Sallie B. Child, October 7, 1870 and October 9, 1870 (Harpers Ferry NHP).

12. Barry, *Strange Story*, 158-159.

13. Tenth Census (1880), quoted in Johnson and Barker, "Virginius Island," 47. *Harper's Ferry Mill Company vs. Thos. H. Savery and others* ("Savery Papers," Harpers Ferry NHP).

14. *Spirit of Jefferson*, April 28, 1885, p. 2, c. 2, quoted in Johnson and Barker, "Virginius Island," 49; *Virginia Free Press*, June 6, 1889, p. 2, c. 3.

15. *Virginia Free Press*, April 10, 1880, p. 2, c. 5.

16. Chas. H. Fitch to James H. Burton, December 5, 1882 (James Henry Burton Papers, Manuscript Group #117, Reel 2).

17. "Abstract of Title, Properties of Harpers Ferry Paper Company, on the Potomac and Shenandoah Rivers at Harpers Ferry, West Virginia, under purchases from the United States Government," August 3, 1929 (Hagley Museum and Library, Accession 1534, Folder 4). Due to factual errors in the description of the Musket Factory lot, Savery received a new deed to this property on April 12, 1887, including "the water power entire of the Potomac river" and "the buildings waterwheels, and other machinery and all the building stone and other building material on the ground."

18. *Report of Water Power*, 46-49.

19. *Report of Water Power*, 46-49. Several attempts were made to re-open the Shenandoah Canal after the Civil War. "An Act for the Improvement of the Navigation of the Shenandoah River," passed in 1868, authorized the installation of new gates in the locks at Strider's Mill and the U.S. Rifle Works, but it is not known if the work was performed. The *Shenandoah River Navigation Company*, formed in 1872, raised $5,000 and awarded contracts for canal improvements two years later. Whatever work was accomplished, however, was destroyed by the Flood of 1877, and the canal never functioned again. (Trout, *Shenandoah River Atlas*, 98).

20. William Luke also helped form the *West Virginia Pulp & Paper Co.* in Allegheny County, Maryland, in 1888. Here Luke's three sons pioneered the commercial use of chemical digesters for the production of wood pulp. "Chemical wood pulp" became the basis for the modern paper industry, and their company was a forerunner of *Westvaco Corporation*, which still manufactures paper in Luke, Maryland.

21. To what extent the *Shenandoah City Company* improved this site is not known. Whatever improvements had been made were wiped out by floods in 1870 and 1877. In 1890, Lieut. Col. Peter Hains of the U.S. Army Corps of Engineers wrote that "Shenandoah City exists only on paper." (Trout, *Shenandoah River Atlas*, 98).

22. Jas. D. Butt to Thos. H. Savery, January 19, 1885 (Hagley Museum and Library, Accession 1534, Folder 4).

23. Hunter, *Waterpower*, 151-155.

24. *Harpers Ferry Mill Company v. Thos. H. Savery and others* ("Savery Papers," Harpers Ferry NHP).

25. Diary of William Savery, August 25, 1887 and February 1, 1888 (Hagley Museum and Library, Accession 330, Box 1). The Child & McCreight flour mill ceased operation after the Flood of 1889. Although abandoned for several decades, the building remained standing until the Flood of 1924.

26. "Savery Papers," Harpers Ferry NHP.

27. Thomas H. Savery to The Dayton Globe Iron Works Co., February 22, 1892 (*Catalogue of the New American Turbine Manufactured by The Dayton Globe Iron Works Co. Successors to Stout, Mills & Temple. Dayton, Ohio, U.S.A.* 1892).

28. E.A. Flanagan to Thomas H. Savery, June 3, 1908 (Hagley Museum and Library, Accession 1534, Folder 4).

29. Hunter, *Waterpower*, 347-348.

30. *Globe Iron Works* catalogue (Dayton, Ohio, 1884).

31. *Catalogue of the New American Turbine*, 1892.

32. Hunter, *Waterpower*, 384-385; Daniel W. Mead, *Water Power Engineering* (New York: McGraw Hill, 1915), 518.

33. "Savery Papers," Harpers Ferry NHP.

34. "Savery Papers," Harpers Ferry NHP.

35. Mead, *Water Power Engineering*, 268. The draft tube was first introduced by Austin and Zebulon Parker in 1840. *See page* 78.

36. "Manager's Report," July 27, 1922 ("Savery Papers," Harpers Ferry NHP).

37. "Manager's Report," December 28, 1921 ("Savery Papers," Harpers Ferry NHP).

38. Joseph H. Wallace & Co., "Report on Examination of Property Owned by the Jefferson Power Company, Shenandoah Pulp Company, Harpers Ferry Paper Company, Harpers Ferry Electric Light & Power Company, all of Harpers Ferry, W.Va.," September 16, 1919 (Hagley Museum and Library, Accession 1534, Folder 4), 2-3; "Savery Papers," Harpers Ferry NHP.

39. William Savery to Thomas Savery, Jr., October 9, 1922 (Hagley Museum and Library, Accession 1534, Folder 4).

40. Wallace, "Report," 3; "Manager's Report," July 27, 1922 ("Savery Papers," Harpers Ferry NHP).

41. *Spirit of Jefferson*, June 4, 1889, p. 2, c. 2.

42. Diary of Thomas H. Savery, May 7, 1889 (Hagley Museum and Library, Accession 291). Flanagan to Savery, June 3, 1908.

43. Wallace, "Report," 5.

44. Minutes of Harpers Ferry Paper Company, Feb. 6, 1890, quoted in Dean Herrin, HAER No. WV-61, "Potomac Power Plant" (Washington, DC: Historic American Engineering Record, 1999), 16.

45. L. Victor Boughman to Thomas H. Savery, October 1, 1885, "Harpers Ferry Paper Company to Potomac Light and Power Company. Examination and report on water rights on Potomac and Shenandoah Rivers at Harper's Ferry, West Virginia, together with land titles to property owned by the Harper's Ferry Paper Company and Conveyed to Potomac Light and Power Company" (archives of the Potomac Edison Company, Hagerstown, Maryland).

46. "Harpers Ferry Paper Company to Potomac Light and Power Company."

47. "Abstract of Title," (Hagley Museum and Library, Accession 1534, Folder 4).

48. "Abstract of Title."

49. Wallace, "Report," 5.

50. Herrin, HAER No. WV-61, 8; Victor S. Clark, *History of Manufactures in the United States, Volume 2, 1860-1893* (New York: Peter Smith, 1949), 486.

51. Flanagan to Savery, June 3, 1908.

52. *Spirit of Jefferson*, March 22, 1898, quoted in Herrin, HAER No. WV-61, 17.

53. Herrin, HAER No. WV-61, 19, 31; Sanborn Fire Insurance Map, 1907 (Harpers Ferry NHP).

54. Minutes of the Shenandoah Pulp Company, Bk. 999 (archives of the Potomac Edison Company, Hagerstown, Maryland).

55. Flanagan to Savery, June 3, 1908.

56. "Savery Papers," Harpers Ferry NHP; "Savery Family Material, 1869-1938" (Hagley Museum and Library, Accession 1534, Folder 4).

57. Wallace, "Report," 6; Herrin, HAER No. WV-61, 20.

58. Herrin, HAER No. WV-61, 20, 31. A surviving blueprint for the *S. Morgan Smith Co.* turbine and General Electric generator, dated December 29, 1922, specifies a turbine of 850 H.P. and 120 R.P.M., and a generator of 500 KW and 120 R.P.M. The actual turbine installed during the summer of 1923 was rated at 900 H.P. (Hagley Museum and Library, Accession 1534, Oversize Material). *See Chapter 5 for the subsequent story of the Potomac Power Plant.*

CHAPTER 5

1. Thomas H. Savery, Jr. to William H. Savery, April 14, 1922, quoted in Herrin, HAER No. WV-61, 21.

2. Duncan Hay, *Hydroelectric Development in the United States, 1880-1940* (Washington, DC: Edison Electric Institute, 1991), 34.

3. Clark, *History of Manufactures, Vol. 2*, 533.

4. Hunter, *Waterpower*, 343.

5. Hunter, *Waterpower*, 490, 492.

6. T.H. Savery to The Dayton Globe Iron Works Co., Feb. 22, 1892 *(Catalogue of the New American Turbine, 1892)*.

7. E.A. Flanagan to Thomas H. Savery, June 3, 1908.

8. *Farmers Advocate*, February 23, 1918, p. 2, c. 2; March 20, 1920, p. 1, c. 5; October 16, 1920, p. 1, c. 2.

9. Herrin, HAER No. WV-61, 16.

10. Herrin, HAER No. WV-61, 16; Patricia Chickering, David T. Gilbert, and Bruce Noble, "Potomac Power Plant: A Summary Statement Concerning History, Architectural Integrity, and National Register Eligibility" (Harpers Ferry: National Park Service, 1995), 7.

11. Herrin, HAER No. WV-61, 16, 22, 28.

12. Chickering, Gilbert, and Noble, "Potomac Power Plant," 14; Herrin, HAER No. WV-61, 35. William H. Savery, who superintended construction of the Harpers Ferry Paper Company, described the firm's planned use of old Armory building materials: "We . . . will tear down all the rest of the old works and use the brick in our new mills." (*Spirit of Jefferson*, Oct. 2, 1888).

13. Herrin, HAER No. WV-61, 33-34. There are no company records as to the disposition of the original pulp mill turbines following the January 15 fire.

14. Letter signed by Eugene Bready, March 13, 1925 (archives of the Potomac Edison Company, Hagerstown, Maryland).

15. Thomas H. Savery, Jr. to William H. Savery, April 4, 1922, quoted in Herrin, HAER No. WV-61, 21.
16. Herrin, HAER No. WV-61, 24-26. The power plant is referred to in various company records and newspaper reports as the Harpers Ferry Hydro Plant, Harpers Ferry Power Plant, and Potomac Power Plant.
17. Minutes of the Shenandoah Pulp Company, Bk. 1002 (archives of the Potomac Edison Company).
18. See David T. Gilbert, *Where Industry Failed* (Charleston, WV: Pictorial Histories Publishing Company, 1984).
19. Smith, *Harpers Ferry Armory*, 23.

BIBLIOGRAPHY

PRIMARY SOURCES

Manuscript Materials

"A Journal of Accounts, &c, Thomas Harbaugh, with, the Potomac Company, and Others. From 1803-1833." Hagerstown, Md.: Washington County Free Library.

James Henry Burton Papers. Manuscripts and Archives, Yale University Library.

"Explanation of the Plat," 1807. Map drawer, Harpers Ferry NHP.

"Harpers Ferry Paper Company to Potomac Light and Power Company. Examination and report on water rights on Potomac and Shenandoah Rivers at Harper's Ferry, West Virginia, together with land titles to property owned by the Harper's Ferry Paper Company and Conveyed to Potomac Light and Power Company." Hagerstown, MD: Archives of the Potomac Edison Company.

"Map of Harper's Ferry Shewing the Location of the Winchester and Potomac Railroad." Drawn by Lieuts. White, Allen, and R.S. Smith, U.S. Army, under the direction of James Kearney, Lt. Col. and T.E., 1835.

"Plan of Part of Weverton," surveyed and drawn by Wm. Dawson, Jr., 1849.

Savery Family Material, 1869-1938. Wilmington, Del.: Hagley Museum and Library.

Savery Papers. Harpers Ferry NHP.

Sawmill ledger. HAFE-283, artifact collection, Harpers Ferry NHP.

Will of Robert Harper, September 26, 1782. Transcript on file, Harpers Ferry NHP.

Public Documents

Land Records of Jefferson County, Virginia. Charles Town, West Virginia.

Land Records of Virginia. Richmond, Virginia.

Trowbridge, W.P. and Charles H. Fitch, *The Manufacture of Fire-Arms.* Washington, DC: Department of the Interior, Census Office, 1883.

United States Bureau of the Census, *Report of the Water Power of the United States.* Washington, DC: Government Printing Office, 1885.

Printed Sources: Catalogs, Memoirs, Travel Accounts

Catalogue of the New American Turbine, Manufactured by The Dayton Globe Iron Works Co., Successors to Stout, Mills & Temple. Dayton, Ohio, U.S.A. 1892.

Catalogue of the New American Turbine, Manufactured by The Dayton Globe Iron Works Co., Successors to Stout, Mills & Temple. Dayton, Ohio, U.S.A. 1895.

Cather, Thomas, *Thomas Cather's Journal of a Voyage to America in 1836.* Emmaus, Pa.: The Rodale Press, 1955.

Globe Iron Works (catalog). Dayton, Ohio, 1884.

Kilburn, Lincoln, & Co., *The Fall River Turbine and Other Machinery.* Fall River, Mass., 1874.

Taylor, James E., *With Sheridan Up the Shenandoah Valley in 1864: Leaves From a Special Artist's Sketchbook and Diary.* Cleveland, Ohio: The Western Reserve Historical Society, 1989.

The Pusey & Jones Company, Paper Makers' Engineers and Builders of Pulp Mill and Paper Mill Machinery. Wilmington, Del: circa 1901 catalog.

Trowbridge, John Townsend, *The South: A Tour of Its Battle-Fields and Ruined Cities.* Hartford, Conn: L. Stebbins, 1866.

Newspapers

Constitutionalist (Harpers Ferry, Virginia) 1840.

Farmers Advocate (Charles Town, West Virginia) 1918.

Frederick Examiner (Frederick, Maryland) 1849.

Spirit of Jefferson (Charles Town, Virginia) 1846-1898.

Springfield Daily Republican (Springfield, Mass.) 1858.

Virginia Free Press (Charles Town, Virginia) 1832-1885.

SECONDARY SOURCES

Articles

Becker, Carl M., "James Leffel: Double Turbine Water Wheel Inventor," *Ohio History* (Vol. 75, No. 4, Autumn 1966).

Lincoln, Jonathan Thayer, "Material for a History of American Textile Machinery." *Journal of Economic and Business History* (Vol. IV, No. 2, February 1932, 259-280).

Books

Bacon-Foster, Corra, *Early Chapters in the Development of the Potomac Route to the West.* New York: Burt Franklin, 1912.

Bale, M. Powis, *Saw-Mills; Their Arrangement and Management; and the Economical Conversion of Timber.* London: Crosby Lockwood and Co., 1883.

Barry, Joseph, *The Strange Story of Harper's Ferry.* Woman's Club of Harpers Ferry District, 1903.

Battison, Edwin A., *Muskets to Mass Production, The Men & The Times that shaped American Manufacturing.* Windsor, Vt.: The American Precision Museum, 1976.

Clark, Victor S., *History of Manufactures in the United States, Volume I, 1607-1860.* New York: Peter Smith, 1949.

Clark, Victor S., *History of Manufactures in the United States, Volume 2, 1860-1893.* New York: Peter Smith, 1949.

Darley, Pat Peele, *Harper, Journey of Faith.* 1988.

Davis, Charles Thomas, *The Manufacture of Paper.* Philadelphia: Henry Clay Baird & Company, 1886.

Dilts, James D., *The Great Road, The Building of the Baltimore and Ohio, The Nation's First Railroad, 1828-1853.* Stanford, Ca.: Stanford University Press, 1993.

Evans, Oliver, *The Young Mill-wright and Miller's Guide.* Philadephia: Lea & Blanchard, 1850.

Francis, James B., *Lowell Hydraulic Experiments.* New York: D. Van Nostrand, 1868.

Hindle, Brooke, editor, *America's Wooden Age: Aspects of its Early Technology.* Tarrytown, NY: Sleepy Hollow Restorations, 1975.

Hindle, Brooke and Steven Lubar, *Engines of Change, The American Industrial Revolution, 1790-1860.* Washington, D.C.: Smithsonian Institution Press, 1986.

Hodges, Kerry, editor, *Chesapeake Bay Communities, Making the Connection.* Washington, DC: Environmental Protection Agency, 1996.

Hounshell, David A., *From the American System to Mass Production, 1800-1932.* Baltimore: The Johns Hopkins Press, 1984.

Hunter, Louis C., *Waterpower.* Charlottesville, VA: University of Virginia Press, 1979.

Huntington, R.T., *Hall's Breechloaders.* York, Pa.: George Shumway Publisher, 1972.

Jackson, Donald and Dorothy Twohig, editors, *The Diaries of George Washington, Volume IV, 1784-June 1786.* Charlottesville, VA: University of Virginia Press, 1978.

Jefferson, Thomas, *Notes on the State of Virginia.* Edited by William Peden. Chapel Hill, NC: University of North Carolina Press, 1982.

Johnson, Allen and Dumas Malone, editors, *Dictionary of American Biography.* New York: Charles Scribner's Sons, 1930.

Lowell, The Story of an Industrial City. Washington, DC: National Park Service, 1992.

Mead, Daniel W., *Water Power Engineering.* New York: McGraw Hill, 1915.

Montgomery, James, *Cotton Manufacture of the United States of America* (1840). New York: Augustus M. Kelley, 1969.

Nelson, Lee H., *The Colossus of 1812: An American Engineering Superlative.* New York: American Society of Civil Engineers, 1990.

Smith, Merritt Roe, *Harpers Ferry Armory and the New Technology, The Challenge of Change.* Ithaca, NY: Cornell University Press, 1977.

Stone, Orra L., *History of Massachusetts Industries, Volume 1.* Boston: The S.J. Clarke Publishing Co., 1930.

Trout, William, *The Shenandoah River Atlas.* Richmond, VA: Virginia Canals and Navigations Society, 1994.

Wayland, John W., *A History of Rockingham County.* Dayton, VA: Ruebush-Elkins Co., 1912.

Wellman, Manly Wade, *Harpers Ferry: Prize of War.* Charlotte, NC: McNally of Charlotte, 1960.

Williams, T.J.C., *History of Frederick County, Maryland, From the Earliest Settlements to the Beginning of the War Between the States.* L.R. Titsworth & Co., 1910.

Zonderman, David A., *Aspiration & Anxieties, New England Workers & the Mechanized Factory System, 1815-1850.* New York, Oxford University Press, 1992.

Unpublished Manuscripts

Bergstresser, Jack, HAER No. WV-35, "Virginius Island: Water Powered Industrial Village." Washington, DC: Historic American Engineering Record, 1988.

Chickering, Patricia, David T. Gilbert, and Bruce Noble, "Potomac Power Plant: A Summary Statement Concerning History, Architectural Integrity, and National Register Eligibility." Harpers Ferry: National Park Service, 1995.

Hannah, David, "Archeological Excavations on Virginius Island, 1966-1968." Harpers Ferry: Job Corps Civilian Conservation Center, 1969.

Herrin, Dean, HAER No. WV-61, "Potomac Power Plant." Washington, DC: Historic American Engineering Record, 1999.

Johnson, Mary Edith and John Barker, "Virginius Island: Transformation of a Small Industrial Community, 1800-1936." Harpers Ferry: National Park Service/ University of Maryland Cooperative Agreement, 1993.

Kissling, Herbert H., "United States Musket Factory, 1796-1835." Harpers Ferry: National Park Service, 1961.

Raber, Michael S., Patrick M. Malone, and Robert B. Gordon, "Historical and Archaeological Assessment, Tredegar Iron Works Site, Richmond, Virginia." South Glastonbury, CT: Raber Associates, 1992.

Snell, Charles W., "A Compendium of the Commercial and Industrial Advertisements of the Business and Manufacturing Establishments of Harpers Ferry and the Island of Virginius, 1824-1861." Denver: National Park Service, 1973.

Snell, Charles W., "A Physical History of the U.S. Musket Factory Plant, 1794 to 1885, U.S. Armory at Harper's Ferry, Virginia, Volume I, 1794-1841." Denver: National Park Service, 1981.

Snell, Charles W., "History of the Lower Hall Island and of Captain John H. Hall's Rifle Factory, 1751 to 1841." Harpers Ferry: National Park Service, 1981.

Snell, Charles W., "The Musket Factory Buildings and Grounds, Harpers Ferry Armory, 1859-1860." Harpers Ferry: National Park Service, 1959.

Stinson, Dwight E., "The First Railroad Bridge at Harpers Ferry." Harpers Ferry: National Park Service, 1970.

ABOUT THE AUTHOR

David T. Gilbert first discovered the myriad waterpower ruins alongside the Potomac and Shenandoah rivers at Harpers Ferry while working as a professional river guide between 1977-1986. His interest in 19th century industry and hydraulic technology has since taken him to such far-flung places as Millwood, Virginia; Washington, D.C.; Wilmington, Delaware; New Haven, Connecticut; Lowell, Massachusetts; Springfield, Massachusetts; and Windsor, Vermont.

Dave presently works for the National Park Service at the Interpretive Design Center in Harpers Ferry, West Virginia. He is also author of *A Walker's Guide to Harpers Ferry, West Virginia*.